THE BADGE BETWEEN US

THE BADGE BETWEEN US

Duty, Marriage, and Family

TERRENCE P. DWYER

BLOOMSBURY ACADEMIC
NEW YORK • LONDON • OXFORD • NEW DELHI • SYDNEY

BLOOMSBURY ACADEMIC
Bloomsbury Publishing Inc, 1359 Broadway, New York, NY 10018, USA
Bloomsbury Publishing Plc, 50 Bedford Square, London, WC1B 3DP, UK
Bloomsbury Publishing Ireland, 29 Earlsfort Terrace, Dublin 2, D02 AY28, Ireland

BLOOMSBURY, BLOOMSBURY ACADEMIC and the Diana logo are trademarks of Bloomsbury Publishing Plc

First published in the United States of America 2026

Cover design: Sally Rinehart
Cover image © Douglas Sacha/Moment/Getty Images; iStock.om/mrgao; iStock.com/vkulieva

A catalog record for this book is available from the Library of Congress.

ISBN: HB: 979-8-8818-4255-0
ePDF: 979-8-216-27781-1
eBook: 979-8-216-27782-8

Typeset by Deanta Global Publishing Services, Chennai, India
Printed and bound in the United States of America

For product safety related questions contact productsafety@bloomsbury.com.

To find out more about our authors and books visit www.bloomsbury.com and sign up for our newsletters.

To those who make policing a career and understand the sacrifices, but mostly to those who love and support them.

To my children, Brian, Siobhan, and Deirdre, who always give me happiness, joy, and love.

And, most of all, to Joan, who never complained. Your love is all I ever need.

TPD

"This is the greatest job on the planet."

—Every cop whoever put on a uniform

"The job sucks."

—Also, every cop whoever put on a uniform

CONTENTS

Author's Note ix
Prologue x

PART I **THE JOB** 1

1 Married to the Job 3
2 Excelsior 9
3 Line of Duty 17
4 Close Calls 25
5 Mobbed-Up 35
6 Funhouse Mirrors 45
7 Bad Mood Rising 55
8 After 9/11 63

PART II **THE GANG** 73

9 Partners 75
10 Crazed Killas Mafia 83
11 The Bosses 91
12 Integrity Issues 97
13 Enterprise Corruption 105

14 Ambush 113

15 Night Terrors 119

16 Hit Squad 125

17 Dope Rodeo 131

18 Stray Bullets 137

19 Manhunt 145

20 Officer Down 153

PART III **THE FIRE** **161**

21 Family Massacre 163

22 Big T and D 171

23 Meeting Sam 177

24 Final Shift 183

25 Recovery 189

Acknowledgments 195
About the Author 197

AUTHOR'S NOTE

The events within are true, subject only to the fallacies of memory and my personal impression of events but otherwise fortified by extensive records maintained from my career. The characters within, other than my family members, public figures, and a few whose criminal records are public knowledge, are provided with fictional names. Some characters are based on a composite of actual people, and some backgrounds are also blended and disguised to provide a degree of anonymity. Specific geographical locations in Part II are vague for the same reason that I have replaced the real names of individuals, for purposes of anonymity and privacy, since several are now enjoying productive, private lives. Conversations are based on memory, notes I kept, or recreated to provide the sum and substance of what occurred.

PROLOGUE

With perfect script in a twenty-five-year-old journal entry, my wife Joan summed up her greatest worry as a police spouse: "The job will ruin us." Always referred to in the vernacular of New York police officers, saying "the job," like a secret code, signified membership in a club. While being in the club came with its perks, the dues paid along the way were costly. The job, as much as it provided for me and my family, also became a repeating contentious element in my marriage. Of course, I only saw this occasionally, never as clearly as Joan did.

The mundane task of clearing out a bedroom closet began a gradual reliving of past events that eventually led me to her journal entry. Three large plastic file boxes on a shelf, pushed out of sight behind pillows and blankets, held twenty-two years of memories. What began as a scrapbook, one Joan made for me while I attended the State Police Academy decades earlier, became a record-keeping obsession. The boxes held numerous newspaper articles, court documents, internal memorandums, commendation letters, case files, and, during the last four years of my career, detailed daily notes on each shift worked, including the weather and investigative activity. I had been a meticulous chronicler of my work, a helpful trait when called upon to testify.

To get to the boxes, we removed high school and college yearbooks, family photo collections, and scattered pennants, certificates, and trophies awarded to our children during their middle and high school years. These relics shared some parallel histories. While my children studied in school or played on the athletic fields earning their awards, I worked on the cases contained in those boxes.

Joan watched as I lifted the first container from the shelf and then, like archeologists, we assessed the ancient contents. It had been sixteen years since I'd read through the old files. Notepads, photographs, audio recordings, trial transcripts, grand jury minutes, and arrest reports recounted my police career.

While searching the boxes, we aligned documents and the investigations recorded with events in our lives: the birthdays of our children, a school function, or a family trip. Many memories were happy, but we had sad ones too, including those that brought back times of stress from the job, affecting our marriage and family life.

Going through each file brought a different recollection for Joan. If I pulled a news clipping of an arrest made and retold the circumstances leading to it, she recalled the overtime it entailed and the missed dinner or family celebration. For every report detailing arrests and investigations, her memory filled in the absences.

Joan resumed the closet organization while I hunched over the boxes, going through records from the last few years of my career. Page after page in my journals, week after week in my investigative reports, the contents reminded me not only of the amount and nature of work I undertook as a police investigator but also the lack of support received from ranking officers. Documents outlining potential corruption issues, personal attacks from supervisors, and safety concerns distressed me. Later, while lying in bed and rehashing events from long ago, my anger increased as the night lengthened. Betrayal, a breach of faith, had once again wounded me. The anger gave way eventually to fatigue and, finally, sleep.

The next morning, preoccupied with the information contained in the files, I vented to Joan. She listened and watched me pace the living room, hurriedly moving from one document to another, speaking quicker and louder when aggrieved by something found in the files. At one point, while I stopped to find an old document, Joan gently spoke up.

"You never processed it."

She might as well have spoken to me in a different language. What the hell did that mean, and what did it have to do with my present anger?

Her tone and serious look let me know she was about to be brutally honest.

"You never let it go, and it nearly destroyed you. . . ."

I didn't want to hear what I instinctively expected to follow.

". . . and it nearly destroyed us."

Her eyes glazed over, always a prelude to tears, and her lower lip quivered.

"I always worried whenever you went off to work." She paused, took a deep breath, and before she could say anything else, I tried to cut her off. "It's long behind us. Past history."

Joan shook her head, "No, let me finish." She wiped her eyes.

"I prayed and told myself you were safe. Nobody ever prepared me, or you, for the other ways in which you could get hurt."

She grabbed hold of my hands.

"So many times, I thought I'd lose you, and it wasn't just when you went to work. Later, when they assigned you to Major Crimes, I worried about how the job impacted you from the inside—emotionally and psychologically. No matter how much you believed retirement placed it behind you, I knew it hadn't."

For several days afterward, we talked more deeply about my police career than we ever had before. Urged by our sharing, Joan gave me her journal to read. It contained entries from when she was at her lowest, moments usually instigated by me and the demands of the job.

"I love you and always have. At times, though, I didn't like you," she said while sliding her right hand along the side of my face.

"Don't take what's inside as anything more than what I felt at the time."

I spent the next half hour reading through her private thoughts. There were fewer entries than expected, though more than should have been made. The absence of entries after my retirement brought me some relief, although it did highlight something I had missed all along. I had failed her in many ways when working as a police officer, and in doing so jeopardized what I valued most: our relationship.

Later in the evening, we talked again. The word "sorry" ended every sentence of mine. "I don't fully blame you," she said. "Somewhere along the way, the job caused you to change. It's taken a while to find your way back." I opened her journal and pointed to the five words she'd written long ago. Joan closed the cover. "We're together. It didn't defeat us. Nothing else matters." Still, those words clung to me, "the job will ruin us." I tried to remember how we got to that point and, more importantly, how we defied the odds working against us. The boxes held half the story; we were the rest of it.

PART I

THE JOB

1
MARRIED TO THE JOB

The closing minutes of his life energized me. Rhythmically, I pressed my interlaced hands down, up, down, up, down, up against the notch below his sternum in synchrony with the paramedic's grip and release of the Ambu-bag. Every compression seemed to force blood from a severed artery into his chest cavity like a burst sewer line spewing water into the street.

The dispatch had been unhurried and emotionless: "shots fired, 800 block, in front of Lincoln Towers. Two down, suspect fled on foot, last seen running west toward the river." I keyed the mic, "Four-zero en route." Fred made an abrupt U-turn toward the Towers. Again, I keyed the mic, "Any description of the shooter?" The vacant staticky voice responded, "Negative, will advise further."

We arrived amid the chaos, cries, and shouts accompanying a shooting. Two local city police officers already on scene tried to keep people away. An ambulance pulled up alongside our State Police unit, and a paramedic jumped out while calling for me to follow him toward one of two bodies sprawled on the sidewalk. A massive housing project loomed over us as a crowd gathered. Fred checked with the city cops for a description of the shooter while I began chest compressions on a Black male in his early twenties, shot twice in the upper torso. The paramedic looked over at me and half-whispered instructions, "You're doing good, keep at it; this is mostly for show until we get him in the rig; he's not making it." The crowd inched closer and became louder.

Crack cocaine, or rock, the free-based solid form of the powdered drug, inundated low-income corners and housing projects in five-dollar red, yellow, blue, and green-topped vials. Ten dollars bought a jumbo with two extra pieces. New York City stood at the epicenter of the national crack crisis; except this was not New York City. This hot June evening, I was in northern Westchester County, thirty miles from the city line, in an area plagued by a scaled-down epidemic of crime and violence occurring in the Bronx and larger Westchester cities of Mount Vernon and Yonkers. Dealers loved the product because the fast, intense high quickly passed and brought addicts back for more. A cooked eight-ball of coke yielded three times the street price of powder. The stuff was pizza dough for dealers, and turf wars raged.

Sweat rolled across my forehead and raced down my back and chest under my ballistic vest. Less than three months out of the academy, my first shooting call came in the middle of an evening shift. Every sound around me became amplified: sirens from different directions racing toward us; angry shouts from the crowd; arriving cops yelling at onlookers to move back; the whoosh of the Ambu-bag's forced air with every squeeze of its rubber bladder; and my own heart pounding, reverberating through my arms and into the victim's unresponsive chest.

My knees dug against the sidewalk. Small granules of concrete and bits of broken glass poked at me. The paramedic nervously eyed the growing crowd while keeping time with my compressions.

"The second rig should be here soon," he said, "help me load him up and then I'm getting out of here."

I looked toward the crowd. An older Black woman stood near the front. She watched intently while mumbling to herself. Her right hand shot out from her side and moved upward. I hesitated, then fell back into rhythm. She made the sign of the cross and continued to watch. I worked on the victim, whom I only knew by his street name Zag, for another thirty seconds until the second ambulance crew arrived and took over.

As I stood and brushed off my uniform pants, rivulets of both victims' blood intersected with three discarded, blue-topped vials by my feet. A slight breeze blowing eastward from the Hudson River spread over me, cooling the beaded moisture along my neck and arms. All sounds blended. The vulgar, intense beauty of the night engulfed me.

Fred's voice snapped through the air like a whip. "Shooter's been spotted, let's go." We ran down the street to a decaying multifamily building and, with guns drawn, entered a darkened yard, then scampered up a narrow path to a wooded area. A chained Rottweiler behind a flimsy wire fence in a neighboring yard snarled at us. "The shooter's somewhere in here," Fred cautioned.

My heart raced as we slowly inched along the path, attentive to the slightest movement in the dense brush. Every instinct told me to leave and find safety, but the adventure enthralled me. I followed Fred deeper into the wooded area until shouts from the street notified us the shooter was in custody. A city officer grabbed him coming out of a yard at the other end of the overgrown lot. A separate search commenced for the gun.

My baptism as a police officer occurred on that heat-saturated street. The gathered blur of faces and thrumming voices promised another side of life I wanted to experience—one filled with raw, hurried, frightening, and intoxicating moments. I vowed then to always be at the center of the shitstorm so I could make things right. If I couldn't make it right, I wanted to be the one to put handcuffs on whoever made it wrong. This is what it meant to be a police officer and what a trooper did best. My police academy training and instructors had assured me of this notion. Heedlessly, I rushed forward, not knowing then what lay ahead of me or how the job would change me. By the time my oblivion gave way to cognizance, I'd already been blindfolded. For twenty-two years, I kept tightening the knot so the blindfold wouldn't fall.

*

The notice to report to the New York State Police Academy in Albany contained an enclosed invitation for family members to attend a half-day Sunday orientation to acclimate them to the State Police and to provide a primer on navigating the future as the loved one of a police officer. Throughout the auditorium sat recruits like me, mostly male, with mixed looks of anticipation and doubt, wearing a jacket, tie, and short hair, which the next day local barbers lining the gymnasium cut even shorter.

The State Police operated differently from other police agencies. This created a collective uncertainty among us recruits. Stories about their toughness, the respect they garnered, and the discipline demanded by the organization intimidated even the surliest people I knew. The guys in my Bronx neighborhood became New York City cops, and I hoped to follow suit by taking two civil service tests and placing high on separate hiring lists. If the NYPD called me first, I'd join their academy class, but deep down, something about being a state trooper appealed to me. After taking their test, I desperately wanted them to choose me, and they did.

Next to me in the academy auditorium sat my newlywed wife, Joan. We held hands, as we did at the movies when dating, listening to the family orientation officer, a lieutenant assigned to the academy. Earlier in the day, we went to Mass together, prayed for a good training journey ahead for me, and took communion. We were both products of Catholic education from elementary school through college.

Despite my excitement at being there, I sensed Joan's anguish. A recalled conversation from college kept invading my thoughts while trying to focus on the lieutenant at the podium. It was a discussion among a group of friends regarding relationships after we heard about the engagement of a classmate to a police officer. Joan blurted out that she would never date a cop, let alone marry one. We'd been dating for only a few weeks.

"Even if you loved that person?" one of her girlfriends asked. For Joan, the reasoning was singular; she wouldn't want the worry of someone she loved getting seriously injured or killed at work. "Anyone at any time could get messed up when working," one of the guys said.

"Not as likely as it is with the police," she responded. "I'd never want to have those worries."

And yet, she sat by my side, four months married, a little over three months pregnant, and ready to enter a world she never cared to embrace.

When we later said goodbye in a hallway featuring a wall containing pictures of State Police members who died in the line of duty with the dates of academy entrance and death under their names, she cried. I felt horrible and tried to console her. "This is a great career," I said, while fighting off my own doubts. I bent down, kissed her belly, and held her for as long as possible.

"You should get back to the auditorium for your next session," she said. I didn't want to let her go knowing she'd return to an empty apartment. "Stay at your parents' house for the night." "No, if I don't sleep at our place tonight, I never will." We kissed one more time, and then she walked alone toward the parking lot. Thus began her journey as a police spouse. We were twenty-three and twenty-two and didn't know any better than to put our trust in the future and one another.

*

What motivates someone to become a police officer? Answers are as varied as those who enter the profession. For me, I didn't like bullies. My mother warned me about them when I was six or seven.

"Don't let him push you around," she advised in response to a neighbor two years older who terrorized the block and me.

"Even though he's physically bigger, you can't show any fear."

The lesson was further ingrained from watching my father, a child of immigrant Irish parents who, as a Korean War Navy veteran, used the GI Bill to educate himself through college and law school. He often represented Davids in fights against Goliaths. I learned my ideals of justice and fairness from him. Criminals were bullies picking on the vulnerable. They had to be stopped. Others needed protection.

Violence in New York City was a recurring news headline during my youth. The infamous, though made-up, quote attributed to iconic ABC sportscaster Howard Cosell of "the Bronx is burning" during Game Two of the 1977 World Series between the Yankees and Los Angeles Dodgers at Yankee Stadium established the image of a city out of control. Early in the game, television cameras panned away from the ballfield to a helicopter camera's overhead view of the brightly lit stadium and moved southeast over darkened neighborhoods to a blazing glow illuminating the dim corners of the South Bronx. An abandoned elementary school building burned. Five times during the two-hour game, announcers Keith Jackson and Cosell offered play-by-play commentary on the blaze until it was extinguished. Cosell said the fire occurred on "the same ground President Carter trod a few days ago." The reference was to Carter's historic impromptu visit to a neighborhood considered to contain the worst urban blight in the nation, the Charlotte Street area of the 42nd precinct. A reporter covering Carter's visit said the South Bronx resembled Dresden after the allied bombing in 1945.

My Woodlawn neighborhood, only six and a half miles north of that urban blight and a quick fifteen-minute drive on the Major Deegan Expressway, might as well have been in Canada. The mostly Catholic, Irish American enclave of city workers—cops, firefighters, sanitation, and correction officers—remained relatively calm compared to the rest of the borough. Weekend bar fights, car larcenies, and the occasional burglary were the extent of urban incivility, though the bordering Wakefield section, separated by a ribbon of parkway running between the two neighborhoods, promised more of an unruly criminal element, as did the southern Gun Hill Road section.

South of Woodlawn malefaction reigned over the rest of the borough. Subway crime, neighborhood shootings, and the ravaging impact of heroin were endemic. Residents accustomed to crime discussed it like the weather, as if robbery and murder, along with rain and snow, were an environmental certainty. The most significant evil to grip the city back then, one making stick-up men and pimps appear as milquetoast, was the Son of Sam killing spree from 1976 to 1977.

For eighteen months, a phantom stalking human prey in quiet neighborhoods held the city terror-struck. A note left at the Bronx shooting of two of Sam's later victims contained descriptions of the author's bloodlust. His reference to Beelzebub, an alternate name for Satan, disturbed even the most calloused New Yorker when the note's contents were released in June 1977. I became hooked on the *Daily News* columns of Jimmy Breslin, with whom the killer had communicated, and his coverage of the hunt for the Son of Sam.

During a summer of playing basketball at concrete city courts and hanging out at night with friends, we often joked among ourselves that one of the many cars passing by our street could be driven by the evil Sam. While we exuded youthful bravado, the adults were vigilant. I still recall my mother's concern. She stopped sitting in our car at night talking with friends after school PTA meetings, cut her hair short because the shooter targeted women with long hair, and insisted I walk in groups of three or more at night. Sam's return to the Bronx, after several shootings in Queens, and his letters taunting the NYPD, heightened the fear women like my mother lived with. On those sultry summer evenings of 1977, few New Yorkers were unaware of the monster roaming the streets.

The Son of Sam investigation became a significant catalyst for me becoming a police officer, a calling I knew something about. Two of my father's friends, one an NYPD undercover officer, the other a US Treasury Department special agent who always arrived in a yellow cab he used for surveillance, often stopped by our 236th Street home. They both worked at night when most people were asleep. I wanted to join their secret world. As much as I also wanted to be a writer, a path my father tried to divert by encouraging me toward law school, the thought of becoming a police officer excited me. In part, I viewed it as my way of helping the borough reverse its downward spiral, but only as a limited sojourn, a prefatory experience upon which to build a writing career. Still, the thought of helping others and the adventure it'd bring was galvanizing. Individual action spurred on by mercy and spirituality, I learned through my high school and college Jesuit educations, made the world a better place. Thus, a combination of adulation of police officers and idealism placed me on the stage at the Albany Center for the Performing Arts in March 1986, when our academy class graduated, and I received my commission as a New York State Trooper from Governor Mario M. Cuomo.

Danish theologian, philosopher, and poet Soren Kierkegaard said life could only be understood backward but must be lived forward. By my twentieth year with the New York State Police, I had been lying to Joan for the prior fifteen years. The deception wasn't deliberate or planned, though I gradually became aware of it and did nothing to change the circumstances. The deception resided in my subconscious, and I was content to let it remain there rather than confront my complicity. I had made many promises to her to leave the job only to become further seduced by a career I felt good doing.

Joan went along, patiently and lovingly, even toward the end of my career when I undertook a new assignment, ultimately testing our relationship as much as the prior twenty years had. The new assignment nearly cost me my career, my marriage, and my life. But that was just the job. Wasn't it? I could only answer this question by looking back.

2
EXCELSIOR

After our family members left the academy on that first Sunday, we were called back to the main lecture hall and split into four companies—Alpha, Bravo, Charlie, and Delta—based on the alphabetical order of our last names. Sergeant Forrest Curtis walked to the podium as soon as we sat in our company assignments. His close-cropped steel gray hair, hollowed-out cheeks, and sinewy build gave the impression of a Marine drill sergeant. He hadn't been one, though he did a tour in Vietnam as part of the 5th Marine Regiment in Hue City. Sergeant Curtis grabbed both sides of the podium, leaned forward, and instructed us as follows: "Look to your left, then to your right. Look at the person behind you and the person in front of you. Do it now!" When we finished and faced the stage, he continued,

"Of the four people around you, the odds are fifty percent or better one of them will not be on this job in 20 years when the rest of you can retire."

Silence.

"Many will not make it through the next two weeks let alone the whole academy curriculum. Others will quit once they get to their stations and realize the job is not for them. Others will get injured and forced into disability retirement. Some will get fired. Others, possibly one or more of you sitting here, will die in the line of duty."

When done, he scanned our assembled group like a hawk over its prey. He then introduced another sergeant standing to his left. A bald, spit-and-polish Black man with a pencil mustache and the build of an NFL fullback stepped to the podium. Former Army drill instructor Sergeant Lawrence Talbert introduced himself as our BMO, Behavior Modification Officer, a distinct State Police way of telling recently sworn-in Recruit Troopers that our former selves no longer mattered. Modification awaited us; forget the military emphasis on drill and instruction.

Twenty-four weeks of physical stress and mental sharpening ensued from Talbert's introduction. Every day began with a run and physical training (PT) at 5:30 am. Classes started at eight and continued until four in the afternoon, followed by more PT and then dinner. We continued in the evening with mandatory study hours, remedial class instruction and PT sessions for those struggling. Drills, academics, more PT, and constant harassment from academy staff often interrupted our study, making the evening hours no less stressful than the daytime.

Whenever we assembled in the academy's main lecture hall, what would otherwise be called an auditorium, the State Police emblem greeted us at the podium base on stage. Regal in its round blue background with bright yellow lettering, the words "New York" curving downward along the top, and "State Police" upward along the inside of the circle, the emblem protruded toward us like a fist in the face. The state seal, with the "Excelsior" scroll spread across a picturesque setting of a river, distant mountains, and a rising sun, positioned the state's motto between two figures: the Goddess of Liberty, to the left, and the Goddess of Justice, on the right. Often, during the evenings, while standing at attention, I'd stare at the center of the seal, transfixed, possibly envisioning future heroics and accolades as a state trooper, while mentally preparing for what usually came next: hours of punishment drills for some alleged infraction by the whole class or a targeted few responsible for the pain the rest of us were to endure. During the first week of the six-month residential academy, we learned to dread the evening announcement of "All recruits, all recruits, report to the main lecture hall in PT gear. Forthwith!" This began a mad scramble along the academy's two housing wings as we recruits hustled to change into issued royal blue shorts with gold piping and gray t-shirts with the academy logo on the left breast. Once assembled, we learned our fate for the evening which usually entailed an hour or longer of grueling physical training, then returning to the housing wings to find the contents of our rooms tossed in the hallway.

"Room change!" a counselor announced after blowing a whistle as we crossed the catwalks connecting the main building to the housing areas. We had ten minutes to find the new room with our name card on the door while gathering our belongings. Clothing, issued gear, and books had to be placed in proper order for inspection by academy staff. How well the class did in getting everything squared away determined whether we'd be back in the gym for another hour or allowed to settle down to sleep for the night.

Attrition in the academy first focused on getting rid of the obviously weak recruits and then those who faked their resilience. The method became clear to us in week three when the lead physical training instructor, a sergeant whose physique looked like a mold from an ancient Greek sculptor's concept of the ideal warrior, gathered us around him at the end of a morning's physical training. "Pay attention!" he barked.

"These past few weeks we got rid of the cunts. Over the next two, we're going to get rid of the real ones," he snarled. A chorus of "Sir, yes sir" and primal grunts filled the gym, even from the four remaining women of the original twelve who began training. Everyone understood the message's subtext; the only thing worse than a woman attempting to become a trooper was any man who failed to possess the required level of testosterone. The next two weeks we got our asses kicked so the instructors could gauge our worthiness to wear the uniform.

Group dynamics quickly came to the forefront. No one in our class wanted to associate with a recruit caught within the crosshairs of the academy staff. Guilt by association was real. During our rare downtime, we gathered along the back stairwells of the housing areas for "spit and polish parties." We talked freely without academy staff oversight while polishing our leather gear. Shoes, work boots, and duty rigs all had to shine. "Make 'em glisten like glass so you'll be able to see your ugly ass faces," a training counselor instructed us during week one. We'd dutifully rub our gear with our index and middle fingers wrapped in cloth covered in black polish until our fingers were numb. All the while we'd complain about the counselors—uniformed troopers who took time away from their station assignments to serve as academy staff for one or two classes—or talk about our fellow recruits by betting on who would wash out or who would obtain the highest academic average. Every discussion during those sessions favored strength, confidence, and devotion to the State Police. An attitude of toughness, competition, and conformity had to be developed, otherwise a recruit risked loss of trust and camaraderie. The academy staff purposely left us alone during those moments for us to bond and learn to "eat our own," a key survival tactic, I'd later learn, for a career in policing.

During week 16, Nolan, one of the guys in A Company, voluntarily resigned. Mid-week he woke up, drilled, and after morning chow, went to the administrative office to sign out of the academy. Within an hour, he walked out the door in civilian clothes, escorted by two staff troopers. He hinted he might resign after returning Sunday evening from weekend leave. Nolan served eight years in the Marine Corps before entering the academy, had a wife and three boys at home, and at twenty-eight, was older than the rest of us. We tried to convince him to stay.

"There are only eight weeks to go; we're two-thirds done. You can't leave us," one recruit implored. We huddled around Nolan at the lunch table two days before his decision.

"You were in the Corps, man. You got this," another offered.

"Fuck this shit," Nolan said. "The Corps busted your nuts for ten weeks to earn your eagle, globe, and anchor, then two weeks later you graduated. The shit here doesn't stop."

Nolan lived in western New York and talked in a way I'd never heard. He sat on his long A's, and his W's felt like a windstorm. He hailed from Cheektowaga, a town outside of Buffalo. Whenever he said the name of his hometown, it sounded like a male Canadian goose sending out a mating call. Guys from downstate, those of us who thought our Bronx, Brooklyn, and Long Island dictions were normal, always got a laugh from his accent.

"I don't see it getting any better," he said the morning of his final decision, as our group finished breakfast. "It's different with this organization."

Maybe he knew something we didn't. Regardless, Nolan had committed the worst violation imaginable in our narrow academy world—he abandoned his company and the rest of the class. By then, our intolerance for anyone not upholding the company ethos had set in. How dare he choose the comfort of his home life in place of suffering here with everyone else. We immediately labeled him a piece of shit unworthy of our consideration.

Meanwhile, my home life moved on without me. Five and a half days of the week I stayed at the academy with 119 other recruits as Joan's pregnant belly expanded and her train commute from our Westchester apartment to her job in midtown Manhattan became increasingly difficult. My short weekends home on leave lasted from 8:00 p.m. Friday night until 4:00 p.m. Sunday, when I'd meet up with classmates and carpool north. Lamaze classes, shopping for our baby, helping Joan around the apartment, and studying for upcoming academy exams consumed my weekends. I also bathed in pain relief cream that Joan rubbed on my upper and lower back, shoulders, and legs. "Will you survive long enough to graduate?" she teased me one evening. "What happened to the big strong guy I married? You walk around here like an old man." If I were not so sore, I would've turned around and playfully held down her arms while kissing her all over the face and neck. "You should see the others; some of them are worse off."

When I returned home for Christmas leave, my appearance shocked Joan. Bruises dotted my legs and arms from various physical training activities; my right eye's once robust black, blue, and red coloration now had a fading yellowish hue, and I weighed twelve pounds less than when the academy began. Nonetheless, I felt great, physically and mentally hardened to academy life. Joan, though, showed signs of the fatigue that, by the end of January, placed her on bed rest for the remainder of her pregnancy.

One evening after the holiday break, a Troop C uniformed lieutenant, an Army reservist attending an in-service school, invited some military friends from the local bar to observe training. At 10:00 p.m., the familiar announcement to report to the gym in PT gear summoned us to a command performance of extensive calisthenics for the amusement of the lieutenant and his pals. After an hour of drilling, in just our shorts and t-shirts, the lieutenant attempted to order our sweaty selves outside for fifteen minutes of calisthenics in the snow and howling late January winds. He had a lot of pride in the State Police and wanted to show off to his reservist buddies. The assistant PT instructor quashed the idea.

Collectively we didn't care. Our sweat for their enjoyment meant nothing to us. We were tough. Pain from pushups, rope climbs, crunches, burpees, boxing, wrestling, defensive tactics, and constant sprints had become a source of pride. Long runs in the morning, becoming increasingly longer and faster over time, only ensured we'd be ravenous by morning chow call. We gritted it out while silently repeating our various mantras to get us through. I prayed the Hail Mary. A Miraculous Medal hung around my neck since childhood, and, except for the six months at the academy, I only took it off to sleep. Raised as a devotee to the Blessed Mother, I found resolve and comfort in my prayers to her.

We recruits developed an unspoken "fuck you" attitude—we refused to break individually or collectively. I guess their plan worked because the training kicked in. Let the weekend warrior bosses come in and have their fun. It didn't matter. We'd go out and do the push-ups, sit-ups, and any other bullshit they wanted in the snow. NCAA Hall of Fame basketball coach John Wooden said, "Intensity makes you stronger. Emotionalism makes you weaker." During training, we engaged in competitions of a different kind, but his words still applied. To make us an integrated whole, the State Police Academy staff tore away our individuality in the name of the organization. It wasn't personal, and any recruit who thought otherwise and let emotion control them didn't last long.

The Wooden quote became a motto throughout my career. I didn't get mad on the street; I got even. Troopers never lost. As much as the training sucked, I never doubted its worth. Training saved lives—yours and others. My injuries in the academy—concussion, severe ankle sprain, black eyes, a sliced right ear, unending muscle aches, and contusions—were warrior badges. No one wanted to be labeled a pussy. Step up or leave. Reputation meant everything, not just among your fellow troopers and sergeants but later when assigned to our patrol areas. View everyone as a potential adversary and take no shit. A trooper must be respected and feared.

*

Radio communications training came late in the academy curriculum. Our instructor, a tobacco-chewing trooper from the Adirondack region of the state, was a "woodchuck," a term reserved for those who grew up in the smaller, woodsy upstate towns where ice fishing and snowmobiling in the winter, hunting in the fall, and bass fishing in the summer were the norm. It was a lifestyle different from many of us downstate recruits raised in more populated city centers and suburban towns.

The most important radio call to remember, if we ever find ourselves in situations where we need immediate emergency assistance, the instructor told us, is radio call Signal 30.

"It's in the Field Manual, under patrol communications. It's your call for help. You give the signal, and the cavalry will arrive."

A recruit from the second row raised his hand. "What do you mean by the cavalry?"

The instructor looked at him and proudly proclaimed, "Every trooper who hears the call will come to help you. You'll never be without backup or abandoned on this job. Someone will always be there for you."

*

My decision to follow a police career was a major life choice and a path to chart a future radically different from what Joan expected when we first began dating. She had to adapt to being a police spouse. Nothing, though, shifted our life in as meaningful a way as having our first child.

A week before graduation, I completed the last phase of the street survival course. Another recruit and I partnered for a mock car stop scenario. My partner was "shot" upon his approach to the car. I drew my gun and shouted orders for the shooter to drop his weapon and kneel on the ground. While doing so, the driver's female accomplice who I didn't see, snuck up from behind and "shot" me in the back of the head. This was a sobering lesson. Tunnel vision "killed" me. I had lost situational awareness. The small female accomplice, barely visible during the stop, slid along the rear seat and exited out of my sightline on the rear driver's side of the "suspect's" car. While I confronted the male suspect, she crouched along the troop car and came up behind me. The unforgettable feel of her mock pistol against the base of my skull and her words—"Bang, you're dead"—provided an indelible lesson.

Shortly afterward, a staff trooper came by and directed me to follow him to the administrative sergeant's office. A message from my mother-in-law awaited me. Joan was in labor. The prior week she'd been admitted to the hospital for pre-eclampsia and dosed with phenobarbital to prevent seizures. I had two weeks left in the academy, and she wasn't due for another four. After leaving her hospital bedside to return to the academy, I cried for most of my drive back to Albany. Her health and that of the baby distracted me throughout the week. Now, as I stood at attention before him, the sergeant asked if I wanted emergency temporary leave from the academy. In the moment the question seemed absurd and six months earlier my response would have been sarcastic, but I'd now become an obedient and disciplined recruit.

"Sir, yes, sir!" I replied. The sergeant prepared paperwork allowing me to skip the last five hours of Friday training prior to the class being dismissed for the weekend. I signed the leave forms, ran to my room to grab my duffle bag, and then exited the rear of the academy building to the parking lot.

I drove two and a half hours to White Plains Hospital. Four hours later, Joan and I were the proud parents of a son, Brian. The day we brought him home from the hospital, I had to return to the academy for my last week of training before graduation.

The three of us now comprised a family. I also gained a work family, a proud police family upon academy graduation, although I still had to prove my worth on the street. After three weeks of field training, I received my full investiture as a trooper when approved to patrol solo. My commitment to the mission of the New York State Police—to protect and serve the people of the state—and the academy ethos, Excellence through Knowledge, resulted in earning my police officer status. I was on "the job" and launched along a career path I'd come to love while hoping to exemplify the state motto, Excelsior, or Ever Upward. The only flaw I later realized was that, unlike Joan, the job would never love me back. But why should it? I often heard other cops complain about the job in this way as if it withheld affection from them. This was an infantile view. What I looked for wasn't love. I wanted to be supported. I wanted to go to work each day and know the job always had my back. Years later, hardened by experience, the misleading nature of the senior trooper's statement during our radio communications class that "someone will always be there for you" became evident to me. Depending on the situation, "always" had its limits.

3
LINE OF DUTY

Joan and I spent 1,160 shared hours together, a little more than 48 days, during my 24 weeks of academy training. We were apart for nearly half our first year of marriage. After my graduation, our reacquaintance competed with other commitments and responsibilities. Our first child had entered our lives; I worked alternating shifts with every seventh weekend off, we became strangers to our single friends, and time alone together was at a premium. We were young parents, barely out of college and into our working lives with the sobering demands of parenthood. A new challenge then complicated our situation. My mother died from liver disease six weeks after academy graduation. This came as a shock to us. We didn't know the extent of her illness. My father and she decided to keep her prognosis private and not burden us with it. Even my brother, still in high school and living at home, didn't know. Although upsetting, we acknowledged the old-school Irishness in their approach to life. They decided that we had enough worry with a new baby and a new job than to add her illness into the mix. Their strange logic didn't make much sense at the time. Only later, through the lens of being a more experienced parent, did it become clearer to me.

I was the last one, though, who should have critically gauged the sense of someone else's actions, let alone my parents' decision. I worked midnight shifts around my mother's wake and burial. Physically exhausted and emotionally drained, I went to the barracks, opened my locker, put on my ballistic vest and uniform, then went out on patrol. Indoctrination into the culture and the invincibility of being a state trooper had scrambled my priorities to the point that my own personal heartache and loss could not keep me from going to work.

Aside from mourning the death of my mother, the physical and spiritual center of my family life, Joan and I had to adjust our plans. My mother was going to watch Brian during the day while Joan went to work. She had a month of maternity leave left, and our options were limited. I took a big pay cut from my prior job to join the State Police. We planned to rely on Joan's salary as a cushion until my contractual pay raises brought us financial stability. Our co-op apartment loan, car payment, and cost of Joan's monthly train ticket to New York City, coupled with the expenses of a new baby, including daycare, left nothing from our paychecks. If we eliminated the monthly train commute and daycare expense, the numbers oddly worked in our favor, but not by much. Joan quit her job and became a stay-at-home mom. "Everything will work out," I told her, echoing a similar conversation when saying goodbye on my first day at the academy. It became a repeated remark as the years rolled by, our family grew, and the demands of the job increased.

*

We met during the fall semester of our sophomore year at Fordham University. Joan, a former business major, switched to Biology, and I studied English Literature. Joan's college friend Mary dated a grammar school classmate of mine, and Joan was in theology class with two of my high school classmates. I'd sometimes see her around campus and exchange a passing hello.

Our story together began at a spring dorm party on my twentieth birthday when Joan, frustrated by my flirting but lack of action, decided to kiss me very deeply and passionately. "Here's a birthday gift no one else will give you tonight," she said. I had been kissed plenty of times. No other kiss felt as meaningful as my first one with her.

"I see you two with a bunch of kids, a dog, and a cute little house with a white picket fence around the front yard," her friend Anna said a few months later at a campus party. From then on, we became referred to as the "white picket fence couple" by friends and classmates.

When we began seriously dating, Joan presumed I would work for a magazine or newspaper while studying journalism at Columbia University as a graduate student. My plans dramatically changed. Despite her aversion to marrying a cop, I decided that a few years as a police officer would provide plenty of experience, material, and contacts to begin a writing career. Plus, my ardor as a teenager of wanting to help and protect others didn't dissipate. We were dating less than nine months when I entered the New York City Department of Correction Academy and began working as a correction officer at Rikers Island, at that time the largest municipal detention facility in the United States. She knew by then of my original plan to join the NYPD. Still, she accepted my marriage proposal ten months later. Joan said she changed her mind about marrying a cop because my blue eyes "sparkled with dreams and held a vision of our future together." My falling in love with her matched. Every time we embraced, it felt like home, and I never wanted to let go.

*

Arrests of individuals for drugs and weapons came easily during my first two years in uniform. My monthly DWI arrests and tickets, the numbers the sergeants cared about, were also high. Unlike some states where the state police are solely a highway patrol, the New York State Police is a full-service agency providing regular police services in municipalities throughout the state, in addition to highway patrol. On any given shift, I responded to and investigated domestic disturbances, felony assaults, burglaries, robberies, larcenies, assisted the Bureau of Criminal Investigation (BCI) with homicide canvases for witnesses, and learned a lot about what happens when the human body suffers a violent death. Fatal car accidents, suicides, and murder scenes provided a graduate education for a young trooper. I worked a mix of rotating day, evening, and midnight shifts in a busy patrol area. Brian was a toddler when Joan became pregnant with our second child, Siobhan. Joan settled into being a police spouse, even though in those first two years she experienced more than expected, beginning with my first night on patrol.

An hour into the shift, my field training officer and I stopped a car with three individuals we eventually arrested for cocaine and heroin possession. One was a recently paroled murderer, another was on bail for armed robbery, and the third had an extensive criminal record. The arrests came after wrestling with one of them who didn't want to be handcuffed. I arrived home shortly before midnight, excited and pumped up about the arrest and eager to tell Joan. Midway through the story, I realized she was upset. The remote idea of the type of people I'd come across was no longer hypothetical for her.

Five troopers lost their lives in the line of duty during my initial two years in uniform. One from our troop, Robert Dunning, the brother of an investigator from my station, was killed by felonious gunfire from an AR-15 when responding to a domestic disturbance call. Shortly after Dunning's death, I stood alongside the hospital gurney of a fellow trooper in a local emergency room. While on a car stop, another car struck him and fled. I was sent to the hospital to check on him. He looked shaken and pale with cuts and bruises on his hands and face and described having a searing pain along his right hip where the car struck him. As he waited for x-ray results, we talked about what happened. "I didn't see or hear the car coming. Next thing, I'm face down in the road." His description captured the reality of police work. Danger came without warning.

The same could be said of death. It entered your patrol shifts like a fog rolling in and blanketing an ocean town. You learned to make your way through the fog until it lifted, knowing it would return. A week before the trooper was run down, I worked a Saturday midnight patrol and tended to a young woman trapped in the twisted wreckage of a small sports car wrapped around a tree. She was nineteen, blonde, and stunningly beautiful even with blood running across her face from a deep gash along her forehead. She wore a short sequined black dress and matching high heels, dressed for a night out she never got to enjoy. Her skin smelled of sandalwood perfume, and her radiant red lipstick contrasted with the darker blood caking into her hair. She didn't survive long enough to make it to the emergency room. A paramedic filling out a run sheet told me at the nurse's station that she coded in the ambulance. The ER doctor, a lanky resident in a blue checkered shirt and skinny cloth tie under a white lab coat, said her sternum fractured on impact with the steering wheel and a broken rib punctured her right lung.

As quickly as the fog rolled in, it rolled out and then in again. A week after standing bedside the injured trooper, my schedule went to 3-11s, and I responded to the suicide of a woman who so viciously hacked at her veins that blood covered her bathroom floor, tub, and toilet; then to the unattended death of an elderly man who collapsed in his garden and whom I helped carry to the medical examiner's van; and finally the scene of a beaten prostitute found along a secluded park road used as a lover's lane, where crack addicts also escaped to fire up their pipes. Death's fog blanketed some patrol shifts more than others.

Academy classmates also became victims of violence, particularly gunfire. The first incident occurred twenty-seven months after graduation. During a midnight shift, Trooper Peter Alano and his partner came upon a hitchhiker who shot at them as they exited their patrol car. Bullets pierced Peter's left arm and leg. One to his chest lodged in the ballistic webbing of his vest. They returned fire, killing their assailant. Peter and I partnered on a few midnight patrols at our first station assignment before he transferred to another troop and I left for a different station. He was a good cop who, prior to joining the State Police, worked undercover with a county sheriff's narcotics unit.

A few days after Peter's gunshot injury, I worked a midnight patrol with another academy classmate, and we discussed the shooting. "Pete's lucky he had on his vest," Gio Lucero said as we cruised through the parking lot of a rowdy bar. I told him Peter's partner wasn't wearing his vest, and they'd switched positions just before the stop. Peter had been driving. "That's God looking out for his partner," Gio said. I listened while checking out a dark Camaro with its interior light on and two individuals huddled together inside. I drove around a row of parked cars. "All I know is, whenever on patrol this Kevlar is always on me." Gio tugged at the corners of his uniform shirt and the visible outline of his ballistic vest.

I shut off our headlights and let the troop car roll to a perpendicular meeting with the rear bumper of the Camaro. Within thirty seconds, we had the two occupants spread-eagled across the hood of the car. Two lines of cocaine on the center console provided immediate probable cause for their arrest and subsequent car search. Gio found three dime bags of coke in the passenger's pocket. I pulled a spring-powered ballistic knife from under the driver's seat. The weapon's detachable blade, released by a trigger, could travel upward of sixteen feet. New York Penal Law section 265.01 classified it as a deadly weapon. Its purpose was singular: to penetrate a bulletproof vest.

Gio and I became friends when we began weekly Sunday carpool rides to the academy. Morris Calvert, a former college football defensive end and track athlete, and Chad Stoltz, a fire department EMT, joined us. Joan knew Gio and liked it when we partnered on midnight patrols. We not only worked well together but also became good friends. Friends, she believed, who would take extra care in protecting each other.

Thirteen months after Peter's shooting, another academy classmate was shot. This time it was Chad Stoltz. Five hours before Stoltz's shooting, I arrested a twenty-three-year-old male for assault and criminal possession of a weapon. He used a shovel to split open the head of an associate he had a dispute with over a car. We struggled briefly before I handcuffed him and retrieved the bloody shovel. I had two more evening shifts left before heading into my first weekend off in seven weeks, and looked forward to it. Joan and I had planned to take Brian and Siobhan to the Bronx Zoo and visit her parents in Yonkers during my days off. Our plans changed with what occurred over the next few hours.

When I arrived home after lodging my assault suspect in the county jail, Joan was already asleep. I soon joined her by quietly sliding under the covers shortly before midnight. Twenty minutes later, Stoltz and his partner were ambushed by an assailant posing as a federal law enforcement officer who called the local barracks and requested assistance. He lured them to a secluded area and shot them as they walked toward him. A bullet grazed the side of Stoltz's head. His partner was less fortunate and suffered a career-ending throat wound.

I hadn't heard about the shooting until arriving at work the next afternoon. The morning's media coverage of the story uncharacteristically slipped by me. Gio sat in the locker room changing out of his uniform pants from the day shift.

"D'ya hear about Stoltz?" Gio was animated, and his voice began to quaver as it did whenever he was excited.

"I read the teletype."

"They were set up," Gio continued.

"By who?"

"Some wacko who wanted to take out cops."

During the day, Gio made calls to Stoltz's station to get more information about the shooting and check on Stoltz. He had been treated and released from the hospital; his partner was still in critical condition.

"Crazy shit, huh?"

Gio was shaken.

"Yeah. Sure is," I replied.

"We still gotta throw on the uniform and ride though," Gio said.

"It's the job."

I pulled the Velcro straps of the ballistic vest across my chest, fastened them to the breastplate, and turned to Gio. "Anything happen on your shift?" Gio stared into his locker while I finished buttoning my uniform shirt and gathered up my gear. He finally responded, "Nah. It was quiet. You be safe brother."

I was barely twenty minutes on patrol when dispatched to a report of a man menacing a delivery driver with a handgun. As I pulled up the incline driveway to the location, an agitated man walked toward me with a large .44 caliber revolver in his right hand pointed toward the ground. I exited the troop car, leaving my door open for cover, and drew my weapon while shouting instructions for him to drop the gun. He continued moving forward, yelling loudly, while keeping the gun pointed downward.

"Fuck being nice anymore," he yelled. "It's always the same thing. No one cares."

"Drop the gun!"

"No respect for people. This shit is tiring," the man continued.

"State Police! Drop the gun!"

He continued walking toward me, gesturing with his free hand, waving the gun side to side, though still pointed downward. I repeatedly commanded him to stop and drop the gun. I yelled louder, my gun aimed at his chest. "Drop the fucking gun!" He suddenly stopped, placed the gun on the ground, and raised his hands.

When I handcuffed him, the man apologized. "Sorry, didn't realize I still had the gun," he said. "You could've been shot," I told him. "I was annoyed. The delivery guy was rude." The dispute started when a delivery van accidentally drove onto freshly sodded grass, and the driver didn't apologize to the property owner. "Threatening him with a gun isn't the answer."

"It's unloaded," he said, as if I should have known. I pulled him to his feet and patted down his clothing. "Is the gun registered?" He looked at me for a moment. "Good question. I'm not sure. It belonged to my father." Milliseconds away from being shot, and he had a calm I wouldn't regain until well-past the end of my shift.

A police officer's line-of-duty death is something you never get used to, although you come to expect them. You suppress the thought it could ever be you or someone close to you. The possibility is always there, lurking. Joan mourned every time she heard about a police officer's line-of-duty death. After hearing about Stoltz, whom Joan also knew, and my own encounter later that day, she decided it'd be better to stay home during my weekend off and play in the yard with the children rather than drive the half hour to the zoo. "You sure? The kids will get a kick out of seeing all the animals."

"Yes, let's stay home. I'll invite my parents over and we can have a barbeque." I agreed without giving it any further thought.

One day, after attending another trooper's funeral, I came home and told Joan if anything happened to me on the job, she and the children were to be stoic and brave. "Don't cry. Keep your composure. People will be watching. Give the ceremony the dignity it deserves."

"Don't be ridiculous. Of course, I'm going to cry."

"Please don't. Promise me. Stoic and brave."

The idiocy of this request matched my foolish rookie belief, fostered by the rough-and-tumble nature of the senior troopers working at my first station assignment, that calling for backup would be a sign of weakness. "You don't call in for backup here unless you're getting your ass kicked," a senior trooper warned me. "And if that happens," he continued, "you might as well not show up to work the next day." The drilled-in sense of toughness from the academy went past physical endurance and the non-stop hectoring of academy staff; it now meant surviving real encounters.

"You're not going anywhere on us. We won't allow it," Joan commanded.

"Not planning on it . . . just saying. Besides, I'm too ornery for anything to happen to me."

Joan laughed, "Yes, you are."

So began our little joke, ending similar discussions of mortality throughout the remainder of my career. Joan knew by then that her worries as a police spouse might not last too much longer. I was a week and a half away from finishing my first year of law school at night. When classes began earlier in the fall at Pace University, I had a tentative plan that gave Joan hope I'd retire early and practice law. The events of the next two years accelerated her hope that my career change would be more imminent.

4
CLOSE CALLS

My decision to attend law school took Joan by surprise. I did not consider becoming a lawyer until entering the State Police Academy. By then, it made sense to join my law enforcement career with law school and use it to leverage an advanced rank as a commissioned officer. Even though a higher rank never came to fruition due to my remaining a street cop, having a law degree benefited me in other ways throughout my career.

During my second year of law school, Joan became increasingly confident I would apply for an assistant district attorney position in Westchester County. Her confidence was likely peppered by my passing comments about the prestige of being with the US Attorney's Office and how sharp local prosecutors made the leap after a few years in the trenches. While her hope grew, so too did her concern about the subtle change she began to see in me. Law school added to the stress of work. "You don't have to figure it all out at once," she said one Saturday while I studied before an evening shift. Law school classmates increasingly failed out or quit after my 1L year, and I didn't want to join them. Studying around my shifts had become harder and competed with my ambition to attain the rank of investigator in the Bureau of Criminal Investigation. This meant arrests, overtime, and working felony cases before turning them over to station investigators. I wanted more for our growing family and for myself. Law school, the job, and family obligations pulled me in different directions, demanding my time and sapping my energy. Then my being named a defendant in a federal civil lawsuit for alleged excessive use of force added one more stressor.

On an early Saturday morning, a potential domestic disturbance call during the last hour of a midnight shift sent me to the residence of a woman who reported that her boyfriend, on his way back from a night of drinking, threatened to kill her. My arrival coincided with a taxicab's drop off of the intoxicated boyfriend, who greeted me with, "What the fuck do you want?" Things got worse when the girlfriend invited me into their cottage after opening the door for him. The boyfriend pushed me, took a roundhouse swing, missed, and I countered with a left hook, sending him sideways toward the front door. A backup trooper came in as the boyfriend continued to fight me. By then, his girlfriend straddled my back and choked me. I restrained him while tossing her to the ground. She grabbed my right leg, felt my .38 caliber backup gun, and tried to remove it from my ankle holster. A quick side kick of my leg pushed her off against a wall, and I resumed wrestling with her boyfriend until the other trooper, aiming for the boyfriend's shoulder, struck him with a baton along the side of the head as the boyfriend lunged to throw another punch at us. That ended the battle. The boyfriend suffered a five-stitch wound to his head along with a broken nose from my punch. We arrested both and filed the incident away as just another domestic. Six months later, we were served with lawsuit papers. For over a year afterwards, depositions, trial preparations, and then a one-week civil trial in the Southern District of New York added to my already busy work and law school schedule. The jury found that we used appropriate force. A second lawsuit filed against me and three other troopers less than a year after the first one, this time by a convicted sex offender who alleged an unlawful entry into his home during a family dispute, also ended with the jury finding in our favor.

The favorable trial verdicts were a relief, but Joan noticed I'd developed a harder edge afterward, with less tolerance for people and an increasingly brooding nature. Since childhood I always preferred my solitude and was happy with a book and often drifted off into my thoughts. The pressures of law school and the job, including my relentless efforts to make more arrests and solve assigned cases to better push ahead my plans for promotion to investigator, led to an increased self-absorption. Joan also noticed my growing lack of trust in others.

"Not everyone is a criminal," she said after seeing me pause in a local mall to keep watch on two young men.

"Everyone's a perp until proven otherwise."

Joan shook her head and wheeled Siobhan's stroller through the children's section while I took Brian and followed the young men out of Macy's toward the food court. When I caught up with Joan a few minutes later, she was putting shoes on Siobhan.

"Find anything, Dick Tracy?"

"Don't be funny. Last time we were here a guy I arrested for burglary hung out by the jewelry counter. Remember?"

"It doesn't mean everyone is up to no good."

"You know nothing. Don't try and tell me stuff you have no idea about."

Thus began a tense afternoon between us on my day off.

My growing distrust of others was not limited to the public. Within my first three years as a trooper, aside from having two classmates shot, two others were convicted and sentenced to prison for felony drug charges. One of them assisted suppliers transporting drugs along the interstate; the other made multiple drug sales to an undercover officer. At my initial barracks assignment, I encountered other misconduct. A senior trooper who came into work habitually drunk escaped from a detox facility where the union sent him. Two weeks later, he was back on patrol and still drinking. Another trooper, already a suspect in a Bronx armed robbery, lost his job for stealing money from motorists. A commercial burglary case I investigated led to a trooper in my squad being the chief suspect. I interviewed him while we worked a day shift together. He initially thought I was joking, but when he realized I was serious, he stopped talking to me. Years later, he was convicted and subsequently fired for involvement in a ticket-fixing scam for pay. And then another trooper, who patrolled with me on several midnight shifts, lost his job after an arrest for possession of crack cocaine. These unsavory elements of the job were not discussed at the academy. As bad it was to learn of police officers committing crimes like burglary or robbery, what distressed me more was the fact that co-workers could be drunk or high while on-duty. On midnight shifts we paired up on patrol and they were the people I had to rely on.

Occasional gratuitous beatings of arrestees, mostly initiated when someone talked back to a trooper, also took place. One morning while entering the station to change for work, a senior trooper from the previous shift handed me blood-stained paperwork on an arrestee he had handcuffed in the squad room. "Here you go, the arrest is yours, I'm going off duty," he said. The arrestee, a frequent flyer at the station, had bruises on his face and lips and the early colorings of two black eyes. His prior multiple arrests for assault, drugs, weapons, and disorderly conduct were remarkable considering he was only twenty-one years old. The senior trooper became upset when I turned down the arrest.

"What's wrong, are my arrests no good for you?" he hissed as he puffed out his chest and moved toward me.

"I don't need the activity. My numbers are already high for the month," I replied while bracing for a confrontation.

He backed down, seeming to accept the explanation, and completed the arrest paperwork. Before leaving, he warned the arrestee against lodging a complaint for his injuries, gave him a desk appearance ticket, and asked me to drive him home. Later, in the car, the arrestee, normally a talkative type, sat quietly until I began to pull out of the station parking lot.

"Where are we going?" he asked.

"I'm taking you home."

He paused as he considered his next words.

"You're not going to beat me too?" he asked with a bit of surprise.

"No, I'm taking you home. Just don't give me a hard time and in the future wise up." For the rest of the ride, he said nothing.

*

My first station assignment was like the Wild West. A hard-drinking core of older troopers, some Vietnam vets, and others from the neighborhoods of the Bronx, Queens, and Brooklyn who wanted to escape the city, only to return later in their careers to work drug, counterterrorism, or organized crime cases, made up the duty rosters. There were bar fights, foot pursuits, lots of domestic violence calls, and drug arrests. Car chases were plentiful too, with wrecked marked units and fleeing vehicles meeting in bent metal and bloodied suspects, some injured from the crashes, others from the beatings troopers inflicted upon them. One chase during the early part of a midnight shift began with a car stop on a main road in a municipality we patrolled. The driver pulled off as soon as we approached, nearly sideswiping my partner and running over his feet. The chase soon went the wrong way onto a short stretch of parkway running through the city and abruptly ended when the driver crashed into another car. Luckily the other driver wasn't injured, but our suspect's car leaked gas and sparks flickered from severed wiring. He violently resisted and fought with us as we pulled him from his potentially flammable vehicle. Our ride to the station soon became nastier than the belligerence he previously displayed. "What the fuck is that smell?" My partner turned to me as he continued, "It's like dead ass." I didn't know what it was but let down the window for some night air. Then, looking up at the rear view mirror, my partner said, "Oh no, you didn't!" From the backseat, the arrestee calmly replied, "Yeah, I shit myself."

There were also occasional wrestling matches with suspects while driving them to the station. One individual I arrested, who, despite being cuffed behind his back and belted into his seat, got his legs up and futilely tried to kick out the front window of the car. On a different occasion, another arrestee, a large boisterous individual whom I had handcuffed minutes earlier, went berserk in the car and banged his head against the dashboard and passenger door window, then crashed into me to force me off the road. I wrestled him with one hand while steering with the other until reaching the station. As soon as we got there, he calmed down because he realized where he was. The station had a reputation, and arrestees usually behaved once inside.

The patrol area was physical. Locals liked to make their mark by fighting a trooper. They challenged you, and force had to be used. I accepted the need to use reasonable force when necessary and did so on many occasions. However, the beatings other troopers sometimes inflicted on arrestees were neither necessary nor lawful. I couldn't tell anyone other than Joan. Notifying a commissioned officer in the troop or internal affairs would label me a rat. In policing, this was a fate worse than death.

I quickly identified troopers to avoid working with and, as added protection, rarely socialized with anyone outside of work. Joan knew my discomfort and how it affected me. She felt helpless. All she could do was listen and try to understand the added pressures these situations brought.

We had other, more immediate concerns. As young parents, we balanced the responsibilities of two toddlers, a move from our small co-op apartment to a bigger one with increased mortgage payments, along with law school tuition, coursework, and class scheduling. She knew my stress over everything going on at the station; meanwhile, she contended with stress of her own as a young mom. Whatever happened at work, I tried to handle and keep her worries to a minimum, despite my increasing difficulty separating myself from work at the end of the day.

The need to transfer out of the station became apparent when I had been there for over two years and realized the place was headed for serious future problems. I didn't want to be around if that happened. The commander of a station on the other side of the county offered me an open slot, and I took it.

Because of law school, at the new station I continued working either day or midnight shifts during the fall and spring semesters. The sergeants accommodated my schedule requests. They did so because I produced good numbers—DWIs, tickets, and arrests—rather than their benevolent view toward my studies. While the days could be busy, the 3:00 p.m. to 11:00 p.m. and 11:00 p.m. to 7:00 a.m. shifts promised the most unusual activity. Since transferring to the new station, I mostly partnered on the overnight shifts with my academy classmate Gio. The station commander liked pairing us together because we produced numbers and didn't shirk any calls. Ironically, as busy and rowdy as the patrol area had been at my first station, Joan came closest to losing me in two separate incidents during overnight shifts on the other side of the county.

*

"You could've shot him. You know that, right?"

I hesitated, still amped from the early morning incident, before answering the sergeant.

"It would've been a good shoot," he continued. "Why didn't you?"

The sergeant's eyes focused on me like two searchlights looking for a lost boat at sea.

"There wasn't an immediate threat," I finally said, feeling like I'd fucked up and done something wrong. During my background investigation, a lieutenant asked whether any moral or religious reservations prevented me from using deadly force if the situation required. I immediately and confidently replied, "No."

The magnitude of the question though isn't apparent until you're pointing a gun at another human being. "He had guns," the sergeant pressed on. "I didn't know at the time," I sheepishly replied.

It had been a busy night for Gio and me, with two DWI arrests, a drug arrest, a bar fight, and a domestic dispute, mixed in with a prowler call, an attempted car larceny, and a minor car accident. Late in the shift, a bit after 4:00 a.m., we attempted to stop a car for speeding in a commercial part of town. The driver didn't pull over, and we followed him for a half mile until Gio passed and cut off the gray Jeep Wrangler. Our marked unit sat sideways in the road. I exited the passenger side with my flashlight ready to illuminate the Jeep. As I held up my hand for the driver to stay put and began my walk up, he placed the Jeep in gear and sped forward, forcing me to jump on the trunk of the troop car to avoid being hit. The Jeep veered onto the narrow shoulder and continued down the road. Another chase ensued, this time toward the Connecticut state line.

Less than a quarter mile into Connecticut, Gio again accelerated ahead of the Jeep and cut it off, placing our marked unit across the roadway. The Jeep stopped at an angle in the driving lane. I sprang from the troop car, gun drawn, and shouted at the driver, "Show your hands! Show your fucking hands!" The driver had a faraway, unconnected expression. He rolled down his window. "Hold on . . . have to get something," he said and abruptly turned to his right. I began a short sprint to the car with my gun pointed at the driver's head. "Show your fucking hands, goddammit. Show your hands." "Wait, wait, there's a . . ." The driver didn't finish because I'd opened the door, grabbed him by the collar with my free hand, and tossed him to the ground. Something banged against the steering wheel and then fell with a thud onto the seat. "Don't move. Stay face down," I said while holstering my gun. Gio stood to my left with his gun pointed at the suspect. I handcuffed him and went back to the Jeep. On the passenger seat was a loaded Remington sawed-off shotgun. A loaded 9mm Smith & Wesson handgun rested on the driver's seat.

I turned toward the suspect, knelt beside him, and grabbed his collar. "What the fuck were you planning to do with those guns." He looked at me and smiled.

"You motherfucker!" I released his collar and walked away while Gio called in the arrest.

Since we were in Connecticut, we turned over the arrest for weapons possession to their responding State Police unit. He'd have to be extradited for the charges in New York, which included attempted vehicular assault and failure to comply.

"It's best you handled it the way you did," the sergeant relented. "The paperwork and investigation of a shooting would've kept us all here until late afternoon." The driver, now Connecticut's problem, faced two counts of weapon possession there. My station's duty BCI investigator who caught the case, Matt Doyle, downplayed the attempted felony assault charge in New York.

"You had no injuries, and it'd be a pain in the ass to file the extradition paperwork," he said.

"The guy lives in New York, though."

"He'll get more on the gun charges in Connecticut," Doyle insisted. I soon realized the reason for his hesitancy: Doyle was studying for the lieutenant's test and couldn't be bothered. It gave me an early glimpse of the complacency of rank. Doyle had the final say even though I'd been the one in danger. Years later, I would witness another example of Doyle's complacency when, as a major and troop commander, he took a lax attitude toward corruption. Policing to people like him was a corporate ladder climb. Corruption issues tended to interfere with promotion and always ended up too messy. All I ever found out about the guy who tried to run me down and then reach for a gun to do God knows what with it was that he faced a two-year minimum in a Connecticut prison.

The other incident, several months later, happened on Halloween night. Gio and I investigated a one-car accident on the northbound interstate. We had to cover the interstate post as well as calls for two municipalities because two troopers called in sick. When we arrived at the accident scene, a slim, older gentleman stood at the rear of a limousine in the northbound lane. The left front tire was wedged into the mangled guardrail and its concrete mooring. On his way home from an evening drop-off, the intoxicated limo driver fell asleep, struck the center median's embankment, bounced off, and then plowed into the guardrail.

We stood with the driver behind the limo in the left northbound lane. I turned toward the troop car to run a registration and license check as Gio and the driver stepped ahead of me toward the guardrail. It was close to 4:00 a.m., and the interstate had minimal traffic. The few cars passing us northbound stayed to the right upon seeing our patrol car's flashing roof lights.

Bare seconds after the three of us moved, a thundering bang followed by a shower of glass, plastic, and metal spreading across the hood and roof of the troop car startled us. A Chevrolet Caprice drove past me, narrowly missing our car after hitting the limo. The Caprice continued southbound in the northbound lane with its lights off. I ran to the troop car, put it in reverse, then made a half turn into the middle lane of the interstate. Gio jumped into the passenger side. I pointed to the limo driver and told him to stand by the guardrail. We chased the Caprice southbound, hoping no cars would come north.

A mile down the interstate, the car pulled into a cut-off separating the north and southbound lanes. The driver, dressed in a zombie costume, asked if anything was wrong, oblivious to the fact he had struck another car while driving in the wrong direction. Drunk and under the influence of drugs, the driver told us he was the lead singer in a band and was returning home from a gig in Danbury, Connecticut. We arrested him and left his car in the pull-off for a tow truck to pick up.

Upon our return, the limo driver dutifully sat along the highway median at the original accident scene. While waiting for the limo's tow off the interstate, I asked our wrong-way arrestee the name of his band. "The Boneheads." During our ride to the barracks, he provided unsolicited samples of his evening's song list. His full rendition of each verse of "Rose Tint My World" from the Rocky Horror Picture Show caused Gio to explode.

"Stop the fucking car! I'm gonna beat the shit out of this guy."

Gio had been quietly seething until this point, trying to keep his rage under control. I could always tell when he got wound up. His face contorted around his lips, and the muscles along his jawline protruded like a blowfish.

"Now the only thing that gives me hope / is my love of a certain dope / Rose tints my world, keeps me safe from my trouble and pain," our Caprice driver crooned from the back seat. His fellow passenger slept and snored through the show.

"Shut the fuck up, asshole. I swear, I'm going to break every bone in your dumb face if you don't shut up," Gio screamed at him.

The Caprice driver continued singing as if performing a set on stage. Gio screamed louder at him.

"Relax," I said, between laughter.

"You think this is funny? This prick nearly killed us." I could barely contain myself. "No, but this is a good song."

Gio then likely wanted to hit me more than the singer. I checked intermittently to my side until Gio's jawline eased up and a slight smile broke from the corner of his mouth.

"He ain't got a half bad voice."

The remaining few minutes of the ride, we listened to more verses and then the beginning chorus of "Monster Mash." Our singer had no idea how close he came to killing three people.

The incident shook me. We booked both arrestees, got them rides home, and impounded the vehicles. When morning sunlight broke through the station's front window, I grabbed the state and national flags and stepped into the crisp morning air. Posting the flags was normally the desk trooper's duty, but I needed a diversion and time alone. My hands trembled when hooking the flags to the eyelets and hoisting them up the poles. Every morning at the academy, after marching drill, we raised the flags before chow. The difference this morning was that I'd had my second incident in a short span of time wherein I nearly didn't make it to the end of a shift. On my ride home, I debated whether to tell Joan what happened. I decided to wait and sleep on it. There would be plenty of time later in the afternoon while Brian and Siobhan napped, and I had time to think over what to tell her.

Two months later, to celebrate New Year's Eve, we had tickets to see a Billy Joel concert at Nassau Coliseum on Long Island. Joan's parents stayed over to babysit Brian and Siobhan. Joan, overcome with a crippling fear something bad would happen to us, no longer wanted to attend the concert. "It's raining too heavily. All the crazies are on the road tonight." I had never seen her so scared. She insisted we stay home. "You know how it is out there. It's not safe." Even though we'd be with my brother Jim and his two friends, it took over an hour to convince her to go. I didn't realize at the time how my work also impacted her. She had absorbed a lot in the past few months and hit a breaking point. The separation between work and home life had narrowed. In the coming year, the gap closed further.

5
MOBBED-UP

On Valentine's Day 1990, seven months after the car chase and gun arrest, and less than four months after nearly getting run down on the interstate, the station commander called my home around dinnertime while I was at school and told Joan I was promoted to investigator. My four years of aggressive patrol activity had paid off. The new assignment to the Special Investigations Unit (SIU) meant that either drug or organized crime cases awaited me. A year and a half of law school remained. Later that night, after I slogged through a grueling Evidence Law lecture, we discussed whether I should take the promotion or remain in uniform while completing law school. The promotion included a pay raise and an assigned unmarked car. The decision came down to finances—we needed the bi-weekly raise and the money from selling our second car since I'd be driving an unmarked "company car." I had also wanted the promotion to the rank of investigator in the Bureau of Criminal Investigation and worked hard for it since day one.

Even though Joan supported my decision to accept the promotion and the added income it brought, she was apprehensive about the new assignment and schedule, taking me into New York City at all hours. She had good cause. Already, less than seventy-two hours into my new rank, a shotgun and a .357 magnum revolver were pointed at me and another investigator while on an overnight surveillance in the Catskill area. We had information about three Gambino crime family associates from Yonkers who planned to rob a drug dealer. Danny Galvin, an investigator slated to be promoted to lieutenant, and I teamed up in one of four surveillance cars.

We parked alongside a closed commercial building and sat in the dark, watching and waiting. Ten minutes into the surveillance, two men stood by the side of Galvin's door. The older one, a large man in denim overalls with a white mustache and scraggly beard, knocked against the window. He held the .357 magnum, alternately pointing it at Galvin and me. The other, his son, a stocky male with a Dutch-boy haircut and uneven whiskers along the sides of his face, stood behind the driver's side rear door with the shotgun aimed into our car. Galvin jumped when he heard the knock and opened his window. My gun was out by my side, finger on the trigger. Tense seconds followed until the older man lowered his weapon, relieved that we were police and not one of the local drug addicts breaking into his shop.

When nothing materialized from the surveillance, I returned home in time for a Saturday morning trip to the local mall with Joan, who knelt in our bedroom putting pants on Brian as Siobhan sat on the floor playing with a doll. Brian turned four in a few days, and she wanted to get portrait photos of him and Siobhan at Sears.

"You're home sooner than expected. How did it go?"

"Boring. Nothing much happened."

"Good. Now your first week in the BCI is done." She smiled at me, puckered her lips into an air kiss, and pulled Brian to a standing position. "Let Daddy see how good those pants look on you." Two days later, somber news added to Joan's apprehension over my new assignment.

On Monday, March 5, during a drug buy-bust operation on the Lower East Side of Manhattan, Investigator Joseph Aversa lost his life in a gunfight with two drug dealers who attempted to rob another undercover State Police investigator posing as a drug buyer. The gunfight also wounded two NYPD officers. An investigation later revealed Aversa died from "friendly fire." A bullet from an NYPD officer's gun struck him in the head. Aversa had been in the BCI for only six months, promoted on the list before mine.

The Manhattan skyline was to my left, across the East River, as I drove over the Whitestone Bridge from Queens at the end of my shift while listening to the police radio chatter that Aversa had been killed a half hour earlier. I'd spent the day on the streets in Ozone Park and then Canarsie with my new unit, getting acclimated to people and locations involved in an investigation. Upon hearing the report of the shooting, I wanted to drive into Manhattan and see what assistance was needed, if any. I didn't know what to do. Should I head west on the Cross-Bronx Expressway and into Manhattan, or continue home? I reached out to my new partner Smitty on the car-to-car channel.

"Do we go?"

"No, it's gonna be a cluster-fuck. They'll have what they need with NYPD and the guys in his unit."

"What about the shooters?"

"Two in custody. Head home."

Immediately, Joan came to mind. She'd be getting dinner ready for Brian and Siobhan, but if she listened to the news, I didn't want her to hear unconfirmed reports of a State Police investigator shot and killed somewhere in New York City. She'd already gone through an unnecessary scare a few years earlier when

Trooper Dunning was shot. My father heard the news report on his way to work and called our home to speak to me.

"He's at work," Joan said.

"Oh, Jesus!"

"What's wrong?"

"Someone shot and killed a trooper from Troop K. His last name began with a D."

My father had to catch a train, said he'd check in later, and abruptly ended the call, leaving Joan to wonder and worry until she heard a radio news report identifying the trooper and outlining the events from the night before.

I drove to the first exit on the Bronx side of the bridge and found a payphone. When Joan answered, Siobhan cried in the background, and Brian began asking a rapid succession of questions—"What's for dinner?" "Who's on the phone?" "Is Tiny Toons on?" "Do you have any snacks?"

"Hi . . . hold on . . . Brian, no . . . it's Dad." Joan sounded frazzled. "Sorry . . . it's been a day."

"No worries . . . on my way home."

"Okay. Anything else?"

"No, just wanted you to know. See you within the hour."

We said our goodbyes with the rote "love you" and, before hanging up, she asked me to pick up a gallon of milk and diapers.

*

"Kid, I had two years on the job when you were born." These first words from my new supervisor, Senior Investigator Gene "Doc" Loughran, greeted me a week earlier when I reported to his office. Doc reviewed my personnel folder for a few more seconds before closing it and welcoming me to the Construction Industry Strike Force, a small five-person unit working cases for the statewide Organized Crime Task Force.

"Nothing would get built in this city if not for the mob," Doc told me. This was my first lesson on organized crime influence in New York City's construction industry. Doc's insight not only summed up the reason for the high cost of construction but also the mob tax exacted on other industries: garbage hauling, the painter's union, the Teamsters, and the Longshoremen's Union. Money changed hands, and things got done. Otherwise, people got hurt. I saw the latter result shortly into my new assignment when interviewing a construction site foreman who refused organized crime entreaties for a cut of the action in the form of "no-show" jobs. Smitty and I stood on a street in College Point, Queens across from LaGuardia Airport listening to the foreman. A few days earlier, two men with baseball bats attacked him not far from where we stood. They pounded the back of one leg repeatedly and broke the tibia in the other. The foreman, a ruddy-faced, second-generation Irishman living in the borough, refused to cooperate beyond showing us his wounds.

"See these gray hairs," he said while leaning forward and moving his right hand across his scalp. A shaved patch of skin and several stitches from the attack carved a valley among his thick light-gray hair.

"I lost any scrap of original color I had left these past few weeks dealing with those guys. I ain't looking to accelerate the process anymore. I plan on another thirty-five years or more before dying from natural causes." We left the interview realizing we were as unwelcome as the mob goons who attacked him.

Housed in the same third-floor offices as our strike force unit, detectives from the NYPD Organized Crime Control Bureau (OCCB) shared copiers, a supply closet, and a kitchen with us. They were led by an experienced lieutenant, Dan Edmunds. He had been an OCCB detective until he became a sergeant working elsewhere in the city before transferring back.

"Don't trust precinct cops in mobbed-up neighborhoods. Never tell them what you're working on," Edmunds told me at our first meeting a day after Aversa's burial. I had attended the funeral with several hundred other police officers from the State Police, NYPD, and departments across the country.

"You don't know who's getting paid off," he continued. This sobering assessment of the job and those entrusted with public safety made me wonder who could be trusted.

Some days I worked in the Bronx and Queens, others in East Harlem, tracking and surveilling organized crime members or wiring up informants to send into locations for meetings with case targets. We traveled in a shadowy world, and our job was to lurk in those shadows and pick up whatever information we could use in later prosecutions.

I quickly adapted to working in the unit and stayed busy. Meanwhile, the spring semester of my third year of law school at night wound down. Doc, who never scheduled me for evening assignments on class nights, often offered blunt advice on what I should do after graduation: "Leave this fucking job and make some real money." I'd heard the same advice from others. At the time, though, all I wanted was to get through my final year and pass the bar exam.

I again faced down guns pointed at me and my partner, this time two months after the Catskill encounter and while with Smitty on surveillance of a Mafia hangout in Yonkers. Local cops mistook us for a robbery crew, at least that's what they initially claimed. Multiple cops surrounded our unmarked car simultaneously yelling for us to show our hands and threatening to blow our heads off. Smitty cursed under his breath, "Pieces of shit got to be on the local mob payroll." We both sat in the front car seat with our hands up and our shields visible on beaded chains around our necks, sweating out the seconds until the cops lowered their weapons. An unpleasant exchange followed between us and the responding cops. It became clear that the purpose behind their show of force had nothing to do with community safety or police work. A marked police unit followed us out of the area until we drove onto the nearby parkway.

In late June, I received orders to report to the office of Senior Investigator Mark Defriest in lower Manhattan. Defriest, supervisor of the Labor Racketeering Unit (LRU), a hand-picked group working on organized crime cases for the Manhattan District Attorney's Office, had been an investigator at my first station assignment years earlier. We met at 349 Broadway on a Friday afternoon in a small fifth-floor office overlooking Leonard Street.

After wrapping up a two-year investigation into the Gambino crime family and their influence in the NYC garment industry, Defriest's unit moved on to an investigation of Mafia control at the Javits Center, the large convention hall in the Hell's Kitchen area of Manhattan. The State Police undercover from the Gambino case, Juan Jiminez, moved from his position as the "owner" of a small garment sewing shop in Chinatown to a non-union job in the Javits Center. Defriest also had an informant, Robbie, in the Teamsters. A month into the investigation, the bad guys became aware that an informant and a State Police undercover worked alongside them. They tried to ferret out the snitch and the cop. Defriest immediately pulled Jiminez from his undercover role, and the informant left a week later under the guise of going to drug rehab. The story captivated me, but it had no relevance to my work with Doc's unit.

"We have a leak. Someone gave up our investigation and we need to find out who," Defriest told me. Horns honking on the street below, whistles from traffic agents along Broadway, and intermittent distant sirens punctuated the brief silence between us.

"The problem we have is that it's pretty clear the info came from someone on the job . . . our job."

"The State Police?" The crack in my voice betrayed my surprise. Defriest then revealed another facet to the story involving a former high-ranking State Police officer who worked in the Javits Center. James Tansey had been the major in charge of the State Police Manhattan headquarters until his promotion to inspector and assignment to Internal Affairs in Albany. He was later arrested for immigration fraud and served federal time. Tansey had made fake birth and baptism certificates for undocumented Irish immigrants and sold them to a bar owner in Manhattan who in turn sold them to immigrants seeking naturalization. According to the federal government, Tansey made $20,000 to $45,000 orchestrating this fraud while serving as a State Police major. In prison, he befriended a few unsavory individuals, and when released, he rejoined them. At Javits, Tansey was the suspected conduit of the leak. Defriest wanted the source.

"You're assigned to me temporarily to investigate who on our job passed along the info." My mouth went dry for a moment. "Why me?" Defriest said he remembered me as an honest, hard-working trooper, and most importantly, as someone who had no connections or strong loyalties to any State Police bosses in Albany. I appreciated his confidence and trust in me, but the overriding reason he chose me had been that headquarters turned down his choices for a more experienced investigator. When Defriest sent my name to Albany it was already after being denied a lieutenant with an impressive investigative resume and Defriest's former BCI partner, who also had established investigative bona fides. Instead, he got me, a new investigator with just over three months in the BCI and less than five years on the job.

Defriest introduced me to Alexander Dragos, another LRU investigator. He would assist me but wouldn't have access to all the case information. "Only five people in the State Police know about this investigation: the three of us, the Superintendent, and the First Deputy Superintendent," Defriest explained. "From here on, all info about the investigation is tightly controlled. You report directly to me." The situation overwhelmed me.

"One more thing," Defriest said. "And this comes directly from the Superintendent. You can't tell anyone what you're working on. Not even your wife or family. We can't risk idle chatter at a party or anywhere else leading to anyone finding out what we're doing." This last order surprised me. Joan and I didn't socialize with job people, and whenever we did have an opportunity to spend an evening without the children we wanted it to be just us. So, who were we going to tell? Still, due to the nature of the investigation, the Superintendent had his reasons for the order.

I left the lower Manhattan LRU office and spent an hour in Friday afternoon traffic trying to escape the city. It gave me time to think and worry. What in God's name did I get drafted into?

The following ten months led me down paths I never wanted to travel on the job, investigating other cops and keeping secrets from Joan. She knew I was on a special assignment, nothing more. Brian and Siobhan kept her busy and distracted at home, while I was mired in State Police intrigue. As the case wore on, I ached for more time with the three of them. Weekend mornings were my favorite when the kids came into our room and snuggled under the covers with us as we tried to catch a few more minutes of sleep. If we were lucky, they'd both fall asleep between us for another half hour. We'd often end up looking across the bed at each other, smiling, with our arms outstretched across Brian and Siobhan's backs, and our fingers gently caressing each other's shoulders. These moments were when I understood the meaning of love and family. The reality of the job, though, always came back like a two-by-four to the face.

One afternoon Donnie Farrell, the senior guy and best cop in the unit, stopped by my desk. My head was buried in stacks of telephone records. He gave the desk two knocks with his right fist. "Brother, the sooner you realize the job ain't on the level, the better you'll be at it. Be mindful." Farrell then smoothed his Fu Manchu mustache, covered his mop of orange-blonde hair with a Panama hat, and strode out of the room. I thought about what Lieutenant Edmunds said a few months earlier about precinct cops.

I floundered in the new investigative assignment for months. When not reviewing phone records or doing background profiles on several suspects, I met with the assigned assistant district attorney, Laurence Heintz, to discuss case strategies. At first, I didn't like Heintz. He seemed typical of Ivy League-educated lawyers in the Manhattan District Attorney's Office. Heintz boasted Columbia University and Harvard Law School credentials. Lawyers like him used the prestige of the office as a stepping stone to either the US Attorney's Office, a powerful Manhattan law firm, or a position on the federal bench. Heintz stood at barely five feet six inches, wore round tortoiseshell glasses, and had a wave of thinning brown hair combed back to reveal a widow's peak. He always spoke with a schoolmaster's precise and deliberate tone. Heintz was the Organized Crime Unit bureau chief, an important step toward further promotion and financial reward. I viewed him as another highly intelligent and competent attorney in the office who tolerated police officers as a necessary bother. The latter assessment proved to be wrong. The more I worked with him and the deeper the case developed, Heintz became a trusted ally.

Months of surveillance, interviews, and poring through numerous telephone records, including internal State Police phone records, finally yielded results. The investigation uncovered a small network of retired State Police commissioned officers and active bosses still working in Albany, and their questionable relationships with criminals. The most startling find was three calls as part of a chain of calls from our internal affairs unit to a number and subscriber name which meant nothing to me until I looked at the address. My trust in the job suffered a near-fatal jolt.

The address belonged to a Bronx residence I had surveilled during my first two months working for Doc. Genovese soldier Ralph Coppola lived in a downstairs apartment of a house owned by his sister. Coppola, a feared mob enforcer, watched over crime family interests at the Javits Center.

"You're telling me, the day before the undercover and informant are exposed, there's a call from a State Police Internal Affairs phone in Albany to Tansey right before he places a call to the residence of a made member of the Genovese crime family?" Heintz was incredulous. Defriest sat across from Heintz's desk and buried his head in his hands. "This is not good . . . not good at all." I stood alongside Heintz as we looked over a horizontal chart outlining a network of calls. Both ends curled along the edges of his desk like mourning bunting. The calls I had traced to our Internal Affairs Unit went from a payphone near the Javits Center used by Tansey to Coppola's phone back to Tansey and then back to Internal Affairs. Two calls were placed before the undercover operation was exposed and one was afterward.

"I'm going to be sick," Defriest said.

"This is devastating news. We need to discuss how to handle it. And . . . quite frankly . . . whether you need protection." Heintz looked at me. Defriest and I exchanged a quick glance at each other. "This is serious business," Heintz said. "We have a major corruption issue."

"I don't think there's any danger here," Defriest countered. I added the same assurance. "I've got no concerns."

"Very well, you both know best," Heintz conceded. "Keep a sharp eye on things, though. I've been doing this long enough to have worries."

My investigation linked Tansey and Senior Investigator Vernon J. Smith, the person in charge of the State Police unit assigned to the Manhattan District Attorney's Office. A subsequent search of Smith's Long Island home yielded incriminating information relating to grand larceny, official misconduct, and sensitive protected government witness information he should not have possessed, including a witness in one of Heintz's cases who was moved out of state for protection.

Soon afterwards I was summoned to Albany. Ironically, the first trip was to explain the case to the chief inspector in charge of Internal Affairs; the second trip, a week later, was to sit before the chief inspector and one of his henchmen, Inspector T. William Muldoon, and listen to them deny any wrongdoing emanating from Albany headquarters.

Muldoon wore a thin mustache and smiled out of the corner of his mouth. He reminded me of the cartoon character Dick Dastardly. Muldoon had been the troop commander during my uniform days. Something about him never sat right, an opinion shared by other troopers I knew.

"How's law school going?" he asked me toward the end of our meeting.

"Fine, I'm almost done."

"Think you'll make it to the end without any problem?" His dark brown eyes hit me like daggers. The tone of his question indicated more to it than concern for my academic progress.

"Without a doubt," I said. One semester remained. For three and a half years, I worked day and midnight shifts to attend evening law school classes. Nothing was going to stop me, least of all people like him.

I arrived home from Albany disgusted by my trip and told Joan everything about the past ten months and Muldoon's sinister comment. "All the more reason for you to leave once you've passed the bar exam." Her reasoning was unassailable. I was a wounded animal seeking shelter. Joan and the children, my only haven, needed me at home. And I needed them because outside our home, the world made less sense to me.

Smith retired from the State Police the week after we searched his house and found incriminating evidence. A Manhattan grand jury indicted him for official misconduct, scheme to defraud, and grand larceny. The grand jury also indicted Tansey, and both surrendered to the district attorney's office with their lawyers in March, shortly after I completed my first year in the BCI. Both faced a minimum of four years in state prison. My first grand jury testimony and arrests as an investigator didn't involve mob guys, but rather two former State Police members. Smith pleaded guilty, but not before a suicide attempt on the eve of meeting Heinz as part of a cooperation agreement. After release from the hospital, he declined to cooperate and took his chances upon sentencing. Tansey went to trial and beat the rap. Robbie, our informant, was in jail on a robbery charge, and his addled brain from years of snorting coke made his testimony shaky. Despite my suspicions of who in Albany headquarters leaked the information to Tansey, there was never enough for an arrest. I went off to lick my wounds and spent every spare summer moment studying for the state bar exam in August. I wanted to pass on the first try. Afterwards, I'd decide on my future. Joan made sure my studying was undisturbed. She wanted me to pass the exam and leave the job. The investigation into the Javits Center—what Defriest labeled as the Leak Investigation—made me question my career choice. The corruption I had encountered up to then involved individual police officers who made a choice to violate the law. The Leak Investigation showed me that the worst kind of corruption runs deeper than a single officer.

In October 1991, a letter informed me I passed the Connecticut bar exam. A month later, New York's notice came. My Connecticut bar admission ceremony occurred on a cold December morning in Norwalk with Joan, Brian, and Siobhan present. Two months later, in a Brooklyn courtroom, I took my New York oath as an attorney. Defriest let me skip out of work for two hours to attend the ceremony. I changed into a suit, walked to the train station at City Hall, and hopped on the shuttle over to Brooklyn. Four years of law school at night while balancing life as a police officer, husband, and father culminated in a solitary train ride back from the Brooklyn courthouse. As a newly licensed attorney in two states, I still had no idea if practicing law full time appealed to me. My desire to continue working as a police officer also lost some of its appeal. I had a decision to make. Deep down, I knew I'd be breaking my promise to Joan.

6
FUNHOUSE MIRRORS

Police corruption is often handled by ignoring it. My experience was that those in charge will not act unless they have solid assurances of corroboration. Otherwise, a response involves either tangling with unions, drawing attention to problems that may delay promotions, or undertaking the tedious and unpleasant work of investigating malfeasance. Better to sidestep and sweep the problem under the rug. However, when crooked cops are arrested and there's a press conference, everyone wants credit. Bosses line up to thump their chests with righteous indignation and announce their role in locking up bad cops. The tried-and-true myth presented to the public is that only a few bad apples are responsible for corruption; there's never a systemic issue. Most of the time, corruption is either stumbled upon or an investigation begins because public pressure forces police commanders and politicians to acknowledge its existence. When a dirty cop is arrested, bosses stand at press conferences with a "tsk-tsk" look on their faces while shaking their heads in unison and assuring the public how vigilant they were in rooting out corruption at all levels, even when it occurs in-house. It is all bullshit. The Leak Investigation left me embittered and disillusioned. The only bright spot came when Defriest offered me a permanent spot in his unit working high-profile organized crime cases. Over the next few years, we investigated the Bonanno, Lucchese, and Genovese organized crime families, Russian organized crime, and, with the FBI, corruption in the NYC Transit Police Benevolent Association.

After five and a half years of this, I decided to transfer out of the Labor Racketeering Unit to be closer to home. Brian was nine, Siobhan seven, and Deirdre turned two. She perfectly completed our little family. Joan's pregnancy and Deirdre's birth coincided with my involvement in a lengthy Bonanno crime family investigation that had me working afternoon and overnight shifts in Manhattan, Queens, and Brooklyn. The time spent working out of the lower Manhattan office made me realize I needed to be with my family more. My hour-long commute when living in mid-Westchester County increased by another hour when we purchased a house two counties north. The distance and time away from the family grated on me. I had already turned down an offer from the Superintendent of State Police to join the Division Counsel's office as an Assistant Counsel. Even though it meant a big pay increase and the non-civil service rank of captain, it'd be in Albany, an equally long commute north. More significantly, I wouldn't be investigating crimes anymore.

*

Midway through my fourth year in the Labor Racketeering Unit, Defriest left us to take charge of an elite statewide detail of troopers and investigators. I then became the interim unit supervisor, a step toward promotion to senior investigator. The promotion would keep me in Manhattan for another two to three years, maybe longer, and I didn't want to wait. Plus, I didn't want the responsibility for a bunch of grown men until they got home. If one of them crashed his troop car, I'd have to drive to the scene or get a supervisor from another station to cover. Our unit had guys all over the place. They came from Long Island, Staten Island, Brooklyn, Westchester, and points further north.

One evening, such a call came from Angelo Abruzzi, an investigator with a drinking problem. He crashed his unmarked car into a concrete abutment while traveling home to Staten Island. It was 11:30 p.m. I'd just finished putting Deirdre, our night owl, to bed.

"Hey, it's Abruzzi," he slurred.

The smell of booze seemingly came through the phone.

"I had a File 3."

File 3 signified an accident or any noteworthy event sent out through the New York Statewide Police Information Network (NYSPIN).

"Where?"

"On the Verrazano Bridge."

"Any one injured?"

An injury meant the accident had to be reported.

"Only my car," he half-laughed at his joke.

I had a pen and pad ready to take notes and asked what happened.

"A deer jumped in front of me."

"On the fuckin' Verrazano Bridge?" I snapped back.

Abruzzi bounced from one New York City unit to another. He had been a ballsy undercover investigator making drug buys and infiltrating Dominican drug groups when cocaine flowed through Washington Heights in upper Manhattan like Christmas snow. There's a short shelf life to the type of undercover work he did, and it caught up to him. Abruzzi arrived at our unit as a temporary assignment when we needed more bodies to monitor the wire on an investigation. He was a forty-year-old infant we all babysat to ensure he correctly recorded calls from the wire.

"Well, it happened right before the bridge, not on the bridge per se," he countered.

"A goddam deer?"

"Yeah. A buck, possibly. They got horns right?"

"In fuckin' Brooklyn?" The incredulity in my voice spiked.

"Helluva thing, ain't it?" he slurred.

I spoke with one of the NYPD patrol officers on the scene. He had better things to do than lock up Abruzzi for DWI. His partner drove Abruzzi's car off the bridge approach and parked it along Fort Hamilton Parkway. They took him to the 68th precinct to sober up. Doug Mirabelli, one of our undercovers who lived near the precinct, picked up Abruzzi and drove him home. The next morning, Mirabelli took Abruzzi's car to a local police-friendly body shop to have the headlight replaced and the front right fender straightened and buffed. It'd cost Abruzzi $200 and two bottles of whiskey—a minor expense that prevented him from being jammed up. It also saved me from a File 3 investigation.

Abruzzi needed alcohol counseling. Not reporting his accident only delayed worse problems for him later. The learned code from the academy and field training required me to take care of other troopers, even a fuck-up like him, otherwise I'd be a rat. We had a talk though. If he got drunk behind the wheel again on my watch, the ensuing investigation would end his career. The threat helped me justify my perpetuation of the funhouse mirror effect common to policing. We ask the public to ignore our flaws as we sweep them aside and proceed to judge their conduct. Our collective posturing knew no limits.

Individuals like Abruzzi were the exception in the unit. The core was otherwise solid. We'd been through a lot together over the years and stuck by each other. Defriest had built a stellar unit, and, prior to his transfer, he kept us busy, as did Manhattan District Attorney Robert Morgenthau. We investigated complex, lengthy, and media-generating cases prosecuted by political stars on the rise.

The Manhattan District Attorney's Office had no shortage of talented and connected young lawyers. They mostly came from top-tier law schools, and some from well-heeled families. Eliot Spitzer, the future New York attorney general and later governor, fit the Ivy League, life of privilege mold that several of his colleagues shared. A position with the Manhattan District Attorney's Office served as a golden gateway for future private sector or political ambitions, but the competition was tough, and family fame and fortune sometimes topped brains, talent, and hard work. John F. Kennedy Jr. was a perfect example. No one made a bigger news splash after joining the office than the only son of our thirty-fifth president.

I first met Kennedy at a December holiday party Spitzer threw at his Manhattan condo. Spitzer invited our unit along with his colleagues from the district attorney's office. Kennedy arrived at the party with a gorgeous blonde model. He seemed uncomfortable in the crowded gathering and at one point slipped off, leaving his date in conversation with several geeky male prosecutors. Dragos went out on the balcony to smoke a cigar, and I joined him to get air. Kennedy was already there, leaning against the rail and looking out at the city lights.

"Nice view, isn't it John," Dragos said as he lit the cigar. Kennedy smiled, then uttered the most words I'd heard him say while assigned to the DA's office: "Mild too for this time of year."

"We hear you'll be joining us in the Rackets Bureau." Dragos blew a puff of smoke out over the railing and watched it dissipate into the evening air.

"I will. Looking forward."

"Welcome," I said, lifting my beer. "Glad to have you join us."

Kennedy smiled again, then excused himself.

Dragos gave me a sidelong look. "Something I said?" Another puff of smoke wafted over the city street below.

The New York City press hounded Kennedy. Reported sightings, photos, and gossip about him underscored the intense public scrutiny he endured and his reticence to befriend people he didn't know. Everyone wanted a piece of him and a story to bring to the press. For someone always in the news, he didn't appear to actively pursue the publicity.

Spitzer, however, was a different story. He liked the limelight, and he was a brilliant attorney. I watched him prosecute Thomas and Joseph Gambino when Defriest assigned me to observe their trial and report on its progress. Spitzer's opening statement to the jury was, like anything he did, impassioned. Pointing to the defense table where the Gambino brothers sat with their defense attorneys, Spitzer stood and said, "These defendants have an awfully powerful partner. That partner is organized crime." The trim, athletic Spitzer then strode toward the defense table and, while in front of the two aristocratic-looking older defendants, said, "Theirs was a marriage of business and organized crime making millions of dollars each year. They wielded an iron fist inside a velvet glove." I've never seen an opening statement as compelling.

The Gambino brothers and their two co-defendants pled guilty mid-trial in exchange for the forfeiture of twelve million dollars to the government and the divestiture of Gambino interests in the trucking companies at the heart of the case. The indictment alleged, and the undercover operation and videos showed, the defendants ran a shakedown racket forcing garment center businesses to use mob trucking companies. District Attorney Morgenthau, with Spitzer by his side, told the gathered media that his office, in one fell swoop, dismantled garment industry Mafia control going back to the days of Arnold Rothstein, Legs Diamond, and Louis Lepke.

"Yes, we gave up jail time but saved a dying industry," Morgenthau said amid clicking camera shutters and the whir of video.

The Gambino brothers' extortion of the garment industry essentially ended with a hefty fine. Three years later, the pre-trial result of another mob-related investigation our unit worked on had a similar ending: the surrender of twenty-three million dollars and no jail time for any mobsters. The parallels between the money grabbed by the Mafia and the government in each case were unavoidable. It was a different kind of extortion implemented by a government agency exchanging no prison time for pleas with multi-million-dollar fines. Meanwhile, less powerful mom-and-pop business owner tax cheats went to prison. The illogic of these settlements confounded me. The defendants in both cases went on to other rackets and indictments in later prosecutions. With the punitive and removal effects of prison eliminated, the big money of corruption, fraud, and extortion remained too accessible for men like them to resist. The venality of the whole system and the bartering between prosecutor and high-profile perp over eight-figure fines versus prison irritated me and hastened my decision to leave LRU. My frustration with the result in the Leak Investigation and the job's complicity showed me that two sets of rules guided the criminal justice system and, depending on which side of the tracks you traveled, dictated how the system treated you. I didn't want to remain assigned to Manhattan dealing with the same frustrations for several more years. Returning to a troop assignment was best for me and my family. Joan agreed.

Other disturbing events during my time assigned to LRU made me consider whether I should forego the transfer, retire early, and practice law. An academy classmate and another investigator, who had been an instructor during our training session, were arrested for tampering with evidence. They both planted suspect fingerprints on items taken from crime scenes to solve cases. Their crimes were uncovered when my police academy classmate, in a CIA job interview, divulged what he had done to show he could conduct covert-style operations. This led to the biggest scandal in State Police history and prison sentences for both. Then, a sergeant and two troopers from my first assigned uniform station were arrested for covering up a crime committed by another police officer's brother. My waning faith in the incorruptibility of the criminal justice system and the integrity of the job kept being battered.

When I joined the State Police, I found a tribe. But my loyalty and belief in the job were continuously tested, and it wasn't only from what I saw within. Corruption rooted wherever it found fertile ground.

Between major investigations, our unit either tracked down fugitive felons or assisted other Manhattan District Attorney's office investigations. One of the latter involved a crackdown on illegal Joker Poker video games common to borough bodegas. Defriest agreed to assist the NYPD Public Morals Division. A new machine cost $2,500 yet recouped over $1,000 a week. The machines were rigged for higher payouts with less chance of winning. Machine owners, usually Bonanno and Lucchese crime family crews who forced bodega owners to install the video machines, preyed on neighborhood residents. When they won, residents were often denied payment and threatened.

Whenever we raided a bodega, cops carrying sledgehammers busted open the machines, which, along with the money inside, were secured as evidence. We entered with brute force, closed the bodega while searching, threatened to arrest anyone who interfered, and moved on to the next location. We were robbers sanctioned by the authority of the district attorney's office and the laws of asset forfeiture, which had become a popular prosecutorial tactic. Asset forfeiture theory sought to disincentivize the profit motives of organized criminal gangs by taking their money and property. In these cases, though, it seemed the only ones losing money were the local bodega owners who still had to pay the Mafia crews.

The last Joker Poker raid I went on ended my willingness to participate in any others. In a Washington Heights bodega, with three out of four machines busted open, I watched as two NYPD cops began stuffing cash from one of the machines into their jacket pockets.

"C'mon, get in on this," one of the cops said as he looked up at me and Lenny Swiderski, another State Police investigator. We both turned and walked out.

"Whatdya think?" Swiderski asked. He had a nervous tic in his right eye, and his head jerked whenever stressed.

"We stay out of there and distance ourselves."

Swiderski, an Army helicopter crew chief before joining the State Police, pulled out a stick of gum and began furiously chewing.

"Right. Mind our own business."

Roaches scampered out of the machines whenever they were cracked open. A swarm of them fled along the filthy floors behind freezers and food displays. When the NYPD officers grabbed cash out of the gutted machines, they shook roaches off the bills before stuffing their pockets. After we hit the last bodega, in another run-down, greasy-floored storefront, I clocked off-duty and drove to my in-law's house in Yonkers to meet Joan and the children for dinner. Upon arriving, I began to take off my clothes while waiting in the rear vestibule for Joan to bring me a towel. I didn't want to enter the house or go near my children in those clothes.

Joan stood at the lip of the vestibule with a towel for me.

"You look annoyed."

I turned toward the towel knot along my left hip and fumbled at it. I didn't want to give any sign of what troubled me.

"Every filthy bodega we hit today had swarms of roaches. I need a hot shower."

Joan took my clothes and put them in the wash while I dashed up to the bathroom. Soon hot shower water crashed against the back of my neck. For fifteen minutes, the forceful pulse of the water massaged my back, shoulders, and the base of my skull and head. The stink and stickiness of the bodegas washed off while what I witnessed other cops doing clung to me.

Several months earlier, when conducting a search at a mob member's house as part of another investigation, I found $25,000 in hundred-dollar bills rolled up in a boxed new pair of slippers in a bedroom closet. Joan and I were in the process of looking at houses and scraping together money for a down payment. I was alone. The thought of taking the money never crossed my mind. Instead, I called a supervisor so we could count the money, photograph it, and together sign the receipt. I'd been offered bribes while in uniform. One was from a biker with two prior felony convictions whom I'd arrested with two ounces of coke. He offered me $12,000 of drug money he carried. The other bribe offer of $4,000 came from a local drug dealer arrested for possession of cocaine and a gun. In each scenario, the arrest meant more to me than the money. I could sleep soundly after putting a criminal in handcuffs. More importantly, I could face Joan.

The corruption I witnessed while assigned to Manhattan troubled me, but the darkest moment occurred with the line of duty murder of Investigator Ricky J. Parisian from our Special Investigations Unit's White Plains office. He was shot and killed while intervening in a grocery store robbery. Our squad had assisted Parisian a few weeks earlier in a gambling raid in Rockland County. Parisian spent weekdays away from the upstate home he shared with his wife, Deb, to work drug cases in Queens. On his day off, he went shopping with her at an Oneonta supermarket. A masked gunman entered shortly thereafter and announced a robbery. As Deb evacuated customers through the store's rear door, Ricky attempted to disarm the fleeing gunman and died from a shotgun round to the chest.

We were assigned to assist with the murder investigation. I packed for several days away from home and, as the children slept, left in the dark to meet another investigator who lived nearby. Together we traversed back roads to Oneonta. For the next several days, over one-hundred State Police personnel worked eighteen -hour shifts. The killer, Colin Hyde, fled to Colorado where Denver police arrested him two days before Parisian's burial. Hyde waived an extradition hearing and promptly returned to New York escorted by a State Police fugitive team. Another investigator and I met them at Newburgh's Stewart Airport in the evening and brought Hyde back to Oneonta for a late-night arraignment and then remand to the Otsego County Jail without bail. The next morning, we assembled for the procession from the funeral home to the church, and then to the cemetery. Later in the afternoon, I arrived at a local baseball field back home to watch Brian play in a little league game. That night in bed, Joan cradled my head in her lap and placed a cool washcloth across my forehead. We talked until I fell asleep to the rhythmic rise and fall of her breathing.

Our unit didn't have much recovery time. We were called back to work two days later, Memorial Day weekend, with orders to report to State Police offices at Fort Schuyler in the Throggs Neck section of the Bronx. Two convicted murderers, one of them a former Mafia enforcer, escaped from the Mid-Hudson Psychiatric Facility in Middletown, a city in Orange County. They had ties to the Bronx and Brooklyn. The escapees, Herbert Arnold and John Casablanca, got hold of a gun, took a facility employee hostage, and escaped in his car.

Both were violent men originally found mentally incompetent to stand trial. Arnold had been charged with murder and other crimes and Casablanca, a reputed Mafia enforcer, killed two people while on parole for another murder. Again, over one-hundred State Police personnel were deployed, this time to join NYPD officers looking for the escapees. Over the next four days, I zigzagged between surveillances, interviews, and searches in the Bronx and Brooklyn. Finally, a disheveled and confused Casablanca surrendered to two beat cops in Brooklyn who stopped to write a parking ticket. Arnold was found three hours later wandering the same precinct with the gun used in the escape and $11.86 in his pocket. The search and capture of the escapees ended a week that started with Parisian's murder.

The search for the escapees hadn't been without side drama. The employee they took hostage was a retired State Police lieutenant, my uniform zone commander several years back, who left the job under dubious circumstances. The escapee's gun was a missing State Police-issued .357 magnum belonging to one of my academy classmates who claimed the lieutenant stole it from his station locker shortly after an inspection. The bosses didn't believe him and eventually forced him off the job. My classmate, fed up with New York, moved south, went to law school, and became a successful criminal defense attorney. This was another example of the way policing tended to view things through funhouse mirrors—a good trooper was sacrificed because it was believed there was no way a lieutenant would do such a thing. Within five months of that case, Defriest was gone.

My decision to transfer closer to home wasn't without hesitation and regret. Defriest had left me as his heir apparent to run the prestigious unit. Our cases were exciting and interesting, but my overall disillusionment with the job prompted me to leave the unit. The transfer became necessary for other reasons. Hanging out after work became too easy. Sometimes I'd go to a local Manhattan bar with guys from the unit, particularly after a long day that began with morning arrests or search warrants, or I'd get together with a high school and college pal, Steve, who worked on Centre Street in lower Manhattan. He left the uniform services after graduating from law school and took an attorney position with a government agency. We'd park ourselves on bar stools and spend hours bullshitting, which included reminiscing over arrests we made when we worked together in the Bronx as correction officers. Many of our barroom discussions eventually led him to encourage me to leave the State Police for a district attorney position or a law firm. He knew the corruption issues I'd encountered and, as our close friend from Fordham University, he also knew how Joan felt about the job. Most of the time, I went out to drown away a creeping depression. This was not how I. wanted to live. Becoming another cop watching his life pass by in a barroom mirror was not only cliché, but it was also a dead end. I had no use for guys like Abruzzi, yet at times I couldn't claim to be any better. The hypocrisy ate at me. My choices had to change. I turned down a promotion and a pay raise to ensure they would. Nevertheless, a pattern started to develop where periodic drinking became too convenient an escape.

7
BAD MOOD RISING

My transfer from the Labor Racketeering Unit back to a troop assignment after more than five years away was seamless. Even though my time working in New York City was dynamic and offered me diverse assignments, change was needed. I'd rubbed elbows at bars with Mafia capos and enforcers while surveilling them, dealt with a member of the Westies, Hell's Kitchen Irish gang, who worked as an informant, and drove another informant who cooperated in a major NYC policing scandal to his rendezvous with federal witness protection. I'd roamed the streets of the five boroughs investigating organized crime cases, looking for fugitives, and chasing down suspects. This was the fun part of the job that was ruined by the different incidents of corruption encountered along the way. The new station assignment ensured me the freedom to work on my own cases, make arrests, and begin a college adjunct teaching schedule while also building a part-time law practice focusing on real estate transactions and estate planning, something otherwise impossible to do while working in the city.

The new station had a lot of drug cases, scattered armed robberies, burglaries, serious assault cases, suicides, and homicides to work. Watching and listening to renowned pathologists like Dr. Michael Baden and Dr. Barbara Wolf at autopsies taught me much as an investigator. Once again, the job was fun. When not working an evening shift, I made it home for dinner and spent more time with my family. Children grow up fast, especially when you're preoccupied with work. When Brian and Siobhan were toddlers, and I traveled in and out of New York City at various hours while also finishing law school, those years blurred by me. For Deirdre, I was home more. Joan also noticed a difference in raising her. Brian and Siobhan attended school full-time when Deirdre was born. Joan doted on her, and they had more alone time together. In the tumult of our lives over the next few years after my transfer, Deirdre provided stability for Joan. She loved the older two incredibly, but it had been tough dealing with toddlers less than two and a half years apart while I chased mobsters and wanted felons around New York City or sat in law school classes.

Initially I found contentment working at the new station and didn't worry about cops grabbing money on raids or Mafia members having police connections. The feeling soon left after being assigned to supervise the wireroom on a homicide involving a local builder shot at one of his properties. The troop commander pulled several investigators from different stations to listen to suspects' phone calls for two daily eight-hour shifts over a three month period. Among the initial list of people of interest was a State Police investigator within the troop. On the first day's case review, one of our lieutenants threatened disciplinary charges for whoever talked about the investigation and the existence of the wire to anyone on the job. Nonetheless, our suspects knew and openly acknowledged they were being recorded by mentioning the names of the lead investigators and speaking directly to them during monitored calls. Obviously, someone had clued them in. A circle of dirtbags with childhood friends or siblings who were cops muddied the investigation from the beginning. I had never worked such a compromised investigation in my career. Even the Leak Investigation kept some integrity to it. This case was a joke from the start. The murder went unsolved, and I began a rough patch over the next year. Joan saw the darkness moving over me and fought to pull me away from rising anger. Meanwhile, I experienced increased sleep disturbances that first started after the Leak Investigation. Recurring dreams of people coming after me, or violent encounters with an armed adversary, or the more frequent one of a corpse that appeared in different locations connected to my personal life, woke me. Joan didn't know about these sleep disturbances until years later when my reaction to them started waking her too.

*

Corruption in policing is one of the vilest aspects of the job any cop can encounter. Repeated exposure is demoralizing. Whenever other cops naively said cover-ups didn't occur, I laughed at them. Cops and politicians invented the cover-up. My experiences encountering corruption led to self-deception. The lie went like this: instances of corruption are part of the culture, and there was nothing to do about it other than to avoid involvement and do my job honestly. Self-deception avoided harder moral choices, like coming forward to report corruption. Police culture had already compromised me from the start. Whether as a young trooper accepting a sergeant's orders to pick up his free meal at a local restaurant or obeying the lieutenant who shit-canned my arrest because he knew the person, or watching my station commander divvy up a drug dealer's seized weapons among his drinking buddies, the culture had me trapped.

Anger began fueling too many bad moods. Looking back and considering my behavior over several years, mild depression likely shadowed me, which explains much. Freud said depression was anger turned inward. With all the anger stored over several years in policing, I kept plenty of it in reserve for myself. Alcohol may have numbed it, but anger is a persistent pest when left to infest.

Believing that my occasional drinking wasn't a problem became another self-deception. If something at work bothered me, it became easier to have a few beers and forget about it. Otherwise, I tended to dwell on things, unable to filter out the events of my day and move on. A few beers helped me relax. "Isn't that why you run?" Joan questioned me one evening after dinner as I pulled another beer from the refrigerator. Running provided stress relief during law school, and I stayed with it by entering local road races on weekends. The children began running and we signed them up for youth races. At three, Deirdre had already run in her first kids race. Running also prevented me from developing a beer gut and maintaining the outward appearance of having it all together. More deception.

"I run to work out stress," I replied. "This is to relax." She followed me to the dining room where a chess board sat atop the table. I'd recently purchased a chess book and taught myself the French Defense and pawn structure. Learning chess served as an evening diversion while listening to either Beethoven's *Eroica*, his famous *Symphony No. 3*, or the sultry tone of Norah Jones. A contrived innocence encapsulated the whole scene and served as a convenient excuse for drinking. What harm did a bottle of wine or a few beers create, especially at home? A worse option would be to have my ass planted on a bar stool somewhere. I spent my time with Joan and the children. Why shouldn't I be entitled to a drink? Joan discounted my justification. "Stress relief and relaxation are the same thing." I looked at her and spoke in a measured tone. "No, they're different. One is physical, the other is mental." "Which one is mental?" she shot back. The last beer was going to cost me. "They're just different." Joan didn't relent, insisting they were indistinguishable. "You say toe-may-toe, I say toe-mah-tow," I countered in my most charming way. "You'll get a tomato . . . to your face if you're not careful. Please put away the dishes when you're done; I'm helping Siobhan with her homework."

I didn't know if Joan was pissed at me or disappointed in me. Her being pissed I could deal with. Over the years, I'd become proficient at pissing people off, especially my State Police bosses. My churlishness spiked if a supervisor didn't adequately support an investigation. What would crush me was if I ever disappointed Joan. Sadly, that was exactly what was happening, yet sometimes I didn't care. As much as I loved her, I began to hate myself and, at my worst moments, sought to push her away. She watched me become more self-contained and fought to draw me out. When I retreated within, I wasn't fun for anyone to be around.

Siobhan, while in middle school, came up with a term for my moods. "Why is Dad so growly?" she asked Joan one afternoon. "He had a bad day at work. Let him have some alone time." I hated being "growly." The worst part was my children noticed it and learned to avoid me when they detected I came home in a "growly" mood. They accounted for my heart and soul, and the only reason for getting out of bed some mornings. I further detested myself for causing them to avoid me, and I spiraled further inward and down.

Joan worried when the darkness came over me and I withdrew. She saw the need for intervention. After much prodding, she convinced me to see a therapist. I was mid-career and carried enough anger for ten people. "I'm always here for you, but you should talk to someone who can help you in ways I can't," she said. Regardless of my hesitation, I loved her too much to let the job impact us as it had been doing. She found a therapist a few towns away with an office in a large commercial building to minimize any chance of me running into someone I knew, especially from the State Police. The stigma for a cop seeing a therapist was a career-ender. I viewed it as a weakness. It placed a label on you as "mental," causing other cops to steer clear. In the police academy, our instructors said the Employee Assistance Program (EAP) was there for us, yet no one trusted the EAP counselors. Stories made their way around the troop about them divulging confidential information and how bosses forced troopers to medically retire because someone deemed them to have a "psych" issue after reporting a visit to the EAP counselor.

The biweekly therapy sessions lasted an hour. My distrust of authority was so intense that I paid out of pocket so as not to have it on my insurance and risk discovery. Paranoia mixed in with the anger. At first, it felt good to have someone other than Joan to discuss work events and their impact on me. Acute adjustment disorder was a fancy way for the therapist to say that certain work situations bothered me. "Your episodes are short, but impactful. And they do tend to accumulate with people in your profession," he told me. The sessions helped until I abruptly decided they served no further use and stopped going. My patience for the process waned after less than four months. The conversations became redundant and pointless. My periodic drinking had ended. I focused on not stressing over things at work that were out of my control and even tried to get closer to my faith. We still went to mass regularly as a family, but I had no tolerance for the Catholic Church and its inability to acknowledge a deep-seated problem with pedophile priests. Similarly, I thought other religions sustained their own moral failings. However, a deeper dive into faith led me to read *The Story of a Soul: The Autobiography of St. Therese of Lisieux* and excerpts from Thomas Aquinas' *Summa Theologica*, Augustine's *Confessions* and *City of God*. Organized religion no longer held any influence over me, though my faith did, and I desperately held on.

Running, reading, and continuing to teach myself chess remained my other diversionary stress relievers. By all outward signs, I was doing fine. Joan said she noticed changes, although she knew better than to expect a metamorphosis.

"You still have a lot of internal turbulence. My prayers are for you to one day find peace." "When will that day come?" I asked. "When you realize you can't fix everything and not everybody is going to live up to a standard you set."

*

When I transferred out of Manhattan and returned to a troop assignment, I had ten years on the job. In the blink of an eye, after establishing myself as a good and reliable investigator, one whom my supervisors tapped on the shoulder for big cases, my fifteen-year anniversary on the job arrived. As the magic twenty-year mark came closer, Joan still surfed the ups and downs of my moods prompted by work. "If you're so miserable, why don't you leave?" she shot back at me during one of my weekly gripes. "For Chrissakes already, take early retirement and go practice law or teach full-time, work at Home Depot, or drive a truck; I don't care what you do, as long as you stop living like this."

She was mad, not an emotion she often showed. Her comments forced me to see and hear her in a way I hadn't for a while. She was beautiful standing there in front of the kitchen window, hands on her hips, an orange sky glowing behind her. I flashed back to a moment a few years earlier when an interim supervisor came to my desk and said an attractive woman in the lobby asked for me. Puzzled, I went to the front of the station by the dispatch desk. Joan sat on the other side of the glass.

"Thought I'd stop by to say hello and see if you wanted to grab lunch."

I had an informant scheduled to meet with a local drug dealer and needed to prepare before heading out with a trooper to cover the sale.

"Another time then," she said. We walked outside, kissed, and she got into her SUV.

"See you for dinner?"

"Absolutely. Love you."

I leaned in for one more kiss, then watched her pull out of the lot. Upon returning to my desk, the supervisor asked if my visitor was a complainant in a case.

"No, my wife."

"You're lucky you're still married. Mine dumped me four years ago."

I didn't make it home for dinner that night. The case evolved into two more informant drug buys, a nighttime vehicle pursuit, followed by a takedown of two suspects at gunpoint, then an after-midnight search warrant. I arrived home shortly before the children left for school, fourteen hours after they had dinner without me.

"Did you hear me?"

Her question drew me back to the conversation.

"Why don't you leave?" she continued.

"Because I love it too much."

The question of why I didn't leave was often asked of me, and the answer always came back to a late evening on a Bronx apartment building's rooftop many years earlier. Crouched behind a wall for cover with my gun out, and eighteen hours into a workday that lasted several hours more, I waited for a wanted murderer—a street thug desperately seeking entry into a Genovese crime family crew—to come up the fire escape ladder from an apartment below. As I looked over the parapet at the brightly lit Grand Concourse, the daytime July heat, still trapped in the roof tar, rose and enveloped my face. I could feel, bone deep, this was where I belonged. Nothing could remove me from that rooftop, not even Joan. A day later, we had the suspect in custody along with the murder weapon and two more guns recovered from another suspect we arrested. I was as hooked as I had been as a rookie trooper responding to my first shooting, caught up in the miasmic swirl of other people's pain.

Despite being licensed to practice law in two states, there were some solid reasons for remaining with the State Police: the lifetime pension after twenty years, and health, dental, and prescription benefits. The real, less practical reason relied on a much simpler answer that frequently returned me to that Bronx rooftop and the satisfaction of catching a murderer and removing guns from the street. Whenever I told that story, people reacted with confusion. "Is it worth it? You could get hurt." Only other cops understood. The aggravating nature of the job wasn't the work, or the evil shit you encountered. That was expected. The organizational nonsense tore you up. Any cop would say the same thing. The bullshit, pettiness, and disingenuousness from within the department significantly add to the daily stresses of police work.

*

Joan's days, with Brian and Siobhan in school, were spent with Deirdre and working at the many volunteer activities she undertook. She was active in the local PTA, volunteered in the classroom, and taught Tuesday afternoon religious education at our local parish. Deirdre, as a toddler, was often bundled up and taken wherever Joan went. Her routine, like most stay-at-home parents, was nonstop busy and hectic. Most days, she barely had enough time to pick up Brian and Siobhan from after-school events, grab a pizza dinner, and then hustle them off to religious education classes, sports practices, or evening school functions with Deirdre in tow. The weekly pace didn't relent until Friday. Joan kept this schedule for several years until Brian started to drive and split chauffeuring duties with her. By then he and Siobhan were in high school, on the cross country and track teams, involved with student government, and the drama club, and Deirdre was finishing elementary school.

To compound Joan's busy life, she decided to enter nursing school when Deirdre began school full-time. Even though she had a bachelor's degree in Biology from Fordham, she needed nursing courses to become licensed as a registered nurse. She did this while working as a secretary in the law practice I began with my college friend, Steve, who worked full-time while I went to the office either after day shifts or before evening shifts and on the weekends. Joan and I often passed each other coming and going through the "revolving door" entrance to our house.

Joan not only ran my end of the law practice, completed nursing school and her licensing exam, and volunteered where needed, she also took care of the rest of us. Too often, she was more like a single parent when I mentally squirreled away into my own world. Situational depression triggered by the job ate away at me and us. It didn't matter. Work still had to be done; responsibilities met. Whenever my work cell phone rang, I was out the door. Fortunately, drinking no longer served as a crutch. I began training for half-marathons and marathons, pouring my energies into running. Joan described my running regimen as obsessive. The dark periods, those moments of anger turned inward, still came for me. The job, its demands, and the cases were unrelenting.

One bright light and saving grace in my career occurred when Sue Heinrichs became my unit supervisor. Her promotion to Senior Investigator with the permanent rank of sergeant brought her to the station. While working for her, I was allowed to handle my cases without interference and arrange my shifts to accommodate my adjunct teaching schedule and part-time law practice. Joan hoped the teaching and law practice would encourage me to apply for early retirement and, for this reason, she appreciated Heinrichs's handling of my work schedule.

Heinrichs would never be identified as a cop by a criminal. Her soccer mom vibe and business suits made her look more like a realtor. She had a boy and a girl close in age to Brian and Siobhan. Her husband Larry, a six-foot, barrel-chested former military veteran who looked menacing upon first sight, worked for IBM as an engineer. "People see me and think I'm the type to clear out a bar. Sue's the one who's more likely to kill you," he once told me at a station picnic. His comment rang true. All 5 feet 5 inches of her often backed bigger male supervisors into a corner when she defended one of us or disagreed with a ridiculous edict a boss tried to enforce on our unit. She was also an expert shot, never scoring less than perfect at the range. Even from 50 yards with a shotgun, she placed a slug round at center mass. Before becoming a supervisor, she worked on major narcotics cases with the State Police unit assigned to the NYC Drug Enforcement Task Force and then came back to the troop as a station investigator. She also became the first female recipient of the State

Police's highest award for bravery. Heinrichs received the award for a single-handed nighttime takedown of a gas station robbery crew.

This is what made her such a good supervisor. She'd done real police work and knew the pressures placed upon investigators to close a case. Also, as a wife and mom, she knew the demands the job placed on home life. I could not have balanced as much in my personal and professional life working for someone else. In all my years with Heinrichs, I never doubted she had my back. Heinrichs allowed me the freedom to follow through on cases no matter where they led. For this reason, years later, I followed her to the Major Crimes Unit at troop headquarters, but not until other investigations further bonded us.

8
AFTER 9/11

Watching the 9/11 attacks unfold, I understood how a generation felt sixty years earlier when Japanese aircraft attacked Pearl Harbor. After the second hijacked plane flew into floors seventy-seven to eighty-five of the World Trade Center's South Tower at 9:03 a.m., I knew life in the United States would forever change. I watched the attacks on an office television with four other investigators after a sergeant alerted us to the incident. We'd been at our desks for less than an hour when the first plane struck the North Tower.

Our station was seventy-five miles north of lower Manhattan, but we knew there'd be assignments for the investigation to follow. Off-duty uniform troopers were ordered to report to work. I called Joan at home. She graduated from nursing school in the spring, and while the children were at school, she studied for her state nursing board examination.

"Did you see?"

"Yes, the news coverage cut into the end of Good Morning America. God help those people."

"It looks horrible."

"Guess you won't be home until late . . . if at all tonight."

The attacks kept coming. At 9:37 a.m., American Airlines flight 77 crashed into the Pentagon, followed at 9:59 a.m. by the collapse of the South Tower. Fifty-six minutes after being struck by Flight 175, the South Tower collapsed in ten seconds like a Jenga puzzle. An exhale of black and gray toxic smoke rose from where the tower once stood. At 10:03 a.m., the final weaponized aircraft, United Airlines flight 93, crashed into a field in Shanksville, Pennsylvania. None of us had experienced anything of this magnitude before.

The depth of the destruction was hard to imagine. A week earlier, the day before Labor Day, I'd been at the Twin Towers after running an NYPD-sponsored 14-mile training run for the November NYC Marathon. It was my final long run before participating in a different marathon near our home. The training run started at the northern tip of Manhattan at 220th Street and Broadway, by the Bronx line, and meandered through the early morning streets of Washington Heights before veering past Columbia-Presbyterian Hospital down to the Hudson River, where runners proceeded south on the path between the river and the West Side Highway. A ruddy, red-headed runner in his forties came alongside me 10 miles into the run near the Circle Line Ferry terminal at West 42nd Street. I maintained a comfortably quick pace with him. In the distance, through the morning haze of sunshine and car exhaust, the World Trade Center towers stood like sentinels over lower Manhattan. The sun's rays dug into my exposed shoulders, and salty sweat crossed my lips while matching strides with my new companion. He broke the silence and pointed to the towers looming in the distance.

"You always know you're near the end when you see those two ladies."

"Sure do. It's a nice sight at this point," I replied. After some small talk for the next few minutes during which I learned he was an NYPD captain, I ran ahead when his stride slowed. "See you at the finish line," he called out. I gave a wave and didn't see him again. Sitting at my desk, I wondered if he responded to the crumbling towers and if he remembered our conversation from the week before.

After the last plane crashed in Pennsylvania, I called one of my informants, Ted. He'd been working with me for nine months on an immigration fraud case in the county.

"Hello, my friend. Kayf haluk? How are you?" Ted liked to drop common Arabic phrases he taught me into our conversations.

"Could be better. Have you been watching the news?"

"Yes. Yes. Very disturbing." His thick Middle Eastern accent hinted at fear.

"What's going on?"

"I don't know. It's extremely troubling."

His words added to the stress of the day. Ted, an Egyptian national whose full name was Tadros Farog, had witnessed unrest throughout the Middle East and, as a Coptic Christian, endured pogroms in Egypt, which were catalysts for his seeking citizenship in the United States. Now, the horrors he'd left behind were back at his doorstep.

We agreed to meet later in the evening. The rest of the day a hodgepodge of activity spread across the station as off-duty troopers reported back to work, and patrol and investigative schedules were rearranged in preparation for assignments at what later became known as Ground Zero. Station dispatchers and the duty sergeant answered anxious calls from residents ranging from whether the community was safe to how to locate a relative who worked in lower Manhattan, while regular calls for service or to report crimes continued to come in.

Ted met me after 7:00 p.m. at our usual spot, the parking lot of a public golf course two towns over from where he lived and worked. Starting in late January 2001, Ted began meeting multiple investigative targets and recording his face-to-face and telephone conversations, all at my direction. We first met serendipitously when Ted was interviewed by a trooper in connection with a minor incident. He mentioned a name the trooper recognized from one of my cases, and Ted was sent to speak with me. Although he had no relevant information on my case, Ted was chatty and eventually began talking about immigration. He applied for a residency visa and took exception to those he knew had obtained their citizenship illegitimately. With Ted's help, I eventually uncovered an immigration and naturalization fraud scheme centered on recruiting mostly low-income waitresses and prostitutes to marry Middle Eastern males seeking citizenship. Those who were naturalized through the scheme included former Egyptian military communications and ordnance specialists and radicalized members of the Muslim Brotherhood.

The information Ted gathered in the months leading up to 9/11 resulted in several arrests, and his services became more crucial after the attacks. For three weeks after 9/11, I worked with the FBI and other federal agencies knocking on doors and interviewing people as part of the nationwide Operation PENTTBOM (acronym used for Pentagon and Twin Tower Bombing) investigation. My work with Ted identified and located people of interest in our patrol area whom the Justice Department wanted to interview. The FBI took some of those individuals into custody on visa and other immigration violations.

As valuable an informant as Ted was, he caused me occasional aggravation. Two months after the attacks, when the Bush administration bombed terrorist compounds in Afghanistan, the local police in an adjoining municipality questioned Ted after he'd gone into a Kennedy Fried Chicken and became embroiled in a verbal dispute with the Pakistani owners over US military operations in Afghanistan. They took exception to his unabashed patriotism and threw him out of the store. Ted stood in the store's doorway and flashed both middle fingers while yelling at them, "Fuck you. George Bush is going to shove missiles up your asses."

After being interviewed by the local responding cop and told to stay away from the store, Ted called me.

"Ted, you can't do or say those things."

"Why not? It's true, and they were badmouthing America."

"Because you're lucky the police didn't arrest you for disorderly conduct."

I then explained First Amendment protections, giving the store owners the right to express their views, even if they spoke badly about the country.

"Okay, whatever you say."

Before we hung up, he promised not to cause any more scenes and to find another place to eat. A bigger screw-up came a few months later when he boarded an Atlanta flight to LaGuardia Airport in Queens, and a clerk asked him to check an oversized carry-on bag. He did so with an ill-timed attempt at humor. The ring of my cell phone awakened me at eight o'clock on a Sunday morning.

"I'm looking for Investigator Dwyer; this is Sky Marshal Hemmings calling from the Atlanta International Airport," the southern voice on the other end of the line said.

"Speaking. How can I help you?"

"Do you know a Tadros Farog, sir?"

The hard "a" vowel of Ted's first and last name became soft and elongated with the sky marshal's southern drawl.

"He's a registered State Police informant."

"Well sir, we have him in custody right now."

I spent the next five minutes listening while Hemmings took a circuitous route explaining how, after gate-checking his bag, Ted asked the baggage handler if he thought he had a bomb. A sky marshal in the boarding area whisked Ted away to the airport's secure holding area.

"Can I speak to him?"

Ted's voice came on at the other end of the line.

"What kind of stupid fucking stunt did you pull this time?"

"I'm sorry, so, so sorry. My anxiety has been bad lately."

"Well, you're in a jam now."

Ted told me he forgot to take his prescribed medication, and that his nerves about flying got the better of him.

"Sit tight and keep your smart-ass mouth shut. Put me back on with the sky marshal."

After another ten minutes of conversation, the sky marshal agreed to allow Ted to board a later flight to New York. A few days later, Ted met me at a diner where he offered to buy me lunch.

"Save your money. If you do something like this again, it's over. You're no longer an asset; you become a liability, and we're done working together."

After the airport incident, he stayed out of trouble. He continued to gather evidence I used in state prosecutions and other information that I passed on to State Police colleagues in the Joint Terrorism Task Force. He also began translating material from jihadi websites for our Computer Crimes Unit. A third incident, almost a year after 9/11, could not be blamed on Ted.

He went to a local post office to mail a package to his brother in Italy. When he approached the clerk's window, the postal employee, an individual Ted identified as a fellow Egyptian, questioned him about his nationality. Ted, fluent in several languages including German, told the clerk he grew up in Frankfurt. He called and told me the postal employee gave him a bad feeling. When Ted returned two weeks later to pick up a certified mailing, the same clerk spoke to him in Arabic.

"You're not German. You're Egyptian."

"What does it matter," Ted replied in Arabic.

"You lied about who you are. And you're a fucking Christian. I thought we killed you all."

Switching to English, Ted began yelling at the clerk.

"Why don't you speak English so everyone can hear what you say?"

A line of people waited behind Ted, and the post office supervisor came out of the rear office. Ted persisted.

"Go ahead, tell me in English the threats you made!"

The flustered postal clerk quickly retrieved Ted's letter before calling the next customer to come forward. After Ted's first post office encounter, I identified the clerk as a naturalized citizen who'd been with the Postal Service for over ten years. Ted had linked him to other area nationals who were part of the Muslim Brotherhood, a Sunni Islamist international organization mostly centered in Egypt. The Muslim Brotherhood, based on information received from law enforcement sources and Ted, had radical elements. Ted provided the names of other local individuals who belonged to the Brotherhood and socialized with the postal clerk.

One of the locations where they met was a mosque near the post office. I contacted our technical unit in Albany and had a video recording camera installed on a telephone pole near the mosque. Several afternoons each week, another investigator and I monitored the camera live from an unmarked car down the street. Two individuals we picked up on the mosque surveillance were later arrested by the FBI and imprisoned after trial for conspiring against the United States and pledging loyalty to al Qaeda.

Even though the FBI investigation had no connection to my case, the arrests spotlighted potential terrorist activity within our patrol area. I'd already arrested a former Egyptian army tank commander for passing counterfeit twenty-dollar bills at a local restaurant. I tracked the counterfeit currency to a money changer, or a hawala, in Shebin el Kom, an Egyptian city located in the Nile Delta of the Menoufia Governorate. The US Secret Service identified the recovered bills as belonging to a seizure of several million dollars of counterfeit currency seized by police in London and later stolen from their evidence locker. Another individual, a former Egyptian soldier, returned to Cairo when he heard I wanted to question him. International events had become local after 9/11.

Joan passed her state nursing board exam in October and started working as a registered nurse in February 2002. At the same time, I pushed Ted harder to set up and record more meetings with different individuals who came within the ambit of my investigation. Most meetings took place at night in disparate areas of the county. Some were in suburban areas, like strip malls; others were in seedier city sections. The original focus of my investigation into immigration and document fraud had expanded post-9/11 to include other crimes: financial scams, drug offenses, and the sale of forged social security cards and driver's licenses. Joan questioned the type of people I pursued and where the investigation was headed. Her concern, fueled by information about the 9/11 hijackers, was that the investigation had moved into a realm beyond the traditional organized crime cases I had worked on years earlier in New York City. I saw no difference between them. Organized criminal activity, regardless of its motivations, carried on in the same ways. The US had been attacked, and I happened to be working a case with possible value to federal investigations and national security interests. I wasn't going to let up. Heinrichs, though, shared Joan's concerns. She called me into her office one day after reading an investigative report. "Close the door."

She motioned for me to have a seat and then held up the report.

"Do you realize there could be terror cells operating in the county?"

"It's possible. I'm merely following the crimes I come across."

Heinrichs, always a cop's cop as a supervisor, pledged to give me whatever help she could at the station level. Any information I developed not leading to a state charge, I passed on to my contacts in the NYC Joint Terrorism Task Force.

One individual I concentrated on was an Egyptian national who approached Ted to commit crimes with him. This individual, Youssef, wanted Ted, a chemist by trade, to manufacture oxycontin and methamphetamines for sale. Youssef entered the United States through Canada on a forged student visa claiming to be studying at a public university in Minnesota. In New York, he applied for citizenship with a fake baptismal certificate from a Brooklyn Catholic church and a forged New York City birth certificate. In addition to asking Ted to manufacture controlled substances, Youssef began aviation lessons at a local airport and applied for hazardous materials endorsements to his driver's license. He also committed felony forgery on county social service documents. I arrested him on state charges and notified federal authorities. This led to an immigration hearing and detention. Youssef challenged his custody and deportation order until his eventual removal to Egypt two years later.

Ted subsequently gathered evidence leading me to a local Italian restaurant owner who'd been a radio and telecommunications officer in the Egyptian army. I arrested him on felony forgery charges tied to falsified immigration affidavits and state driver's licenses. Federal prosecutors became involved, took over the state prosecution, and transferred the file to the federal court in White Plains. The feds charged the restaurant owner (who called himself Salvatore or Sal and told everyone he emigrated from Calabria) with document fraud. Sal had helped other Egyptian nationals by providing false immigration documents. The feds gave him probation after an assistant US attorney, FBI agent, and I sat down with him and his attorney for a plea negotiation meeting. In exchange for no prison time, "Sal" agreed to work as an FBI informant.

Ted worked harder than most informants, considering he didn't have criminal charges pending against him. With Sal's case transferred to the feds, I continued to balance the larger investigation with other investigative assignments for nearly five years, including after being assigned to the Major Crimes Unit at troop headquarters. Working with Ted dominated my workdays and time off. I often worked alone, and not by choice. Other than Heinrichs and a few investigators who occasionally assisted me, the ranking officers at troop headquarters showed no interest in the case. Instead, the new BCI captain told me to either find a wider conspiracy or pass along the information to the upstate intelligence center in Latham and concentrate on my regular assignments. The captain, Harold Quade, a recently promoted addition to the troop, also threatened to transfer me to a different station if I didn't comply. Referred to as "highway therapy," the intent of such transfers was meant to modify the behavior of allegedly recalcitrant troopers and investigators through longer commutes to work. Despite pointing out to him the crimes my case targets committed in the county and their ties to radicalized individuals and the mosque, my orders were to give my case information to an analytical unit rather than to continue investigating ongoing crimes. In a post-9/11 environment, his order baffled me.

His transfer threat was hollow. I'd grieve it as a punitive transfer and likely win. A greater concern, and one that similarly perplexed Joan, was Captain Quade's disregard for the investigation. "How can your boss not give you the resources needed after what happened on 9/11?" Her question was rhetorical; she already knew the answer, which was that logic rarely controlled police work.

Other registered informants worked for me, but Ted was the most reliable and effective. He traveled easily within the county's undocumented immigrant community. As a waiter in local restaurants, he disappeared into the background, like a potted plant people didn't pay attention to and talked freely around. Ted was a sponge who, as an educated multilingual individual, didn't forget anything once he heard or saw it. One worry of his, though, was other police officers.

"I see bad cops around and know what they do," he said to me one day. "No one can know about us."

"Your identity is protected," I reassured him.

"Even from the State Police? There are bad troopers around here too."

I had no suitable answer to give. His statement later dovetailed with information from two other sources about corrupt cops in the area that another investigator, Heinrichs, and I would eventually investigate.

Meanwhile, late in 2004, Ted told me about a Yemeni national going around a local municipality threatening people and claiming to be linked to terrorists. The individual also unabashedly said he worked for the FBI. I wanted to locate this person, surveil him, and see if a recorded meeting between him and Ted could be arranged. I looked for several weeks with no luck, until one morning while reading the local morning paper at home over breakfast, I found him.

"Holy shit!" My outburst from the kitchen table brought Joan running from our bedroom where she was getting dressed for work.

"What is it? Everything alright?"

"You remember the guy I've been looking for, the one Ted told me made threats about being a terrorist?"

Joan's face scrunched up as she tried to remember the specifics from one of the many job-related stories she had heard.

I placed the paper down and turned the article toward her. She read the front-page Associated Press story about a local man, Mohamed Alanssi, an FBI informant and a key witness in several federal trials, who'd tried to burn himself in front of the White House. Alanssi's FBI handler, a military reservist, had been called to active duty. The federal government paid Alanssi over $125,000 and covered his rent in a nice condominium complex by the Hudson River, yet he claimed to have been abandoned by the FBI, and he began making local threats. Alanssi's wife remained in Yemen, suffering from stomach cancer, and he wanted to travel to see her. Angry over his treatment by the FBI, Alanssi, who'd been in contact with the *Washington Post*, notified them on the morning of November 15, 2004, that he planned to burn his body in "an unexpected place." Later in the day, he set himself on fire in front of the White House.

The FBI took a black eye, and federal prosecutors in the Eastern District of New York had to repair their case after the main witness had set himself on fire in public. His mental stability later became an issue at trial. Nonetheless, I passed the information along with Alanssi's local ties to our troop intelligence unit and forwarded a memo to the troop commander, Major Doyle. The response was underwhelming. Lieutenant Steven Plummer, assigned to troop HQ six months before Quade and responsible for overseeing the Major Crimes Unit, asked me what I sought to accomplish by passing on the information. Major Doyle, the same individual who many years before refused to extradite the motorist who attempted to run me over and pull a gun during a car stop, phoned Sue Heinrichs to ask the same question.

"It's intel. Information our troop counterterrorism unit should be interested in," Heinrichs told Doyle.

The following day, she called me into the office to express her frustration.

"Jesus Christ, when they canvass the troop looking for info and no one has anything all the bosses get pissed. Then, when we bring them something like this, they stare at us like we're morons."

"If it weren't such a tragic way to conduct police work, it'd be funny. I'll still do my thing," I said.

"I know you will; I count on it."

But doing my thing only led to trouble under the new troop headquarters administration. At the time, I couldn't see the developing pattern. The way things were going within the troop, I was racing toward a showdown with Quade and Plummer, more trouble, increased scrutiny, and personal jeopardy. Neither Joan nor I expected the overwhelming strain of the last two years of my career.

PART II

THE GANG

9
PARTNERS

No relationship in police work tops the bond you develop with a partner. Sue Heinrichs became someone I placed a lot of trust in and agreed to follow to Major Crimes when she was appointed the unit supervisor. She and Joan developed an easy friendship, and whenever Sue called the house, I'd usually get the phone after the two of them caught up on what the children were doing, or they made plans to meet up for a run. I worked for many outstanding first-line supervisors during my career, but Heinrichs was the best. If needed in an undercover role, she'd be available to pitch in; she'd often be out on arrests when possible, and she always made sure the investigators assigned to the unit had little interference from the brass. She let us do our jobs while she handled the petty politics and annoyances so common in policing. "If you ever decide to transfer somewhere else, talk to me first because you'll need to have your head examined, and I'll make the appointment. You'll never find someone like Sue to work for again," Joan scolded me one afternoon when I randomly mused about possibly transferring to either the Violent Felony Warrant Squad or the Drug Enforcement Task Force. The only other person to achieve the level of trust and faith I had in Heinrichs was my Major Crimes partner, Juan Limon. A Brooklyn-born Puerto Rican with an in-your-face sense of humor and the build of a prizefighter who favored sports jacket and tie ensembles, Limon had the quirky mannerisms of the television detective Colombo. He counterbalanced my Brooks Brothers and Calvin Klein preferred wardrobe and Bronx Irish temper that could go from zero to sixty in a flash. We were the perfect marriage of police partners.

We meshed on an Operation Impact assignment shortly after my arrival at the Major Crimes Unit. Operation Impact's goal was to target high-crime municipalities and arrest people with outstanding warrants. As we cruised along a main downtown thoroughfare, Limon saw local detectives running along the sidewalk shouting into their radios. Suddenly, a car raced out of a side alley where it hit a city patrol officer assigned to our group, pinning him to the wall. Instinctively, I yelled, "Get him!" and Limon maneuvered our unmarked car around traffic and gave quick chase for two blocks until he boxed in the other vehicle next to a parked car. I jumped out, went to the fleeing driver's door, grabbed and tossed him to the pavement, and handcuffed him in one quick move. Limon stood right by my side with his gun pointed at the suspect. Right then, he proved to me his worth as a partner. We took the suspect, a local Blood-affiliated gang member, to the city police department for processing. After that chase and arrest, Limon and I became inseparable. We worked several big cases, had a lot of laughs, tossed back a few beers, and skirted minor troubles along the way.

*

We were less than two weeks into 2005 when a double homicide required the Major Crimes Unit. The bodies of a middle-aged man and a twenty-year-old woman were found in the trunk of a vehicle in a long-term parking space by the Metro-North commuter rail line. Both bodies, covered by a bloody white sheet and stuffed in the trunk like luggage, suffered single gunshot wounds.

Several hours into a full day of chasing down leads and conducting interviews, we interviewed the female victim's older brother, Gerald, a twenty-two-year-old college senior. What began as background information gathering gradually turned into a suspect interview. During a four-hour interview, Gerald made several bizarre comments. At one point, seemingly unmoved by the violent death of his sister, he stated, "Bad things happen to bad people. They both had an aura of evil about them." When asked to explain what he meant, Gerald said, "You'll find out when you catch who did this." He later inadvertently placed himself at the site of a secondary crime scene where troopers recovered his sister's car. His incriminating statements during the interview, along with forensics from the two cars and the house where he lived with his parents and sister, provided probable cause for his arrest. The investigation pieced together that Gerald's parents were on a Caribbean vacation when their friend came by to return borrowed tools. When Gerald opened the door, he met the older man with a shotgun blast to the chest. He had no reason other than he wanted to. Meanwhile, his sister, upstairs taking a shower, heard the noise, threw on a robe, and came downstairs to find Gerald in the doorway above the body. He turned with the shotgun and placed a round in his sister's chest. After wrapping them both in bed sheets, he dumped the bodies in the trunk of the older man's car, drove to the parking lot, and paid for a week's parking. The next morning, a passing commuter saw blood on the trunk and called the State Police.

I came home late after Gerald's interview and arrest, well past two in the morning, with a raging headache. Limon and I had to be back on the case in a few hours. The little sleep I got didn't relieve my headache. Joan always knew when I interviewed a suspect. The duration and intensity of the interview process, and the concentration required, always left me spent.

"Run the hot water and stand over the sink with a towel over you. Clean your sinuses first," Joan instructed me.

Afterward, she gave me two aspirins and a cold compress for my forehead.

"Drink lots of water and have a good breakfast," were her final instructions before dashing out to drop Deirdre at school then heading to work.

The circumstances of this homicide presented an irony not often encountered. It occurred in an affluent area, and the perpetrator was an unlikely suspect, an upper middle-class college student who had once been a top Division 1 pitching prospect. A mental breakdown during his sophomore year forced him to give up baseball and return home. Limon and I had investigated homicides resulting from drugs, domestic abuse, or gang-related revenge, all involving individuals considered lower class and on the societal fringe. While violence knew no class or economic restrictions, encountering it among affluence always seemed out of place. We investigated another case of this kind in the spring with the homicide of a seventeen-year-old girl from a wealthy family.

We saw her body at the same time as her father when the hospital asked him to identify his daughter. She lay naked, face up on a gurney under the high lumen intensity of emergency room lights. No one had taken the time to cover her before the father entered for the viewing. Speckles of blood joined a constellation of freckles across her chest and abdomen. Her long strawberry blonde hair fanned out across the white hospital sheets. Fourteen puncture wounds dotted her chest, and strangulation marks cut along her neck. The stab marks—closely grouped and patterned the way you chop ice, quick and frenzied—marred her pale skin. A long deep slashing cut along the inside of the left breast stretched toward her belly like an exclamation mark, leaving an intense punctuation of brutality. None of these wounds were fatal. The bandana wrapped around her neck and pulled tighter and tighter until she had no more air to breathe killed her.

The girl's employer, a bakery owner, called her parents when she didn't show up for her scheduled Sunday morning shift, his busiest time of the week. She hadn't responded to his cell phone calls. Her parents went looking and found the SUV she drove parked a short walking distance from the bakery. In the back seat, they found their daughter's half-dressed and bloodied body with the bandana still around her neck.

We spoke to her father in a waiting area near the emergency room. He placed his hands on his forehead and pulled down along his face, as if erasing the image of his dead daughter; then he collapsed into a chair. The father asked if I had any children.

"Three . . . a boy and two girls."

"Cherish them," he said as he let out a guttural sigh.

We took the lead in the case and learned of a mysterious ex-boyfriend the parents didn't like. Other than that, they had little information about him to provide us with solid leads. They had no phone number, last name, or address. Their ignorance as to who their seventeen-year-old dated angered me. No one entered any of my children's lives without me obtaining every bit of personal information about them short of a DNA test. I believed the father failed in his responsibilities as a parent, and it led to his daughter's death. My parenting was much different, though my hypervigilance wasn't always fair to my children. I announced rules and barked commands with little reason or explanation. Only I knew why, and it usually came in response to an incident from work. But my children were safe. As cop's kids, they developed their own fine-tuned radar for people. Why hadn't this father been as vigilant in acclimating his daughter to the evils of the world and the darkness of other people? Nevertheless, I pushed further judgment of the father aside and plowed into the case.

After hours of investigative digging, we uncovered information on the ex-boyfriend, Ramon, an undocumented Guatemalan immigrant with family in the Eastchester section of the Bronx by Co-op City. She had met him at a teen nightclub in Port Chester, not far from her home. He was seven years older than her. Further investigative work by our team brought us to a marginal neighborhood in Stamford, Connecticut, where three-story wood-framed row houses and chain-link fenced-in backyards proliferated among garbage-strewn vacant lots. Ramon hid in the third-floor apartment of a cousin who agreed to drive him to Kennedy International Airport in the morning for an early flight to Guatemala.

When we reached the exterior third-floor stairwell, a slim Hispanic woman in an apron with a dish rag in her hand stood by an open door. Moving toward her apartment, I asked her, "Ramon, aqui?" "Si, si," she said with a smile. "Policia." Bereft of any further Spanish, I motioned toward the door, which she opened for us. We pushed through the kitchen and two small rooms before entering a darkened front bedroom where, on a single bed in the left corner of the room, sat a solitary figure. "Policia, no se mueva," I shouted while pointing my gun at the figure. "Are you Ramon?" "Si," came the response.

Ramon stepped forward with his arms out to the side. As he moved from the shadows of the room into a slant of sunlight coming in from a crease in the drawn window shade, I holstered my gun and handcuffed him.

Limon asked, "Do you know why we're here?"

"Si, I hurt Amanda."

During the subsequent hours-long interview, Ramon admitted to abducting, raping, and stabbing Amanda. He wanted her back and snapped when she refused to reconcile. I left the Stamford police station at close to 11:00 p.m., nearly sixteen hours since first being called in. Pulling out of the parking lot, I called Joan and told her I was on my way home. I made her a promise years earlier after leaving the NYC detail to always come straight home after a bad day.

Joan was my comfort, and more than she realized, my protector and my security. Without her and the children, I wasn't sure what kind of person I would be at the end of days like this.

The year began busy and stayed that way. In addition to several homicide callouts, our Major Crimes Unit worked on a serial rapist case and two different bank robbery crews. The bank jobs, stretching from New York to Fairfield County in Connecticut, went back to being locally handled cases since the FBI's new mandate after 9/11 focused on terror-related investigations. Unless a bank robber had ties to Hamas or al-Qaeda, the FBI no longer responded. This left our Major Crimes Unit with the added responsibility of assisting local departments with bank robberies in a four-county area.

Heinrichs and I were busy with another matter creating a lot of tension in our lives. For over a year we'd been working with another investigator, Robert Bosse, on information he developed about a uniform trooper allegedly dealing drugs and protecting local drug dealers. Bosse developed an informant and went to Heinrichs with information about the trooper and two crooked local police officers. A few weeks later, Heinrichs brought me into the loop because of my network of informants, including Ted, as well as my experience with long-term investigations. The three of us traversed a bumpy road of rejection from the bosses, mainly Captain Quade and Lieutenant Plummer, who questioned our motives. "This seems personal," Plummer said to Heinrichs during a brief closed-door meeting she later described to me. "You don't like the trooper." Heinrichs, incensed by Plummer's comment, shot back, "There's an informant, and the county drug task force has surveillance that raises serious questions." "Nonetheless, we have people to handle internal matters," Plummer countered. "Who aren't fucking competent enough to properly investigate it," she replied. Her words chased after Plummer, who left the office and pulled the door shut behind him. I began preparing an affidavit to eavesdrop on the suspects' phones. A week later, Captain Quade, through Heinrichs, ordered me to stop. Internal Affairs, he told her, now had the case. I went home that evening wanting to climb onto my roof and scream at the top of my lungs for the whole neighborhood to hear. "Nothing is ever on the up and up!" reverberated through my mind. Maybe the time had come for me to go to the press and outline all the shit I'd seen in a police career and now the potential whitewashing of drug-dealing cops. But what real evidence did I have? We'd been stymied in the early phases of the investigation. Turning the case over to Internal Affairs, where police work went to die, was like closing the case with no investigation at all.

Joan had a better way of dealing with my frustration. "Ice cream dinner!" she announced. She'd had a busy day at work too. Brian and Siobhan came in late from track practice, and Deirdre had a big science project due at the end of the week. Ice cream dinners were Joan's way of taking a "time out" when everyone was super-stressed or busy. We piled into her SUV and headed to the local Cold Stone Creamery. My worries eased away while we all sat at a corner table by the store's window eating our ice cream and I talked with the children about school and weekend plans.

Heinrichs, Bosse, and I eventually took our concerns and case information outside of the troop and brought them to the New York City Drug Enforcement Task Force (DETF). We did so after finding out that an Internal Affairs captain assigned to investigate the suspect trooper revealed the specifics of the investigation to his girlfriend, who was the station lieutenant supervising one of our targets. She in turn warned the suspected drug-dealing trooper about the Internal Affairs investigation. The incompetence was astounding. Bosse had already transferred to a drug unit after becoming frustrated with the progress of the case. At one of our case meetings at a Holiday Inn Hotel, a State Police captain assigned to DETF said Quade and Plummer were upset with Heinrichs and me and wanted to remove us from the Major Crimes Unit. We both knew they'd try to do so by jamming us up with disciplinary charges, no matter how petty. The only comfort we had upon hearing the news was the DETF captain's offer to transfer to his detail. "There are two open slots in Manhattan if you want to jump ship," the captain said.

Amidst homicide and bank robbery callouts, Joan had to additionally deal with my cell phone ringing at night and me disappearing for upwards of two hours "to take care of something" relating to the investigation into corrupt cops. This usually meant meeting Bosse to surveil someone or interview an informant. I'd return home, bitch to Joan, and she'd listen. This wasn't new for her. She remembered I had no choice as a young trooper except to transfer away from an out-of-control station and knew how the Leak Investigation clung to me for the rest of my career, and the different job issues since then. I internalized it all. Joan always listened and tried to understand my pain and bitterness. Her unwavering support and love for me endured two decades of testing. She now saw an end in sight. My twenty-year job anniversary in September quickly approached, and, she thought, so did my retirement. And yet, with everything going on with Quade and Plummer and my past experiences, I made a momentous decision as we approached the end of summer. In the middle of another homicide investigation, this one a "who-done-it" dump job in the woods, I had the temerity one evening to announce a shift in my retirement plans.

"I want to stay for my twenty-five years," I said while washing up for dinner. Joan stood in the bathroom doorway devoid of a response. I rambled on, excited about my decision. "The extra five years will boost my pension, it'll give me more time to build the law practice, and Brian and Siobhan will have graduated college."

"I thought you were miserable," she finally said.

"Only because of the fucking bosses and the shit they overlook. Not the work; that doesn't bother me."

"If your bosses are the problem, why would you stay?"

I had made no plans for an exit. Despite my law practice side hustle, I ran hot and cold as to whether it was for me. "I've got seniority, number two in the unit, and no one fucks with me," I reassured her. This was part of my continuing self-deception. For twenty years, Joan lived with the badge between us. It existed as an invisible wall we stood on either side of—Joan originally not wanting to be a police spouse and me unable to leave the pull of the job. My multiple promises to leave didn't amount to anything other than talk. Now, with my retirement in sight, Joan once again lost out to the job. "Limon's the best partner I've had; we work well together. Plus, Heinrichs and I have unfinished business with these allegations of corrupt cops in the county." My mouth kept running, not once pausing to gauge her reaction. Joan, my true partner, the only consistent and reliable one throughout my career, once more placed second. My self-absorption and focus on working investigations blinded me to her pain. Deep down, she detested the job. She hated what it did to me, how it separated us, and how it changed me. She mourned the loss of the person she first met on Fordham's campus.

By Halloween 2005, I'd been subjected to random inspections to see if any of my work manuals or equipment were out of order and was questioned about my outside employment memo, which had been on file for over a decade. Some days, Lieutenant Plummer pulled me from my caseload and ordered me to assist with evidence inventory or clerical duties with the troop secretaries. Worst of all, he kept me out of the loop on Counter-Terrorism Intelligence Unit (CTIU) briefings and ongoing investigations despite my having the only registered Arabic-speaking informant in the troop. The clear chicken-shit pattern indicated the bosses planned to fuck with me. I contemplated my options, which included a transfer out of Major Crimes. I had a transfer offer from the captain of a statewide investigative unit along with the drug task force offer. Then, on Halloween night, Heinrichs called me. "There's a gang task force being formed by the FBI, and they're looking for someone from the troop." I was in the local supermarket grocery shopping with Joan. Weighing the offer, I wandered down the cereal aisle. The preliminary information sounded good, but I didn't want to leave Limon. "They only want one person right now. The captain said he'd spare you," Heinrichs said. The minimum one-year assignment started the following week. "Sign me up. It'll get me the hell away from the bosses and their messing with me." I caught up with Joan in the bakery department and told her about the new assignment investigating an inner-city drug gang. They called themselves the Crazed Killas Mafia. I already looked forward to the change. "You're crazy. Haven't you had enough?" She pushed the cart a few steps, then stopped. "If it's something you want to do, go ahead . . . but at least think it over some more." I walked toward her with outstretched arms and a goofy puppy dog smile. "Don't come a step further until you promise me you'll reconsider this." Her response startled me. "What's the matter? I thought . . . " "No, you really haven't thought much about anything. You're escaping one situation to go running into another. I fear what you're heading into is not going to be the answer you're looking for." She grabbed a loaf of fresh bread, tossed it in the cart, and continued to the end of the aisle toward the meat section. I'd already committed to the assignment, and, reluctantly, so had she.

10
CRAZED KILLAS MAFIA

Crazed Killas Mafia members committed forty-eight shootings in a twenty-two-day period the previous August. Those shootings and an open gang-related homicide in a neighboring town brought me into the investigation as part of the Department of Justice Safe Streets Task Force. The gang embarked on a shooting spree and terror hold on the city streets over a year earlier and still ran loose, shooting and robbing indiscriminately.

The city, a forgotten industrial burg of 48,000, in a metro area population of nearly 700,000, whose better days remained a half-century in the past, had multiple civic woes: poverty, crumbling buildings, a failing school district, political turmoil, and, of course, crime. The Crazed Killas Mafia, also known as the CK Mafia or CKM, represented a violent fraction of the city's overall crime problem. An overworked, underfunded, and understaffed police department monitored the ongoing urban decay.

I teamed up with FBI agent Tom Adamo and Eddie Hartigan, a savvy and street-smart city detective. The three of us were tasked with building the case from scratch. We started by gathering gang intel, then set up late-night drug buys during the cold nights of late December and January.

Adamo's biggest asset was that he used to be a trooper. For four years, he wore the uniform, so we had a common bond from the same academy training. Former police officer FBI agents not only gained more acceptance from other cops, but they also worked better with them. Special agents who hadn't been cops were easy to sniff out because they generally looked down on the local police they worked with. Criticism of the FBI always centered on their taking credit for investigative successes and quick finger-pointing when things went sideways. Adamo didn't fit this stereotype. He had a proven track record of working with local police agencies, and he shouldered equal credit and blame for investigative success or failure. He had successfully investigated two prior street gang cases with other police departments in the suburban NYC metropolitan area. Adamo worked by identifying trouble spots in cities needing an infusion of federal money and personnel. He compiled crime statistics, city budgets, local police department manpower issues, and then went out and made his pitch to the municipalities where he felt he could be effective.

When Adamo sold an idea, no one said no. At six feet four inches with an athletic build, thick black hair to his collar, and the swarthy good looks of his Mediterranean heritage, he also possessed an undeniable charisma. I first met him at the office he rented as our cover location and thought he'd stepped out of an Abercrombie & Fitch catalog for a middle-aged audience. In his late forties, he wore khaki slacks, a dark blue shirt with thin horizontal white lines, and a sweater draped over his shoulders. Tom Adamo greeted me like an old friend. "How ya doing, T," he said with a firm handshake before pulling me into a bro hug. "Welcome to the team, and by team, I mean you and me, along with city detective Eddie Hartigan." I didn't know Hartigan, which was a good thing because any names I knew of city detectives came to me for bad reasons. Sometimes I heard accounts from Ted and other times from another informant about local police misconduct. "We'll meet up with Eddie tomorrow. He's in court today finishing up testimony on another case." Adamo had a lot of personality to deal with at first, but I detected a genuineness about him. Within half an hour of meeting and talking, it became clear that I could work with and trust him. His investigative pedigree included an undercover stint in Providence, RI, posing as a counterfeiter and fence for stolen property. He worked undercover for eighteen months and did business with New England Mafia crews. He had also worked undercover in the South where he posed as a small accounting firm owner laundering money for outlaw biker gangs and their meth operations. His impressive resume told all I needed to know about him. Behind the bonhomie dwelled a serious and focused investigator.

Disrupt and dismantle, the motto of the Safe Streets Task Force, fed into how I viewed my new investigative assignment. This type of task force model, created in 1992 by the US Department of Justice, provided funding, personnel, and resources to municipal areas plagued by street crime. Combating violent gangs and drugs comprised the core of its mission. I committed to that mission and motto, knowing my prior investigative experience with organized crime in New York City would serve me well.

Eddie Hartigan was less outgoing than Adamo. Upon our first meeting, he kept a guarded distance until he sized me up. I did the same with him. It didn't take long, though, for either one of us to earn the other's trust. Hartigan was one of the best cops I ever worked with. When Adamo put together his task force team, he insisted on Hartigan working with him. FBI resources and money coming into the city depended on the police chief agreeing to assign Hartigan.

The three of us had very different personalities and a combined sixty-five years of law enforcement experience. Such a mix did not generally make for a great working relationship in our world. Personality and ego often bumped up against each other. After our first month, we gelled like we'd been partners for years. Our quick bond benefited the investigation because at the outset we were the extent of the task force. Neither Hartigan nor I knew this entering the case. Adamo explained that we would carry the load until we put together enough of a case for him to request agents from his regional office and approach other local police agencies for manpower. Those terms suited me. I'd been involved before in building cases from the ground up with little to no support.

To his credit, Adamo had established a rapport with Sgt. Ted Buchanan and Detective Arturo Taglieri from the County Drug Task Force. Taglieri, a veteran narcotics investigator and technology whiz, served as second-in-command to Buchanan, who effectively guided his people on the streets as they made cases. Both became invaluable assets for coordinating drug buys into the CK Mafia. However, Hartigan was our biggest asset on the street. He knew everyone in the city who needed to be known and had an encyclopedic memory of gang members and what group they ran with. He even knew their arrest records without consulting state databases. From my vantage point, Hartigan had a gift that couldn't be taught. He not only treated people fairly and earned their trust, but he did it in a way that put him on par with the local pastor. If a shooting or homicide occurred, Eddie Hartigan got a call from the streets. "Detective Eddie," or "Mr. Clean" among the kids because he had a large shiny bald head atop a stocky frame, was the only city detective who, during the Thanksgiving and Christmas holidays, received invites from people living in the worst sections of the city to drop in for dinner if working. The respect and trust he'd earned first as a uniform patrol officer then as a detective paid dividends when needed. "Detective Eddie" went to funerals of neighborhood murder victims, brought Christmas presents to families with lots of kids but little money, and was the one to whom suspects surrendered themselves. His gruff exterior hid a softie. He revealed this other side whenever he talked about his two daughters, Emily and Annie, both travel soccer players and swimmers, and his wife Tess, his high school sweetheart. Hartigan had only two discernible vices: cigarettes and food. Built like a football lineman, he carried an extra thirty pounds since his rookie days. The added pounds and his chain smoking ruled him out for any foot chases. If anyone ran on us, I'd be the one going after them.

The opportunity to work with Adamo and Hartigan to rid the city of the violent scourge of the Crazed Killas Mafia excited me. Working the streets presented less hazard than the politics and drama at troop headquarters and dealing with the inflated egos and demands of bosses like Quade and Plummer. The old guard in charge retired, and a new breed of police supervisors, my generational peers, micromanaged us. They ran investigations from the daylight comfort of their offices and second-guessed decisions made by seasoned and competent investigators. Captain Quade, a career ladder climber, fit the mold. The troop BCI command amounted to another assignment en route to his next promotion. Police corruption issues tended to stunt a supervisor's career path, but taking a swing at it and missing also had repercussions. Integrity and ethics were easily subordinated for the next promotion and currying favor with a higher-ranking commissioned officer. It was an all-too-common scenario I encountered from supervisors like Quade.

Three weeks into the CK Mafia investigation, three days before Thanksgiving, my first taste of the continuous grief I would endure throughout the following year came when Adamo and I joined the city police in a search warrant for the house where a CK Mafia soldier lived. The city police Neighborhood Recovery Unit had made three crack-cocaine buys from a resident there. We went along for the ride at Hartigan's invitation to see what investigative leads might develop. Embarrassment greeted my arrival when a city police sergeant held up a State Police uniform shirt found in the living room among powdered cocaine and packaging paraphernalia strewn about the coffee table. Hartigan found more uniforms and a State Police-issued Glock 9mm handgun in a bedroom. The owner, a female trooper, lived there with her twenty-one-year-old son, who openly sold crack cocaine from the house while other CK Mafia members hung out cutting and bagging product. The city cops took photos and tagged the uniforms and gun as evidence. Their lieutenant at the scene made notifications to troop headquarters, as did I. Later in the day, Quade and Plummer summoned me to troop headquarters and admonished me for not securing the uniforms and gun.

"You should've brought them to us," Quade said.

"It's the city's case. I had no role other than to observe and pick up intel." They both reluctantly acknowledged my limited authority at the search scene. "It makes us look bad," Quade said, still not happy with the outcome. The female trooper's close connection to gang members worried me. When I asked about her status, Plummer said Internal Affairs would handle the investigation. Years later I discovered they allowed her to stay on the job after a short suspension, and she retired after twenty years with a full pension and benefits.

One night in early December, after dinner with Joan and the girls, I called Adamo and asked to meet him at a commuter parking lot adjoining a state parkway near his home. Joan, talking on the phone with Brian, checked on his exam schedule and when he planned to come home for Christmas break. He was in his second year of college and had just begun indoor track season. I scribbled a quick note—"Going to meet Adamo, back in an hour, tell Brian hello, love him"—placed it on the end table next to where she sat, blew her a kiss, and left.

I met with Adamo to tell him about suspected police drug dealers in the county, the potential ties to a trooper, and how our Internal Affairs Unit mishandled the investigation. "We supplied information to the New York City Drug Enforcement Task Force," I told him. "No one above the field level took the information seriously enough to do anything about it." The recent development with the female trooper and her son heightened my concerns. I wanted to be upfront with Adamo and let him know the situation so he could decide if he wanted to continue working with me and the State Police.

"Keeping case information contained worries me. There are people on my job who have too many connections to bad dudes," I said. For a few seconds, he stared off at the oncoming lights of northbound traffic zipping up the parkway.

"Every agency has issues," he finally replied.

"I'll understand if you want to cut me loose from the case."

"Don't you think I fully checked you out before we teamed up? You, my friend, are the only one I want to work with." Relieved to hear those words and happy to continue working with him, I suspected we'd come across more potential police issues as the case progressed and let him know. Undaunted, Adamo assured me we'd work through it. Driving home, I focused solely on how to build a case against the CK Mafia. The best way was to aim for the top.

*

Sonny C, real name Gregory Josepha, the handsome, charismatic leader of the CK Mafia, started building his reputation as a drug dealer and gang leader while in high school. He took on the name Sonny C as homage to the *Godfather* character, Sonny Corleone. Despite Sonny Corleone's brutal murder in the movie where he is trapped at a toll booth and shot by rival mobsters, Hartigan heard Josepha admired how Sonny Corleone took no shit and fought whoever stood in his way. Sonny Corleone had one other admirable quality Josepha liked: he fucked every woman he could seduce.

As profane and misogynistic as he presented himself, I subsequently learned of a different side to Sonny C. He never spoke of or to one girl, Anila Lee, with anything in his voice other than love and respect. She was the mother of his daughter, eight-month-old Jasmine, who lived on the north side of the city with Anila and her parents. He and Anila were high school sweethearts but broke up before knowing she was pregnant. Sonny gave Anila cash each week for Jasmine and sometimes accompanied them to doctor's visits. This revealed the most decent part of him. Otherwise, he was nothing more than a cold-blooded killer who poisoned his neighborhood with drugs.

Sonny C's top two partners went by the street names Domino and Squid. Each one was violent, though only Sonny C had a known homicide and a suspected second to his credit. Squid came close sixteen months earlier when he ripped off a coke dealer and shot him twice, once in the car from the passenger seat and then a second time after he pulled him out onto the pavement, stood over him, and shot him in the chest. It turned out Squid had shot his cousin, someone he vaguely recognized as a relation and spent time with at family picnics by the river. That didn't stop him from pulling the trigger a second time and fleeing with his victim's cash and coke. The cousin would spend a month in the hospital and another month convalescing at home. He also later became our informant.

The gang had two main enforcers, Darlin Porfenoit, a/k/a Manic, and Jesus Malpica, a/k/a Halfway. Despite his diminutive size, Halfway struck fear in many around the city. He'd draw a weapon and pull the trigger without remorse. Of the many shootings in and around the city, we connected him to a dozen or more. Manic, also prolific with a pistol, fired his gun less randomly, though no less lethally. Malpica earned his nickname while slinging crack at a northside housing project bordering the town line as a 15-year-old. An older dealer tried to move him along, and when threats didn't work, he resorted to making fun of Malpica's size. As soon as he told Malpica he was only "halfway grown and shouldn't be playing with adults," Malpica pulled out a knife and stabbed the rival dealer in the gut and then slashed him across the face. His reputation for instant violence was spawned along with his street name.

Halfway earned his reputation by pulling off his retaliation in the courtyard of the Stacks, the nickname given by locals to the city-owned northwest housing complex. It earned its name from the ventilation and exhaust pipes on the roofs of each building. The large black and rusted red cylindrical pipes, one local cop noted, looked like the smokestacks of an old ocean liner. He alternately named the complex the Titanic because "very few get out alive," and the name stuck among some city cops. The housing complex's reputation for violence led the city police to enter a mutual aid compact with the neighboring town to send patrols as backup on calls there.

The four x-shaped brick buildings stood only six stories high, unlike the twenty-floor Westview Apartment housing project further west by the river, which was also a gang hangout. The Stacks, configured like a maze, had car access through a side street that dead-ended next to the drab green wrought-iron fencing around the main walkway to the courtyard. It looked like an entrance to a prison, which it ended up being for many. Residents with cars, considered a luxury by those who lived there, had marked diagonal parking slots along the narrow dead end. Most residents relied on the city bus stop on the other side of the housing complex for transportation.

We needed to identify the different gang members. As many as sixty claimed to be CK Mafia, but getting to know the leaders was crucial. I'd learned from working NYC organized crime cases the importance of getting inside their heads and learning to think like them. Delroy Jenkins, tagged with the street name Squid due to his gangly build and long arms, was an enigma as a gang member. He had a steady girlfriend and never seemed to cheat on her. He also had a good home life. His father drove a truck for a local waste company where he made a decent wage, had insurance, and a pension plan. His mother worked at a local nursing home. Squid had been a good student. Hartigan pulled his high school file with assistance from a detective in the juvenile bureau. Solid SAT scores, B-B+ average throughout high school, and three credits from a community college course he took during his senior year showed his academic potential. At twenty and only a year out of high school, Squid's college future halted quickly two years before. A six-month jail bid for a strong-arm robbery held him back in school. He'd snatched gold chains off the neck of a football player from a rival school as the other team's bus loaded up after a game. The bid caused him to lose a school year, half of which he spent drinking and smoking weed after his release from the county jail. But he was a thinker and more reflective than other CKM members. Squid also liked history and, as our later phone recordings of him showed, occasionally peppered his conversations with references to different wars. World War I was his favorite, but his fascination with military history wasn't for the pure quest of knowledge. Squid viewed the CKM as an army, a guerrilla-type outfit, and he took his role as Sonny's co-leader seriously. He was the tactician of the group to the extent that any approximation of tactics could be claimed by them. They were mostly opportunists, street predators, like hyenas ready to move on wandering gazelles, except their gazelles were other dealers, anyone who had cash, and the drug fiends who craved the product they sold. Because he thought things out and planned, we were concerned Squid had the capacity for worse violence than Sonny C who, like his fictional *Godfather* hero, was impulsive. Squid acted more like Michael Corleone, who instilled more fear because he controlled his violence and revenge. As I'd done when investigating Bonanno and Genovese mobsters many years earlier, I inhabited the CK Mafia leaders' lives to the point where I knew them better than their own families, and, sometimes, better than my own.

Joan and I always maintained a close relationship with Brian, Siobhan, and Deirdre. As they got older and became teenagers, I felt even closer to them during driving lessons, running together, and having discussions about problems at school or with peers. However, as the gang case progressed, especially during the following summer, I often checked out. Our collective life as a family moved quickly as Joan's nursing duties increased, Siobhan finished her last year of high school, Deirdre prepared to move up to middle school, and Brian's college education reached the halfway point. Most of the time, I played catch-up with what was going on in their lives as the gang investigation consumed my time.

11
THE BOSSES

If Squid was the more cerebral and methodical side of the CK Mafia, Yasim Thomas, street name Domino, typified its brawny physicality. As a high school freshman, he benched 240 pounds and squatted a full stack on the weight machine. By sophomore year, as a promising running back and starter for the high school football team, he gained interest from some colleges, but he liked collecting greenbacks more than piling up yards on the gridiron. He'd been immersed in the city's gang culture since middle school, and his two years on the varsity football team with a demanding coach and the potential for a college football scholarship did nothing to allay his gang connections. The street was his home. It held an allure unlike anything else. In a different context, I understood this part of Domino better than anyone.

Squid and Domino represented two different approaches to street violence. Squid believed violence served a purpose and should be used strategically and sparingly. Domino viewed violence as fun. He liked it. From the information we gathered in the first few months of the case, I worried Domino would commit a homicide during the investigation. He was eighteen and extremely dangerous.

The investigation moved through the winter months with either Adamo, Hartigan, or me joining the County Drug Task Force on informant street buys from lower echelon gang members. Alternately, Adamo and I surveilled CK Mafia drug corners and picked off buyers on car stops several blocks away from the site of the sale. If we flipped someone, we sent them back a day or two later to make a drug buy for us. One night, we got lucky and picked off an associate of the gang leaving Domino's house. He was a local high school senior who went by the name Smokes. We pulled him over for a loud exhaust and no inspection sticker on his windshield. Smokes had no license, and when we had him step out of the car, a gun lay on the driver's seat. Bingo! Another nick in the CK Mafia armor. Smokes bought the gun from Domino. It was late February, and in addition to the gun, we had multiple drug buys involving gang members, including two buys into each of the top three, Sonny C, Domino, and Squid, but we were still short of getting the investigation where it needed to be and the goal of establishing an enterprise corruption charge against the gang members.

Enterprise corruption, the state charge equivalent to the federal RICO (Racketeer Influenced and Corrupt Organizations) Act used against the Italian Mafia, presented a potent weapon for dismantling criminal groups. To effectively build this kind of case against the CK Mafia, we needed to show a structure with a hierarchy of responsibility and predicate crimes committed by members of the organization in furtherance of its activities. Enterprise corruption prosecutions hadn't been used much outside of New York City, and never against a street gang.

Early on, I proposed building such a case to Assistant District Attorney Stan Burghoff, who oversaw the investigation for future prosecution. I had to first convince him of our case's legal viability, assuming we'd be able to link other crimes to the CK Mafia. Burghoff, an experienced and aggressive prosecutor whose features called to mind an English Bulldog, cautiously relished the challenge of building a state RICO-style prosecution against the CK Mafia.

"My main concern is being able to tie the predicate offenses together," he said. "Gangs operate much more loosely than traditional organized crime groups." I assured him we'd link individual crimes to concerted gang activity and deliver him a one-of-a-kind case.

Months of investigation yielded inconsequential results, nothing to get us close to making the type of case needed to go forward with an enterprise corruption indictment. From my experience, I knew we needed eavesdropping warrants to listen to the main players' cell phone calls. The best evidence for an enterprise corruption charge would come from those calls and where they led us. We were still a long way off, and my bosses, Captain Quade and Lieutenant Plummer, became impatient with the progress of the case and with me.

Plummer could be decent and easy to chat with at times, but he was mercurial. It earned him the derisive monicker "Napoleon." His appearance contributed to the nickname. Plummer stood at 5 feet 9 inches with a broad build. His jet-black hair kept short at the sides and back, with a fuller slicked-back growth on top, contrasted with his pale complexion. Plummer rose quickly through the ranks to lieutenant. He was a "company cop" who never found a flaw in any edict or policy coming from Albany headquarters, what those of us in the field referred to as "the puzzle palace." When it came to police work, he was a dilettante, claiming to know more than he did about how to make a case. Plummer never worked as a BCI investigator. He wrote tickets for three years before taking the sergeant's test and then spent another three years as a sergeant busting troopers' balls until he took the lieutenant's test. He scored high enough to be pulled up to the Inspection Unit as a noncommissioned officer until promoted, followed by a trip to the FBI National Academy. Plummer could be complimentary and funny when relaxed and not seeking to impress everyone. Those moments with me were too few to generate prolonged affection for him as a supervisor. By the time he became our lieutenant, I'd had my share of good bosses who took care of their people and didn't let their rank—those single silver or double brass-plated butter bars they wore on their shoulders—go to their head. The younger generation of commissioned officers were ladder climbers, or rocket ship cops, who disdained actual police work and rode their careers from behind a desk. You could always tell which bosses had done real police work; they were the ones who let you do your job and made sure you had the necessary support. Plummer fit somewhere in between. He gave free rein until his ego intruded and he felt compelled to insert himself into a case. As Captain Quade's right-hand man who oversaw the Major Crimes Unit, Plummer hovered over the unit's work more than he did the separate BCI stations scattered around the troop.

Quade was my age. I didn't like him upon our first meeting. Heinrichs' initial assessment cut right to the core, "Geez, he gives me the creeps." Women's instincts, I learned, were always to be trusted, especially when it came to men. I relied on them years later when vetting my two future sons-in-law and asking our daughters' friends what they thought of my girls' boyfriends. Both times the women confirmed my gut instincts, though their confirmations made me feel better. Heinrichs' opinion of Quade reassured me as well. I wasn't wrong about him.

Quade had a habit of trying to look through you as an intimidation factor. His antics didn't faze me. Good bosses didn't act like they hated you from the start. Quade, however, came up in rank when it seemed the supervisor's school taught them to treat subordinates as the enemy. Maybe my understanding of rank's demands failed because I never sought the promotions they did and found my purpose as an investigator. Quade's reputation prior to coming to the troop command was tepid. He'd been assigned to the New York City Drug Enforcement Task Force where he ran a money laundering unit for a year and a half before going back to his home troop on Long Island as the uniform administrative lieutenant. At DETF, he was a hands-off supervisor for the first year, someone willing to let his unit work with little interference, until he started to become more involved as he got comfortable in his role. Word spread that he could be a pain in the ass. The DETF detail commander had enough juice in Albany headquarters at the time to get Quade transferred back to Long Island and into uniform. Quade, though, had cultivated his own Albany connections. As a result, his promotion to captain came quickly, and he received a plum assignment running BCI operations in one of the busiest troop commands in the New York State Police. The troop's proximity to New York City, several busy interstates and state routes, large populated suburban patrol areas, and the smaller, crime-ridden urban centers along the spine of the Hudson River accounted for much of the activity.

I jumped to the Safe Streets Task Force assignment to get out from under Quade and Plummer's constant glare after the way they handled the information about a potentially corrupt trooper and other cops in the county. There are many subtle ways a supervisor can mess with a cop, and their testing me with petty assignments and extra scrutiny of my work forced me to look for a way out. Working with Adamo and Hartigan for the past few months was liberating, but I ran up against more trouble when reporting to Plummer the name of a gang member who had a relative working for the State Police. Shortly thereafter, I reported the recovery of a State Police investigator's duty weapon that his fifteen-year-old gang-affiliated son used in a robbery. Even though the city police contacted him when they arrested the juvenile, I beat them to the notification, and Plummer was not happy. In a clear case of a "shoot the messenger" reaction, Plummer asked if I enjoyed telling him bad news. Had I not notified him, though, I'd have been in trouble. Notification up the chain of command was a big deal to the State Police hierarchy, which was understandable. Supervisors like Quade and Plummer took it to extremes. They wanted a streaming news service of all the news all the time so as to never be caught off guard if a colonel from Albany headquarters called for an update. I didn't control the news; I just reported it, but it seemed to be irksome to them, especially the nature of what I had to report. Considering my prior queries into corruption, I expected to be blamed for every piece of shitty news involving another cop crossing their desk, as if I purposely dug it up. I would have been fine with never encountering State Police uniforms and a duty weapon on a search warrant for drugs or discovering family relationships between CK Mafia and State Police members or reporting the recovery of another State Police firearm in a different arrest weeks later. These events complicated my life. I merely wanted to work the investigation and bring it to a successful conclusion.

"Where's this case going?" Plummer asked me one day when I was leaving the Major Crimes office after stopping in to retrieve old case notes. "The captain's been reviewing your progress reports, and it appears you've got nothing more than low-level drug sales." I hoped to avoid anyone in the headquarters building, especially him. "We're working on something now that'll turn us in a positive direction," I replied. He then told me to stem violence in the city and prevent further homicides like the JJ Williams murder; otherwise, I'd have to answer to Albany HQ. The JJ Williams shooting in the adjoining town was the catalyst for the task force and a focus of its mission. Sonny C killed Williams, a local drug dealer, the prior year after luring him to a quiet local road to buy two ounces of coke. When the moment came to pay, Sonny pulled a 9mm semi-automatic and shot JJ once behind the right ear. "It's on you if any more bodies fall. You hear that? This is coming straight from the captain . . . and now me." Plummer's comment surprised me and, for a rare moment, left me speechless. He turned toward his office, and I made a quick exit out the back door to the parking lot. On my drive home, I called Heinrichs to let her know about the conversation with Plummer. I needed to riff off a string of expletives, and Joan didn't need to catch the brunt of it. She had her own work matters to deal with as a nurse in a busy pediatric practice in the city. My anger level rose incrementally higher each minute after leaving troop headquarters, and I wanted it to come down before reaching home. Heinrichs knew well the natures of Quade and Plummer, having to deal with them every day, and she provided balance to their micromanagement style. "That motherfucker never worked a case like this, let alone any major case," I yelled into my cell phone. "How the fuck am I now suddenly responsible for everything happening on the street?" Heinrichs broke the mood with levity. "But are you having fun yet?" The remainder of the ride home, I thought only about the investigation and outlined plans for the next phase. We had good fortune on our side, and it came in the form of a CK Mafia shooting victim, Squid's cousin whom he'd shot months earlier. The following weeks would get us our eavesdropping warrants, but not before the results of the investigation nearly caused my removal from the case and forced retirement. Not to mention the toll it took on my marriage.

12
INTEGRITY ISSUES

The CK Mafia investigation levied its heaviest toll on me within two weeks of my run-in meeting with Plummer when I registered a local parolee, Tariq Kwame, as an informant. Adamo and I approached Kwame, also known as TK, in January, two months into the investigation. An arrest for drug possession while still on parole threatened his freedom. Kwame aged out of the gang scene at thirty-five yet still retained street cred. His attempt to settle down with his fiancée and baby daughter by opening a convenience store in the city kept being interrupted by gangbangers knocking at his door. A conviction on the new charge would send him back to prison for the remaining three years of his sentence, but he had something we wanted.

Kwame mentored the younger Sonny C. Before prison, he ran the largest drug crew in the area. He arrived in Dannemora State Prison at twenty-three years old to begin a ten-to-fifteen-year sentence for drug distribution. Paroled after serving his minimum bid, Kwame made it through two years on parole supervision until he decided to handle a drug deal for a friend in exchange for a percentage of the profit. Squid, at the other end of the deal, shot Kwame during a rip-off of four ounces of cocaine and cash. Sonny C never would have approved a move on Kwame. We surmised he wrote it off as the price one paid for operating on CK Mafia turf, and Kwame had been in the wrong place at the wrong time.

A.D.A. Burghoff realized Kwame's potential and agreed to hold off prosecution if he cooperated. We all viewed him as integral to gaining enough probable cause to allow eavesdropping on CK Mafia cell phones. For Kwame, the choice didn't require much thought; returning to prison wasn't an option. He wanted revenge. Cooperating with the police ensured he'd get it.

As a confidential informant, Kwame had to sign a formal cooperation agreement. Because of his parole status, we needed permission from the state Division of Parole to use him. The acting commissioner, a State Police colonel laterally assigned to serve in the post until the governor appointed a new commissioner, denied our request. We scrambled to get the denial rescinded.

Burghoff enlisted the help of his boss, District Attorney Walter C. Braden, who contacted the Division of Parole's counsel's office. Adamo contacted the regional special agent in charge of the FBI, and I went to Quade. Albany HQ quickly rebuffed Quade's request.

Adamo couldn't register Kwame as an FBI informant since US Attorney General guidelines were stringent. Agency guidelines required approval from the state Division of Parole, and we already knew they denied the request. The order from the acting commissioner of parole forbidding the use of Kwame as an informant made no sense. I disagreed with his decision and had Kwame sign the State Police paperwork to register as an informant. We had an individual who wanted to trade potential prison time for his cooperation, and I was willing to provide him with the opportunity to do so. Plus, I interpreted our agency guidelines more loosely and ambiguously. My legal training provided an ace in the deck to play whenever it served me. I navigated a precarious position with this move but it needed to be done.

"You sure of this?" Adamo asked while I completed the paperwork.

"Who else are we going to get at this point? He gives us immediate access." I made copies for my files and prepared an envelope to bring to troop headquarters the next day.

"If he notices, I'll be all mea culpa," I said. "Oh, sorry lieutenant, it must have slipped through."

"You're going to catch hell," Adamo said with a grin.

"This will help the investigation. That's all that matters."

I submitted the paperwork to Lieutenant Plummer for endorsement. A week later, Quade's and Plummer's signatures approved my requests with an informant identification number. Kwame became State Police confidential informant KBI-009. Adamo and I quickly went to work getting the County Drug Task Force tech unit to video and audio wire Kwame's place of business. We recorded every meeting in his store with Sonny C, and when Kwame met him elsewhere, he wore a wireless transmitter.

For a month, we worked Kwame hard and arranged multiple meetings with Sonny C. Kwame didn't mind because it meant no prison. He'd be there for his daughter's first birthday in November. Our efforts paid off. In mid-March, Kwame told Sonny C he needed a gun, and Sonny offered one for sale. We set up the buy on a weekday afternoon at Kwame's store. The gun, a 9mm semi-automatic the CK Mafia referred to as "Lucifer," we believed was the murder weapon Sonny C used to kill JJ Williams. It made sense for him to unload the gun and place it in the hands of a paroled former drug dealer like Kwame, even if they were friends. That was the drug game. The week leading up to the sale was tense. We weren't sure if Sonny C would go through with the deal or if he planned to rob Kwame.

With CKM, events could turn ugly in an instant. The advantage of having Kwame wired alleviated some concerns.

When the day of the sale arrived, we sat in Adamo's Tahoe in a parking lot on Main Street across from Kwame's store. Taglieri and Buchanan from the County Drug Task Force set up in the parking lot behind the store in case entry had to be made from the rear of the building. A sedan with two FBI SWAT guys idled at the other end of Main. Hartigan cruised the busy commercial area around Kwame's store to make sure no CK Mafia members waited to stage a rip-off. Robbery remained CKM's calling card, and even though we had no indication this meeting was anything other than a straightforward transaction, we weren't taking any chances.

When Sonny C entered the store, he and Kwame walked to a room in the back and entered an office. In less than fifteen minutes, Sonny C exited onto Main Street with $500 of FBI buy money. He left in a black Monte Carlo driven by an associate named Blade, a CKM soldier and Sonny C's chauffeur and bodyguard. A half-hour later, Kwame met Hartigan, Adamo, and me in a local church parking lot to turn over the gun. Hartigan rushed it to the State Police forensics lab in Albany. Later, ballistic testing matched the gun to the JJ Williams murder and the one used by Squid in Kwame's shooting.

The irony of Kwame purchasing the same gun used to shoot him delighted A.D.A. Burghoff. "These guys are ruthless and smart. It's lucky for us they can also be incredibly fucking dumb," he said. We had an important break in the case; however, it didn't stave off the shitstorm barraging me over the next three days. I had to come clean about the gun purchase, and from Plummer's initial reaction, I knew deep trouble lay ahead.

Captain Quade ordered me to his office the next morning to meet with him, Plummer, and Heinrichs. Much to her relief, I never told Heinrichs about registering Kwame as an informant after the interim parole commissioner's denial. This took her off the hot seat and gave her a stronger position to advocate for me. At the meeting, she staunchly defended my decision to use Kwame as a State Police informant.

"Parole made a moronic call on this one," Heinrichs told Quade.

"The colonel made the decision, and he's in charge of parole right now," Quade snapped at her. "Well, the colonel is an ass. Who the hell else does he expect to buy a gun from a gang member? What're we gonna do, find some legit citizen to do the buy for us? It's fuckin' ridiculous," Heinrichs fumed. She unsuccessfully voiced the same complaints made by others who weeks earlier attempted to change the acting commissioner's decision. His denial was no longer the issue. The topic of conversation had shifted to my violation of the Division of Parole's determination, and, by proxy, State Police orders. Quade sent me out of the room. Twenty minutes later, Heinrichs exited the meeting and took me to her office.

"This isn't looking good; they're mad at you," she said. "They're talking about disciplinary charges and removing you from the case."

"What charges? They'd be hard-pressed to find a violation of any manual sections."

"They're super pissed. They'll find something," she said.

"Kwame was registered in accordance with the Field Manual. Quade and Plummer reviewed and signed the registration form."

"Yeah, that's what has frosted them the most. Their names are on the paperwork approving your use of him as a CI." My self-righteousness began to kick in. "And they read my weekly progress reports and are supposed to know what's going on." Heinrichs smiled. She'd been my BCI supervisor for over eight years and knew I'd arranged things so there'd be collateral fallout if my use of Kwame became a problem.

During the next thirty-six hours, Quade twice ordered me to troop headquarters to meet with him and Plummer. The first time there, I stood at attention in his large office along the corridor leading to the Major Crimes Unit and listened to the revisions he wanted in my memorandum explaining the circumstances of Kwame becoming a State Police informant. Every change he required aimed at minimizing his and Plummer's oversight in signing the authorization. Quade's contempt for me was palpable. I couldn't blame him this time. My reaction would be no different if I were in his position. Nonetheless, I felt justified in doing my job. On the second trip, Quade admonished me by saying that Colonel Arturo Diaz, the head of our Bureau of Criminal Investigation operations for the state, expressed concerns about my integrity and any problems it may cause with the investigation. Plummer stood next to Quade and solemnly nodded his head. I got angry when Quade made the comment. "If the colonel wants to discuss integrity issues in this troop, tell him to come down here and give me an hour. I'll provide him with at least a dozen." I'd had enough. Their nonsense and posturing sickened me. Either take me off the case, suspend me, or fire me. My overall frustration prompted me to take out my shield and slide my holster and gun off my belt. "You know what? I've got twenty years in and something to go to. Here, take these." I held the shield and holstered gun out to Plummer, who clumsily took them. "I'm driving up to Albany tomorrow and putting in my retirement papers." "No, no . . . don't be rash. This is not about . . ." Quade then quickly pivoted, "You're going to be okay on this." He took the holster and shield from Plummer and thrust them toward me. "Take these back. We only had to officially talk with you on Albany's behalf," he said.

While I'd been home pacing, fuming, and planning my next move, Heinrichs mustered the troops. She first called Burghoff. "You know the type of scum this job let's slide with shit," she said. "And now they're going to try and ruin this man's career because he did the right thing!" Burghoff had already been at work on my behalf. At his request, District Attorney Braden called the Superintendent of State Police. Meanwhile, Adamo had the regional special agent in charge call troop and Albany headquarters, and Burghoff made his own calls to State Police brass. Heinrichs also enlisted a few local police chiefs to make calls.

Finding out what Heinrichs and the others said and did on my behalf was overwhelming and humbling. Arguably, I violated orders when registering Kwame as a confidential informant. My actions were for the right reasons, but, admittedly, out of line, and gave Quade a viable reason to come after me. Maybe I wanted to create an excuse to leave the job. Joan and I discussed my exit strategy during those three days in limbo when I didn't know what my future in the State Police held in store. I planned to return to adjunct teaching at a local college's criminal justice program and practice law full-time. My part-time law practice was busy, and it would be easy to open the spigot and bring in more work, especially without the constraints of the job. I still wanted to put in twenty-five years, but Joan was more than ready for me to retire. Leaving would be so much easier and more lucrative.

Joan worried over the possible consequences of my actions. "There are people on the job who don't like you." "What's not to like? I'm a sweetheart," I countered. "You leave some people with a sour taste. If you don't like someone, you go out of your way to let them know it." Her comment surprised me, though it shouldn't have. Years of living with the job provided her with a perspective often lost on me. Phrases like "you don't let go of things," "you're driven more than most," "you strike back when you feel attacked or slighted," and "you don't let people get close to you," bounced around the walls of the room. "The people on the job who like you admire the stances you take. Don't think for a minute, though, they'll stand with you if something goes wrong. Except for Juan and Sue, you're alone at work." Her assessment was 100 percent accurate. This was her way of giving me a wake-up slap across the face. She knew there would be more incidents ahead of me. The next one arrived a few weeks later; only this time I hadn't crossed a line at work; instead, it was at home with Joan, and, like my disobeying orders at work, I wasn't sure we'd come through it intact.

The closest we came to divorce resulted from an argument prompted by my moodiness and anger, and the most trivial of all circumstances. I asked Joan if we had cold cuts in the refrigerator for a sandwich to bring to work. She had just arrived home from a busy workday, and I was preparing to meet up with Adamo for a night of drug buys. "Did you look? I'm barely in the door. Hold on," she said. Something in her response set me off, and a curse-filled invective followed. A trigger had been pulled within, setting me off based on a perceived slight detected in Joan's tone. Irrational is the only way to describe my behavior. I stormed out of the house and drove to CK Mafia territory to surveil our case targets.

A deep frost encircled our marriage and lingered for days. I had snapped at Joan like she was a mutt on the street who didn't show respect. She supported me weeks before through all the trouble surrounding my use of Kwame as a CI and now, I'd pushed her away again. She didn't deserve my anger. I'd fucked up. For several nights afterward, I stayed on the street past my shift, hunting my CK Mafia prey, waiting for them to give me reason to pounce. It was easier than offering Joan another apology.

We fought infrequently, though I gave her plenty of reasons to be angry with me. We loved each other deeply and passionately. I just didn't always feel equally deserving of her love. She deserved love, unlike me, a voyeur and sometime facilitator of the violence, pain, and duplicity I dealt with every day. My sense of complicity and anger led to self-loathing. An accumulated feeling of despair further burdened me. What good did I accomplish? What purpose did any of us serve while on the job except to delude ourselves that we stood for a vague concept of justice and morality? Most people see the world in terms of ordered absolutes, and they set out neat columns of good and bad, right and wrong, rich and poor, love and hate. I viewed the world as a conditional mess, like an intertwined ball of wires that everyone forgot what they connected to. On the surface, I held it together, but what brewed inside me bubbled and burned each day until it had to be released. Too often, the release came when it shouldn't have, and my loved ones caught its wrath.

Our fight resolved a few days later in the waiting room of Yale-New Haven Hospital during surgery on Brian's left ankle tendon. He began having severe pain in the ankle during his college outdoor track season. He made it through a sophomore season of cross country, indoor track, and most of outdoor before we discovered he had a congenital condition where his ankle tendon slid over the bone. I broke the silence between us and asked Joan if she wanted to leave me, scared her response would be "yes." It should have been, even after nearly twenty-one years of marriage. Thankfully it never came to be, but she said things had to change—the anger had to resolve itself. "I'm sorry" had by then worn out its welcome. What else did I have to say to her? Explain the pressure to successfully investigate the CK Mafia, the lack of support from my bosses, the different corruption issues encountered, and my growing distrust of people in my own agency? She knew all of this. I used it as an excuse to sustain my rage.

"Where's this anger coming from?" Joan pleaded. She deserved a response. I looked at her, and not a single word came to mind other than "sorry." Tired, meaningless, and as common as a loose penny, “sorry” meant nothing anymore. “There’s a point when you have to be able to let things go.” She was right. How do I let go, though?

I hated myself for the behavior toward her. Past marital skirmishes suddenly came rushing back, and each memory was the same; I had been the instigator. Joan always forgave me, and we went on like nothing happened, but this last incident woke me up to the fact that I had to fix what troubled me. Self-help only went so far. Whatever needed to be done, though, had to wait. The investigation intensified after the gun buy, and I had to make it through the approaching hot, humid summer.

13

ENTERPRISE CORRUPTION

Months of investigation alleviated A.D.A. Burghoff's initial concerns about building an enterprise corruption prosecution. We had shown the CK Mafia operated with a distinct hierarchy and structure, much like Sonny C's revered La Cosa Nostra. The drug buys, late-night surveillances, and cultivation of low-level street informants brought us closer to applying for eavesdropping warrants on CKM leadership's cell phones, but Sonny C's gun sale to Kwame delivered the needed punch. We now had to make a case tying together all these disparate crimes and placing them under the umbrella of gang membership. According to New York law, every CK Mafia defendant we wanted to charge had to be shown to have committed at least two underlying designated felonies within a ten-year period. Street work only took us so far. Listening to cell phone calls of Sonny C, Domino, and Squid would give us much more. Getting a court-ordered eavesdropping warrant required showing that we had exhausted all investigative avenues and that no other conventional method would yield further results. We met the exhaustion requirement, and Burghoff prepared eavesdropping warrants. I had already begun drafting a forty-five-page affidavit for Adamo and me to sign. My legal background and prior experience with New York City organized crime investigations gave me the confidence to undertake the preliminary drafting of the affidavit.

Burghoff reviewed my work, made additions and some changes, completed his application on behalf of his boss, District Attorney Braden, and in late May took a drive with me and Adamo to the chambers of a state supreme court judge in an adjoining county for approval and signature. The State Police Technical Unit from Albany then installed the listening equipment in a "wire room" where shifts of law enforcement personnel listened to hours of calls. An unused State Bridge Authority building on the opposite shoreline of the city served as the "wire room" or "plant."

Adamo staffed the wire room by getting commitments from the adjoining town police, the city police, his regional FBI office, and the State Police to provide personnel. But they were only assigned to work three rotating shifts to listen to calls and take care of the administrative duties involved with court-ordered eavesdropping on multiple phone lines. Captain Quade authorized two investigators to join us and work in the wire room. We still needed help on the street. Sue Heinrichs requested permission to have my Major Crimes partner Juan Limon join us in the street work. Plummer denied her request. I knew he and Quade were still angry with me over the gun buy with Kwame and accepted this. From my perspective, though, they seemed to harbor another reason. They went hot and cold with me, just like they'd been prior to my joining the Safe Streets Task Force. Admittedly, I didn't always act in a way to curry their favor, was opinionated, and didn't kiss anybody's ass. The latter was often viewed by supervisors as a character flaw for subordinates who wanted to get ahead. I didn't want to go anywhere, though. My satisfaction came from being an investigator, working cases, and going home at the end of a shift. The people on the job who mattered worked alongside me, not the bosses. What annoyed me was being denied help on the street. Nonetheless, we now listened to cell phone calls of Sonny C, Domino, and Squid. The case heated up, and eavesdropping warrants for other phones soon followed.

*

Few police officers get the opportunity to work on an enterprise corruption case. CK Mafia was my third. I knew how to build a prosecutable case, which had been part of my original pitch to Burghoff rather than pursuing conspiracy charges against the gang members. As the initial few weeks on the case rolled by, I worried that the strategy might fail. Things had moved slowly.

The first enterprise corruption case I worked on from beginning to end in the early 1990s involved the Bonanno organized crime family's infiltration of the New York City newspaper delivery system. The Manhattan District Attorney's Office tasked the State Police Labor Racketeering Unit with the investigation after receiving complaints from the *New York Post's* board of directors and other industry executives. Two undercover State Police investigators posing as security consultants were placed in the *Post*. The paper's ownership granted District Attorney Robert Morgenthau investigative access. The undercovers worked the overnight shift when most of the thefts, extortion rackets, and other crimes occurred.

At the time, the *Post* lost circulation numbers, which impacted advertising rates since the lower the circulation, the less the paper could charge for ads. Additionally, management discovered ghost employees on the payroll—Bonanno crime family members and associates—collecting salaries for not working. The ghosts were listed as drivers or "tail men" on the trucks, those who unloaded the papers along the routes.

Complicating matters was the *Post*'s location in a known Mafia stronghold in the shadow of the elevated portion of the FDR Drive. The *Post* fronted on South Street, with Catherine Slip and Market Slip bracketing the building. Water Street ran parallel to South Street behind the building. Across Water Street and a strand of green city park land, the massive Knickerbocker Village apartments, home to several members of La Cosa Nostra, occupied a city block. A social club at the corner of Cherry Street and Market Slip, affiliated with the Genovese crime family, was two doors down from a Bonanno social club. Both nondescript storefronts, painted dark brown with blacked-out windows, harbored ruthless killers, thieves, hijackers, and loan sharks. During the day, heavyset, scowling men sat outside drinking espresso and wine while smoking cigars. At night, Cadillacs and Mercedes-Benzes with tinted windows double-parked on Market Slip across from the clubs. The *Post* was also a short distance from the Paris Café restaurant and South Street Diner, both favorite mobster hangouts. The Fulton Fish Market, another mob-infiltrated industry at the time, sat tucked under the north and south conduits of the FDR Drive, a block and a half away from the diner.

For over a year, I conducted surveillance in Manhattan and Brooklyn, backing up our undercovers, trailing informants when meeting investigative targets, and making nighttime stops of delivery trucks. When not working the overnight shift, I spent my days tracking and arresting wanted fugitives across the five boroughs, identifying individuals photographed during overnight surveillances, conducting interviews on the *Post* case, and reviewing the NYPD 1st Precinct cold case files of a murdered Bonanno soldier in the event our investigation came across any leads.

The newspaper investigation coincided with the Third Colombo War, a rift in the Colombo crime family which, along with the Bonanno, Gambino, Genovese, and Lucchese crime families, comprised the five New York Mafia families.

Over a two-year period, nine bodies of Colombo family members surfaced throughout the city and Long Island. Numerous others went missing. The number of murdered, missing, and incarcerated Colombo soldiers jeopardized the survival of the crime family, and the other four families circled the dying carcass.

We worked the same city streets as the Colombo soldiers during the struggles. The murders, a backdrop to our investigation of the Bonannos, heightened our commitment to keep the undercovers, informants, and each other safe. Mafia violence permeated New York City in the early 1990s. We surveilled gangsters attending baptisms, weddings, and funerals, woke up with them outside their homes, and tailed them until they returned at night. Investigating the CK Mafia and keeping track of their activities years later followed the same routine. The only distinction between them was the way the media and the public romanticized the Mafia and vilified urban gangs. Both deserved contempt as dangerous criminals;

however, in some twisted logic, paunchy middle-aged white men who wore gold crucifixes around their necks and received the Catholic sacraments were treated as modern-day Robin Hoods. Meanwhile, Black and Hispanic young men, and the white kids hanging out with them, who took on similar crime group structures, initiations, and rituals, were labeled hoodlums, thugs, and lowlifes. To me, they were all criminals subject to the same investigative intensity and negative publicity.

In the *Post* case, we focused on the superintendent of delivery, Robert Perrino, a Bonanno associate. Perrino could never be a made member because he had been a cadet in the NYPD Academy until he dropped out for unknown reasons. Nonetheless, mob culture fascinated him, and he got closer to it when he married the daughter of former Bonanno underboss Nicholas "Nicky Cigars" Marangello.

Perrino worked as the overnight shift's leader of a team of mobsters and their associates who infiltrated the newspaper's employment rolls. In addition to no-show jobs, the overnight crew committed fraud, extortion, coercion, loansharking, and firearms sales, all while using the *Post* as their base of operations. Perrino oversaw a racket responsible for defrauding the *Post* of significant amounts of revenue and tens of thousands of dollars a month paid to acting boss Salvatore Vitale, Sr., whose son also had a *Post* no-show job. All together, the rackets being run at the *Post* yielded an annual seven figure payday for the Bonanno crime family.

Along with having two State Police undercovers in the building, we surreptitiously installed a court-ordered video-audio device in Perrino's office. For several months, we had a bird's eye view from the video camera in the middle of the room and recorded conversations between Perrino and Bonanno made members Richard "Shellackhead" Cantarella, Alfred "Al Walker" Embaratto, and Joseph "Joey the Mook" D'Amico, among others.

When search warrants in the case were executed and arrests made, Vitale Sr. became worried about Perrino and ordered his murder. In May 1992, believing he was attending a meeting at the Brooklyn social club owned by Bonanno capo Anthony Basile, two Mafia soldiers shot Perrino in the back of the head and then, realizing he was still alive, stabbed him in the heart with an ice pick. The killers threw his body in a car trunk, drove across the Verrazano Bridge and placed him in a barrel with concrete. They eventually buried him under the cement floor of a Staten Island auto body shop. Years later, as a result of a separate federal investigation, FBI, NYPD, and State Police forensic teams recovered Perrino's body.

In my assignment with the Safe Streets Task Force, almost fourteen years after Perrino's disappearance and my involvement with the arrests in the *Post* case, we began monitoring CK Mafia calls between Sonny C, Domino, and Squid during the first week of June 2006. On a sunny Monday morning, only ten days after we monitored the first CK Mafia call, I sat on the witness stand in the federal Eastern District of New York's Brooklyn courthouse testifying in the racketeering trial of Perrino's killers. My testimony came after weeks of preparation at the US Attorney's downtown Brooklyn office and then driving north to work evening shifts keeping tabs on CK Mafia gang members. Somewhere in the middle of all that was my regrettable and irrational outburst toward Joan. The pressure from my bosses during the CK Mafia investigation and the long days spent in Brooklyn followed by nights in the streets chasing Sonny C, Domino, Squid, and the rest of their gang made me irritable and edgy. I constantly had to remind myself to keep my emotions in check when at home. Family is what mattered to me and they deserved the best side of me, not the job side.

The day before my federal court testimony, Siobhan graduated from high school, and we had sixty people at our house. We celebrated her accomplishment, which included a combined academic and Division 1 track scholarship, with gathered family and friends. When our guests started to clear out, I snuck off to my home office to check with the wire room on the CK Mafia's call activity while reviewing old reports on the *Post* investigation in preparation for my testimony. The timing of the convergence of the two cases was not lost on me. At one point, Siobhan came to my office door holding a small plate with a piece of cake. "I knew you were here alone and thought I'd bring you this." She placed the plate on my desk, and I saw in her smile the same sweetness and nurturing spirit as her mother. "Mom and I are so proud of you. I can't begin to describe a way to measure it. Most of all, we love you," I told her while closing my file and pushing it to the side. Siobhan came around my desk, hugged me, and then stayed while I finished the cake. We talked for a few minutes until she gently slid my plate toward her and got up to leave. "I know you have more work to do before the trial tomorrow," she said. Mutual "I love you" and blown kisses crossed the room before I returned to my files.

The CK Mafia's emulation of Italian mobsters led them to parallel its hierarchical structure of capos and soldiers, along with their treachery and techniques. The CKM bumped off rivals and took out snitches (several open homicides were attributed to gang members) and protected their meeting locations where they met late at night. To be a member of the gang, you had to be either a family relation or have gone to grade school together. They didn't allow outsiders in. Their cliquish nature insulated them far better than other criminal groups I had investigated, but weaknesses are inherent in any plan or organization. The wires would expose some of those weaknesses, while others presented themselves unexpectedly.

The city police arrested the CK Mafia's enforcer, Halfway, on a drug charge shortly after the wire went live and held him in the county jail on $15,000 bail. After two court appearances indicated state prison awaited, he contacted his attorney to make a deal with prosecutors. Burghoff set up a proffer session to sit down with Halfway and trade information and possible testimony for a deal. During a proffer session, nothing a defendant says can be directly used against him in a criminal prosecution. The benefit of the meeting is that it allows the defendant to speak freely. If the prosecutor determines the defendant is telling the truth and the information can be used at trial, an exchange of reduced prison time is made for his testimony against a more important criminal target. Halfway's proffer session was like nothing I'd ever seen before. He arrived at the district attorney's office fifth-floor conference room in shackles accompanied by a sheriff's deputy. He stood five feet six inches, thick across the shoulders, and wore a Caesar cut hairstyle with neatly trimmed chin strap sideburns joining a goatee. Halfway appeared more like a boy playing at being a man, a regrettable mistake many on the street made about him. He was dangerous and lethal. Halfway sat in a large, cushioned leather chair next to his attorney. He looked around the room at the carved oak moldings and then across the long mahogany table where Adamo and I sat on either side of Burghoff.

"Mr. Malpica, I'm Stan Burghoff, supervising assistant district attorney. You're here so we can judge the value of the information you want to offer. Has your attorney explained the purpose of this meeting to you?"

"Yeah."

"And you understand that nothing you say can be used directly against you in court or to arrest you?"

"Yeah."

After more preliminaries, Burghoff introduced Adamo and me before turning on a tape recorder.

"Mr. Malpica, we know you're a member of the Crazed Killas Mafia. What is your your role for them?"

"I get motherfuckers who gotta get got."

Burghoff looked at Halfway's attorney who rolled his eyes.

"Could you clarify what you mean?"

"I body motherfuckers."

"Once again, so we're not misunderstood," Burghoff continued, "can you please explain what it is you do?"

Halfway tilted his head to the side, exhaled a deep breath, and then leaned forward like a teacher imparting a lesson to dense students.

"I shoot motherfuckers." The black coal buttons of his eyes held Burghoff in a prolonged stare.

"Thank you," Burghoff said. "Moving on, let's discuss some of those shootings."

For the next hour, Halfway admitted to three recent shootings, selling drugs, and engaging in robberies. He also provided a list of the various weapons held by CK Mafia and the code names used so no one would know they talked about guns. Now we knew why the gun Sonny C sold to Kwame was dubbed "Lucifer."

"Like Betty is a Beretta .380 we got. If I'm gonna use her it'd be like 'I got Betty with me and taking her to meet that dude.' Anyone in the crew knew I'd be using it to clip some motherfucker." By this point in the interview, Halfway enjoyed his role educating the "dummies" in the room.

We scheduled a second session for the following week so Halfway could sign a formal cooperation agreement. Unfortunately, before the next meeting, the gang's drug wholesaler, a guy named Lawrence Kittles, bailed him out of the county jail. Halfway refused further cooperation. Adamo and I were worried. We didn't like the fact he waltzed away as a snitch and returned to his CKM crew as the tough guy. But his being loose on the street bothered us more.

The wires stayed busy with chatter: drug sales boomed, robberies brought in cash and drugs, and the gang plotted against rivals. Among the monitored calls was a conversation between Sonny C and an unknown subject looking to broker a deal for a retired trooper willing to trade a bulletproof vest for a gun. This was the fourth State Police intersection with the gang since the case began. I delivered the bad news in person to Quade and Plummer at troop headquarters. As usual, Heinrichs stood by my side. Neither of them showed much concern because the trooper was retired.

The investigation moved at a faster pace with the call monitoring, and we considered eavesdropping on the cellphones belonging to CK Mafia lieutenants Manic and Lorens Roberts, another fearsome enforcer with the street name Kango. Heinrichs made a renewed request on my behalf for more personnel to assist on the street. While the wire room was adequately staffed, the street work fell upon Adamo, Hartigan, and me. Assistance from the County Drug Task Force only occurred during the drug buy operations. Because I lived closest to the city center, I was called out the most for the late night and overnight incidents. I went out alone each night, without backup, despite repeated requests for assistance. My sole lifeline was the cops in the wire room monitoring the gang's cell phones. A frantic call one hot August night from one of them likely saved my life.

14
AMBUSH

My cell phone rang as I began to turn onto Esplanade Drive. Prieto, a local city cop working in the wire room, shouted from the other end, "Don't make another pass! Domino spotted your car." "Got it." I hung up and pulled over. I knew better than to make the last pass, but at least one of the two males walking south along Esplanade Drive carried a semi-automatic handgun.

The conversation captured by Prieto between Domino and Squid revealed that Domino and his cousin, AJ, wanted to rob someone. Domino's brooding nature meant trouble for anyone who unwittingly crossed his path. He didn't need a reason to rob; he did it for sport. Someone arriving home from a late work shift or sitting on their front porch enjoying a twilight chat with a friend was prone to his violent rage. Prieto said Domino sounded angry on the call.

The pair walked toward a construction site where Esplanade Drive connected to Marcy Street. Locals used openings in the fence on both sides of the site as a shortcut. Domino and AJ headed toward the opening and the short walk across the construction site from Esplanade to the run-down duplex on Marcy, which had rusted bikes and an old cloth couch on the porch where Domino lived with his mother and sister in a second-floor apartment.

Between rapid text messages and callbacks, Prieto stayed in contact with me while monitoring the conversation between Domino and Squid. Domino, disappointed he didn't find anyone to rob, headed in for the night. He expressed concern about seeing my car to Squid, who sat in another car at the north end of the city with Sonny C. Prieto said Domino and AJ hid behind parked cars, waiting for me to make another pass through. Domino told Squid he'd shoot into the driver's side window. Their plan called for AJ to cross in front of my car so I'd stop, and then Domino would run up to the car while shooting. If Prieto hesitated for only a few seconds before calling, I would have driven right into their ambush. I'd been at the corner when he called, less than a quarter of a block away, ready to make another pass through the street looking for a reason to arrest Domino and secure the gun. Fifteen minutes earlier, shortly after settling into bed, a call from the wire room pulled me away from home. "Sonny and Squid are planning to ambush Pure, and Domino's on the prowl to rob someone," Prieto said. I threw on jeans, a t-shirt, and grabbed my duty rig. "Where you going?" Joan put down the book she was reading. "Gotta check on something. Be back soon." I kissed her, knotted my sneakers, and left. The difference a few minutes or merely a few seconds can make in our lives is uncanny. The incident highlighted the need for more help on the street. We required a dedicated two or three person nighttime surveillance team to cover these guys, otherwise our luck was bound to run out.

Pure, or Marshula Graham, as his mother named him twenty-six years earlier, dealt large quantities of cocaine as a regional supplier. He wholesaled illicit drugs to gangs like CK Mafia. Sonny C and Squid planned to kill Pure and step into his spot. There couldn't be any witnesses. An investigation into Pure's murder didn't concern Squid or Sonny C; they were confident the case would go unsolved. They worried more about Pure's own crew. His alleged $50,000 post-mortem street bounty on the head of anyone who dared to step up against him kept him relatively safe. In the event someone killed him, there'd be mayhem in the streets as everyone fought for a piece of the reward. None of us working on the case knew who administered the bounty or if it really existed. Street rumor always had a way of amplifying the truth of a situation. True or not, the rumor kept Pure operating without much worry. Only the Crazed Killas Mafia was brazen enough to try to remove him from the area drug trade.

I waited in my car, a short distance away from what could have been a tragic outcome to the night, for either me or Domino and AJ. When enough time passed for Domino and AJ to clear the block, I drove to my original destination to thwart Sonny C and Squid from their intended plan of killing Pure. Prieto called back to check on me. Other than Prieto on the phone, I had no backup. Local city patrols were thin and tied up on other calls.

It was midnight when I cruised past the Sailor's Monument at the intersection of Ward and Grocer Streets. The dealers and their customers, usually in the area, were gone. A homeless man sprawled atop the cement lip of the monument fountain was the only one in sight. Drug deals at this hour generally moved to Aronal, the local dance club three blocks away.

I continued to Continental Acres, an apartment complex in the town just over the line from the northeastern corner of the city. Squid and Sonny C hid in a car in the complex's parking lot as a marked town police patrol, which Prieto requested, passed through. We wanted to prevent Squid and Sonny C from ambushing Pure by keeping them on edge. Squid called Domino while lying along the front seat of a tan Acura, with Sonny C stretched across the back seat waiting for the police patrol to pass. They planned to shoot Pure when he arrived at his girlfriend's apartment. From what he picked up on the wire, Prieto said both wore sweatsuit hoodies and bandanas to cover their faces. Squid complained to Domino during the call about the mid-80-degree weather, "That motherfucker Pure gonna get shot just for making me sweat like this."

The marked town patrol stayed in the area until another call demanding the officer's attention pulled him away. I drove into the complex entrance as the marked unit exited. Squid's car idled in a space located across from where Pure's girl Tamarah had an apartment in building 2.

My undercover car, a seized light gold Lexus IS 300 with dark tinted windows and chrome rims, had enough wear on it to look like a city-driven car yet nice enough not to be the kind typically used by the police. This time, though, it needed to be noticed. Squid and Sonny C, already freaked out by the marked unit cruising through the lot, would hopefully see my car soon afterward and decide to try for Pure another night.

Prieto called me again to report another call between Domino and Squid. Domino, now in his room on the south side of the city, listened to music and smoked a blunt. The presence of the marked patrol and then my slow drive through had shaken Squid and Sonny C. They decided to wait a half hour before driving out of the complex and calling it a night. Squid told Domino they'd meet later and create a new plan. They scheduled a meeting for midday at the gazebo by the riverfront park, a private area where side street access went under a state road leading into a tangle of city streets where they could easily disappear either on foot or by car if the police or local rivals rolled up on them.

I pulled out of the complex and set up surveillance at a strip club parking lot down the road. This was the CKM's third attempted robbery of a drug dealer over the past four nights. The continued denial of my requests for help on the street bothered Joan. "They're going to get you hurt or worse, God forbid," Joan said earlier during a rare dinner together. "This would never happen under McNeary." She referred to a well-liked former captain who ran troop BCI operations before Quade came along. Quade hadn't seen a need to add more personnel to the case, not even for a few nights after knowing Adamo had fallen ill and Hartigan had vacation leave. Quade and Plummer grew tired of the investigation and my absence from the regular Major Crimes rotation. They also grew tired of me. Heinrichs heard the scuttlebutt at troop headquarters and kept me informed. "Watch yourself," she warned.

My bulletproof vest rested on the passenger seat, ready for a quick toss over my head and fastening if anything went down. Under the circumstances, the vest should have been on, but the night's heat crawled up through the floorboards of the car. I went without it while waiting and praying Pure wouldn't stop by and crash at Tamarah's apartment. Let it be one of those nights he hooked up with some other woman keeping an open bed for him in the area. If Squid and Sonny C saw his dark blue Lincoln Navigator pull into the complex, they'd take their shot. After many months of investigation, I could predict this with some confidence.

While waiting for their Acura to drive out of the complex, I seethed with a deep rage. I had been purposely left alone to contend with a violent street gang planning to take out a rival dealer. We were nine and a half months into the case, and from what I'd been told, Quade and Plummer had decided to put me in the doghouse and leave me on the street without backup.

"We don't care what he wants or needs, he'll do what we tell him to do," Plummer told Heinrichs when she made a request to at least cut Juan Limon from the Major Crimes rotation to assist me. The comment illustrated Plummer's worst nature. Once he had an idea about something or someone, he fixed it in place. Plummer, I could only assume, held a grudge against me for the number of police corruption issues the case unearthed. He likely believed that I purposely followed up on information Quade told me to abandon more than a year earlier. His added annoyance resulted from my tight working relationship with Adamo and the FBI. Heinrichs told me weeks earlier that he and Captain Quade felt I'd become too independent of them. This was ridiculous considering they assigned me to the task force.

A bit past 3:00 a.m., a few patrons staggered out of the strip club. Two entered a waiting taxi, and four others piled into a minivan. They left in separate directions, the minivan heading north toward the community college a mile up the road and the taxi southbound past the apartment complex entrance. Shortly after the taxi went by, the tan Acura made a fast and sharp turn out of the complex. I followed them on the short ride to Sonny C's Hearth Street residence while calling Prieto. "We're on the move," I told him. "Stay loose, it sounds like they're done for the night." Prieto had intercepted a brief call from Sonny C to Domino: "We out. Need you with me next time." I didn't want there to be a next time. The nightly callouts over the past week wore on me. I worried over what this would lead to.

The Acura pulled across the street from the house, and Sonny C stepped out of the passenger side, adjusted his waistband, and before crossing to his house looked up and down the street while standing alongside the open car door. He then dashed across the street and went inside. Squid pulled off and continued to his mother's apartment near the city's downtown. He too clocked in for the night.

I sat up the street with the car lights off and waited twenty minutes before calling Prieto. He said all the phone lines had been quiet since Sonny C's last call to Domino. Relief spread across my body—neck, shoulder, chest, back, and leg muscles relaxed.

Before driving west along the state route separating the city's north and south ends and heading toward Grimaldi Boulevard, I stopped at an all-night gas station mini-mart and picked up a sixteen-ounce can of cold beer. I parked along the boulevard with a view north to the river and sat on the car's hood. Mosquitoes filled the muggy night air. A three-quarters moon reflected off the water, and the red, white, and blue lights strung along the bridge leading out of the city twinkled in the distance. The beer tasted good, but the better sensation was the cold can pressed to my forehead. I had made it through another night.

My home was a short drive away past neon-colored signs of twenty-four-hour gas stations and brightly lit strip malls with empty parking lots. A town police car sat in a pull-off along the roadway, the silhouette of the officer partially visible in the greenish glow of the mobile display terminal by the dashboard. A tractor-trailer backed into the delivery bay of Price Chopper, and a newspaper truck driver dropped two bundles of papers outside the closed doors of a delicatessen. Whether in the neighborhoods of New York City, southern Westchester towns, or other parts of the state, the activity didn't vary. I knew these routines well. The early morning hours had a pulse and rhythm appreciated by those who worked when others slept.

Like other nights when quietly entering the house, I kicked off my shoes at the door and walked down the hall. Deirdre, Siobhan, and Brian—suddenly grown at thirteen, seventeen, and twenty—slept in their rooms. I placed my handcuffs and bullet magazines in my nightstand's top drawer, then slid the belt from around my waist while holding my holster and gun so they wouldn't fall to the floor. The irregular working hours were exhausting, yet I couldn't fall asleep right away. I needed to wind down. The sounds and smells of the streets clung to me. I wanted to shower and crawl into bed fresh and renewed, but that would wake everyone.

I also wanted to wake Joan, but she had work in the morning. She worked as a nurse at a local pediatrics practice in the city. The same streets I came in from, she'd enter and start her day tending to a mix of children from both the city's large undocumented Mexican population who paid their bills in cash and came to appointments with both parents, the children neatly dressed and scrubbed, and the bordering town's children whose parents' insurance covered their healthcare. She also likely tended to the children of gang members. Hartigan had once spotted Sonny C's baby mama, Anila Lee, going into the pediatric office. I envisioned Joan cooing, smiling, and softly talking to her baby while administering a vaccine or checking vitals, as Anila looked on, unsure and uncomfortably holding her baby girl. "She's young, a sweet girl, overwhelmed with being a mom," I imagined Joan saying. Anila and her baby's future, once we arrested Sonny C and Anila had no more money sent to her, would concern Joan. I often thought she was too trusting at times, and too forgiving of others, including me, and needed to be more critical. But that wouldn't have worked for either of us.

I watched Joan as she slept, jealous of her peace. She drew shallow breaths under a soft glow from the moon creeping in through half-closed shades. I wanted to talk to her, hold her, maybe more. Anything to distract from my night and the past few days. Even with the air conditioner on, Joan had the sheet thrown off in a diagonal fold across her waist. Small beads of perspiration puddled in the cupped hollow of her back. An adhesive heat clung to the room. She appeared so serene, with one leg straight and the other angled, her hips relaxed along the contour of the mattress, and her shoulders streaked with tassels of hair. I wanted—maybe even needed—to tell her about my night. I also wanted to scream, punch something, yell out my frustrations and anger, and then be told it didn't matter because I was home now. Most of all, I wanted to hold her close, nuzzle my lips into the back of her neck, and start kissing her along the spine until she'd wake, turn over, and welcome me back. That was a lot to want from her. It would have been unfair to expect much at that hour. Later. Always later. We had to get through the day first. It still hadn't begun for her, but mine had already been too long. Hopefully, no more interrupting calls would beckon me. Maybe I could get some sleep.

15
NIGHT TERRORS

When sunlight first entered our room the next morning, Joan—already up, showered, and dressed—sat on her side of the bed tying her sneakers. Despite her attempt to silently move about the room, I heard her. She apologized when she saw me awake. "No worries, my alarm goes off in fifteen minutes."

"What time did you get in?"

"Late."

She stood at the foot of the bed.

"You were running in your sleep again last night." I ignored her, hoping she'd let it go. "And you were mumbling . . . at one point I thought you were going to have another night terror." Embarrassed, I wanted to deflect the conversation.

"You've been unsettled the last few nights." She put in an earring and looked at me for a response.

"All good." I rolled off the side of the bed and made my way to the bathroom. Joan straightened the bedspread and called after me.

"The kettle is on for tea. Do you want a cup, or will you be showering?"

I locked both bathroom doors and turned on the faucet.

"I'm working out first," I said over the flowing water.

I was home, in a supposedly safe place, and yet couldn't wait to get out the door, back to the case, the street, the aggravation, the second-guessing, and the unknown outcomes ahead. Lately, the street and all its craziness made the most sense to me. A calm and resoluteness that otherwise eluded me when away from the investigation always reappeared when working. The only way I settled down between callouts to check on CK Mafia threats and regular work hours was by running.

During the investigation, I trained for the Chicago Marathon with Heinrichs and a few other State Police colleagues. We met up for long runs on Saturday mornings. I joined those runs when possible; otherwise, the missed miles were made up later in the day or on Sundays. By late summer, training entered its weekly high mileage period. Running gave me a natural high and a sense of accomplishment each day. My body craved the release of endorphins. The stress level of the investigation and the combined microscopic glare from Quade and Plummer ensured my need for the mood-enhancing benefits of a good run. However, my lack of sleep, averaging only four hours a night, and the increasing sleep interruptions undermined my marathon training. On several mornings, Joan reported my restless tossing and turning and how I talked and simulated running. Occasionally, my screams from night terrors woke Joan. She said I wrestled with my pillow, punched it, and flailed wildly whenever it occurred. The intermittent dreams I had throughout my career started coming more frequently the year before my assignment to the Safe Streets Task Force. Midway through the CK Mafia case, they became more intense, and night terrors began.

Dreams are linked to memory and emotion. They must be because of all they seem to reveal. There's no randomness to them; rather, they're a release for feelings we otherwise shut down during waking periods. Dreams are also about fear, but not overriding crippling fear that makes us unable to function. Instead, it's the fear we suppress and chew on while working through whatever caused it. It's when we are awake that we fool ourselves into believing our true nature is revealed. What we show to others is rarely who we really are. Dreams, one might say, are an abstract painting formed from memory. And memory is the hot coal tossed on a pile of dry leaves. Left long enough, there's a conflagration. Only the fire is remembered, not what caused it. In my sleep, I burned out of control.

The job creates fear, not a fear for yourself or for what might happen on the job but a fear for those closest to you. It's the fear created when you rush with lights and siren to a call of a baby choking at a daycare center only to arrive too late, then have to conduct interviews with daycare workers and the mother until the investigators arrive. It's the fear, after carrying her missing person flyer in your patrol car for over a month, of finding the teenage runaway dead in a wooded area, curled in a fetal position and decomposing from the elements. It's the fear from interviewing a pedophile you've arrested and listening to him explain how he lured his victims as he seeks your understanding and claims he is sick and can't help himself. It's the fear from interviewing the felony robbery and assault suspect you know is a stone-cold predator who will rob and eventually injure someone else if he's let free. This is the fear you carry, knowing all the bad in the world, some of which exist not too far from where you live and where your children go to school that you want to shield them from. Fear invades your home life. You have a responsibility to your family and little patience for explaining the reasons why your children can't go to a classmate's house or ride their bicycles beyond the cul-de-sac or why they must tell you where they'll be at every moment when not with you, and the fear never leaves; it remains as you watch over them first as infants, then as toddlers, teens, and adults.

Maybe the fortitude to engage in police work eluded me. I considered this a few times over the years. The feeling intensified during the CK Mafia case. Perhaps my prior self-deception about corruption on the job extended into thinking that nothing I saw or did at work bothered me. But the thought passed quickly. I was a good police officer and liked the work. Oddly, the evil and fucked-up nature of other human beings drew me in. Upon entering the job, an older cop told me that I had an exclusive ticket to the best show on earth. This has been the perpetual tagline provided to new police officers. Reality is so much more interesting than fiction, even if reality traps us into believing the objective world we inhabit is all we experience. I once read a quote from physicist Max Planck saying, "we ourselves are a part of the mystery that we are trying to solve." Aside from Planck's broader scientific meaning regarding reality, my dreams seemed to tap into my own mysteries. There existed a world within me that remained closed off and unexplored.

*

A recurring dream of mine first manifested itself many years before, coming sometime after the Leak Investigation. The dream's plot, with changing scripts, had me warding off an unknown assailant. In a violent confrontation, the assailant had a gun pointed at me. My gun malfunctioned whenever I aimed to shoot in self-defense. The perpetrator then pulled his trigger, and the gun went off, but I'd wake before anything happened. Sometimes I screamed into the darkness of our room, as had been happening more recently during the case, waking Joan, who calmed me before I fell back to sleep. Most mornings, I remembered the dream, not the screaming and thrashing about.

The confrontation dream became as common as another that followed me in my sleep—visions of a dead body in a shallow grave I desperately didn't want anyone to find. In the dreamscape, I assumed responsibility for the person's death and didn't want my guilt exposed. In later dreams, the body, wrapped in a canvas tarp tied with thick brown manila rope, had moved elsewhere to an unknown dark place, then coffined in a cement burial vault placed deep in flat ground. I'd watch from a distance, ready to prevent discovery if someone got close. Although I never saw the victim's face, it didn't matter because the outcome never changed. I woke up confused and scared. A few minutes had to pass before realizing I'd been dreaming. Running in my sleep and mumbling incoherently also seemed to be the byproduct of the dreams.

An online search for the meaning of hiding a dead body in a dream yielded plenty of entries. The interpretations were varied: an attempt to hide a mistake made, the suppression of feelings of guilt or low self-esteem, an attempt to hide actual emotions, or the concealment of parts of oneself from others. The last two made self-diagnosed sense, except I had no idea what emotions or parts of myself I wanted to hide. None of it mattered because, over the years, I refused to pay prolonged attention to the dreams. Like most encounters in my life, I moved on. The job-related nature of the dreams didn't go unnoticed, though.

At one point during the summer of the gang investigation, I did more research about what dreaming of a gun not firing meant or of being attacked and the combination of both. The results were not surprising: feelings of being threatened by something, loss of power or confidence, or a struggle one is facing. With the internet, I could continue self-diagnosing and disregarding my underlying stress. Whatever troubles came in my sleep disappeared when I was awake. I navigated work like an ice-cutter steadily forcing its way through a frozen sea, making safe passage for others. My sense of invincibility and self-sufficiency fed the false belief that all was okay with me. Forward motion counted for something; keeping pace with my work mattered, anything else amounted to retrograde. An adult functioned this way. My generation's upbringing demanded no other course of action but to stifle emotions, never admit hurt or pain, and act like all was okay. This same kind of faulty credo led to my ass sometimes being planted on a bar stool years earlier or sitting at home drinking while playing chess. My learned behavior was not to talk about problems but to bury them with activity and a façade of normalcy. Running became my new elixir. In hindsight, it may have been more of me trying to run away. It was better than getting caught by whatever chased me.

I made a mental note of my dreams and moved on, treating them like dog-eared pages in a tossed-away book. The dreams faded to irrelevance as soon as I heard Deirdre and Siobhan moving about the house, or Brian heading off to his summer landscaping job, or Joan emptying the dishwasher before leaving for work. A steady routine circled our lives. The veneer of placid domesticity overtook my dreamscapes, but as a police family, we lived a bit differently, and my work often came crashing through our doors and windows in unseen ways. The dreams, and through them my fears, risked being exposed when, in my own home, safety seemed elusive. My dream life and the occasional terrors they brought needed to remain hidden. Most of all, my children could not know. There would be no way to face them as maturing adults, telling them to confront their fears and go out and conquer the world when my own unidentified and ineffable fears chased after me.

Brian, Siobhan, and Deirdre had become sharp students of other people and noticed things their peers didn't. Once, when Brian and Siobhan witnessed an incident while in the schoolyard behind our house, a town police officer interviewed them. When the officer asked their friend, who also witnessed the incident, if he obtained the plate number of the car, he had no answer. Brian immediately rattled off the plate, make, model, and color, while Siobhan provided a description of the driver. As Brian's friend stood in our dining room, mouth still agape, the officer looked over at Joan. "They're a cop's kids." The officer smiled; he knew all too well. Deirdre, for her part, had a habit of locking down the house tighter than a maximum-security prison, double-checking doors and windows after we all went to bed for the night. I wanted them to be safe, especially at home, yet even with doors locked and windows shut my nights could be invaded by these dreams and the terrors they sometimes caused. How long until each child discovered my disguised weaknesses and fears?

*

After my workout, I drove to the wire room to listen to the conversation between Squid and Domino that Prieto monitored hours earlier on the wire. Back at work, in the thick of the investigation, all my fears vanished. The playback of their call reinforced how close I came to being ambushed by Domino.

"Yo, this fuckin' ride's crept by two times."

"You buggin, Dom," Squid replied.

"Nah, man, it's a tinted hoopdie, like JJ's brother's car, gold colored or some shit," Domino said. "He lookin' for payback."

Domino referred to the Streamers nightclub shooting two weekends before that occurred across the river in a bucolic college town where New Jersey, Long Island, and Westchester kids partying through college on their parents' cash spent the weekend getting intoxicated along the main street's crawl of bars. Sonny C, Domino, Squid, Manic, and Halfway jumped in Sonny C's rented Escalade and made the twenty-minute drive across the river. Sonny C and his crew had ventured out from the Stacks to meet girls and make a few drug sales inside Streamers. No sooner had they arrived at the club than JJ Williams' half-brother, Marlon, showed up. Rumor on the street after JJ's murder quickly pointed to Sonny C, and Marlon sought to even the score. There were words in the club, a scuffle that went outside, and then a gunshot. No one was hit. All the players involved had scrambled out of the area by the time the local police arrived.

"That ride is getting lit up next time it creeps around. We setting up now," Domino hissed into the phone.

"Chill, Dom, chill . . . it could be the Ds," Squid reassured him.

Ds was street shorthand for detectives or plainclothes units. Domino's paranoia sizzled through the recording.

"It ain't no D's, it's JJ's bro and his boys. If they looking for somethin' we got it waitin' for them."

"Who you got?" Squid asked.

"Rocky."

We knew from our fleeting June proffer session with Halfway that Rocky referred to a .40 caliber Smith & Wesson semi-automatic in the gang's arsenal. One more of their "pass-around" weapons ranging from a .25 caliber compact to a .45 caliber cannon kept at different locations under the control of the gang.

"Jus' be careful man, if it's the Ds you gonna bring heat," Squid again warned.

"It ain't no Ds."

"Can't be sure."

"Is to."

"How so?"

"Because ain't no motherfuckin' Ds creepin' around these streets after midnight . . . they're nine to five motherfuckers," Domino snarled back.

The phone lines clicked off, and the recording stopped. I desperately needed Limon's help working the streets with me. Maybe the recorded call with Domino threatening to shoot up my car would change things.

One more set of eyes, though, wouldn't be enough. I requested at least three additional investigators. When talking with Heinrichs later in the afternoon, she said she'd see what could be done. But I knew there were limits to what she could accomplish. Lieutenant Plummer had a problem with me, and even a respected Senior Investigator like Heinrichs had little leverage to exert. I wondered how much longer Quade and Plummer would leave me on the street alone, trying to prevent robberies and murders under the night's camouflage. If it weren't real, this would all be another bad dream, but even in those, I didn't have any rest. I never got as much sleep as the gang members, who didn't wake up until ten or eleven in the morning. When I slept, bad dreams inhabited by unknown people chased after me.

16
HIT SQUAD

I had a relatively quiet Saturday night after narrowly escaping my car being shot up by Domino over forty-eight hours earlier. Halfway sold vials of crack by the waterfront gazebo, and we put a buy into him. He also brokered a deal for Domino, who had a .32 caliber revolver for sale. The unidentified buyer said he'd have the money later that week. Otherwise, Squid, Domino, and the rest of the crew laid low on orders from Sonny C. He wanted to figure out if they were being followed. He worried about the CK Mafia's drug-dealing rivals, not the police.

Joan and the girls dressed for Mass as I puttered around the house. Brian attended the evening service with a few high school friends. He slept in. I unapologetically avoided Sunday Mass. A street gang consumed my time, and I didn't have the energy to confront another type of gang, which was how I started to view organized religion. I'd already given up on people when gathered in groups. They didn't seem to behave well. Organized religion in general and the Catholic Church in particular irritated me. Nietzsche famously said, "In individuals, insanity is rare, but in groups, parties, nations, and epochs it is the rule." I realized what he meant. To me, the State Police had moved into the insanity category next to the Catholic Church.

"Again, with the running and talking in your sleep. What's going on with you?" Joan looked at me from her dresser mirror while rubbing moisturizer through her hands. I had come back to our bedroom for my watch, and her question caught me off guard.

"Who were you running from?"

"No one. Just trying to catch you."

I tackled her onto the bed. We spent a few playful moments kissing, then she sprang up, smoothed her dress, and put on lipstick.

"Aw, c'mon," I complained while reaching for her.

"Stop. You're being fresh." She was equally playful, though undeterred from arriving at Mass on time. I pouted.

"The girls are in the next room," she said.

"How do they think they got here?"

"Now you're being really fresh." She leaned over, kissed me, then shooed me off the bed so she could straighten the covers.

"Are you heading in this morning?"

"Not until later. We have something going on tonight," I told her.

"Dinner?"

"I won't be around."

"Remember to check the ceiling primer in the family room before you leave. It looks like there are a few splotchy areas. It may need to dry some more; if not you have a few touch-ups to do."

Amid everything going on, we decided to remodel the family room. To save money, we did the painting and molding ourselves. I didn't tell her the work would be delayed a few weeks, maybe longer.

"Will do. Going for a run first. A real one this time." I grabbed my sneakers and headed for the hallway.

"We still have to talk about what's going on in your sleep," she called after me.

*

As much as running offered me an escape, it also served as my form of penitential prayer. Each foot strike on the road amounted to a kind of self-flagellation as in "I . . . am . . . truly . . . sorry . . . my . . . Lord . . . for . . . the . . . transgressions . . . I . . . have . . . visited . . . upon . . . my . . . soul." I don't know why I always felt so penitent. Maybe being Catholic meant being constantly sorry for something. The rote lessons of childhood adhered faintly. Prayer still lingered in me even after no longer favoring the ritual of the Mass. I hadn't yet lost faith, although my tenuous hold presaged a break from a community of the faithful. I viewed my faith as something more personal and less communal. Group participation never worked for me. Why go to church when at my parish I'd run into a convicted child molester distributing communion as a Eucharistic minister or an unabashed adulterer standing at the lectern reading a Bible selection? Being a police officer gave me too much information about other people to pretend to gather in shared Christian values.

The trails and river paths I ran became my altar instead. The trees, sky, and distant hills served as the cathedral. My sweat served as an offering in sacrifice. Unburdened and alone, I raced along wooded paths, with the river to one side, and the roots, rocks, and ruts of the trail the only obstacles to traverse. Whenever my running shoes struck the smooth, soft dirt, it felt like an embrace for me to fall into with arms outstretched. A free float onto a flat, forgiving surface to hide, wrapped in a warm cocoon of soil, leaves, and the sound of my breathing, steady and calm, before falling off to sleep. Instead, I ran, and ran, and ran, without getting anywhere. I couldn't run past the present and couldn't turn back, as much as I wanted to. The limits of time reminded me of my own limits, which is why, under a warm sun, I needed to feel the hammering of my heart, the air filling my lungs, and the sweat on my skin. Dreams of confrontation and the dead had too frequently interrupted my sleep. And sleep, what was needed most, came in fits and spurts. Even then, I ran.

*

At the wire room, two task force members manned calls in the front office area. Everyone else gathered in the back room of the building. Adamo returned from his bout with a stomach bug, and Hartigan banked his vacation days when he learned of the planned hit on Pure and my near run-in with Domino. Detective Taglieri and Sergeant Buchanan from the County Drug Task Force also met with us.

While home sick, Adamo reached out to federal colleagues and found a DEA warrant for Pure. They wanted him in connection with a drug sale. The warrant had been indexed under a different street name and a misspelling of his last name, explaining why a prior DECS (Drug Enforcement Coordinating System) check came up empty. We wanted to place a buy into Pure, but it became increasingly harder to accomplish with him being hunted down by the CK Mafia's hit squad, with whom we were now in a race to get to Pure first. None of our informants could locate him, and our checks of his relative's addresses throughout the county came up equally empty. We decided, with the blessing of A.D.A. Burghoff, to pick up Pure on the DEA warrant and get him off the street. Otherwise, his days were numbered.

I'd been out of the house since shortly after Joan and the girls returned from church. After my run and shower, Adamo called and said he had the DEA warrant in hand. We began to formulate a plan to arrest Pure. First, we had to find him. We split up around the city—Adamo and I in his black government-assigned Chevy Tahoe, Buchanan and Taglieri in their county car, and Hartigan in his unmarked city unit. Other County Drug Task Force officers checked Pure's hangouts and rousted informants. We were nearly two hours into the search when Johnny Ackert, one of Sergeant Buchanan's Drug Task Force officers, received information that Pure and his girl had booked a week-long getaway. Ackert's informant didn't know where. When asked the name of Pure's girl, the informant came up blank on that too. We hoped it was Tamarah, who lived in Continental Acres, where Squid and Sonny C had waited two nights ago for Pure to arrive. We made a collective decision to surveil her apartment. Ackert and his partner set up surveillance at the Stacks in case Pure went there. The rest of us focused surveillance on Continental Acres and waited for Pure. If he had a different girl on his getaway calendar, we wasted the day, and Tamarah had a lonely week ahead of her.

Adamo and I set up at the strip club lot on Kahl Road where I had previously sat alone trying to figure out how to thwart Pure's murder if he showed up. Hartigan took the direct eye in the parking lot of Continental Acres near building 2. Buchanan and Taglieri parked at the other end of the entrance watching traffic heading north on Kahl Road from Pekoes Avenue toward the complex. The cops in the wire room listened for any chatter among the CK Mafia as to Pure's location. Then, we all waited.

This is the tedious part of police work rarely shown on television or in movies: countless hours of boredom and often dumb luck. If it weren't for the CK Mafia's desire to rob and kill Pure, we wouldn't have known of the DEA warrant. Adamo solved a dilemma we had in the case—do we preserve the investigation's confidentiality, or do we save Pure's life?

We couldn't let anything happen to Pure. His murder would be our fault if we ignored preventive measures, yet we didn't want to burn the wire. I worked under the onerous warning from Captain Quade through Plummer that any killings by CK Mafia were my responsibility. Despite the investigation being a multi-agency effort in which all case decisions went through the District Attorney's office, I still couldn't believe Lieutenant Plummer said I'd have to account to the bosses at troop and then Albany if a body dropped. With this crew, he might as well have said I'd be responsible if sunshine turned to rain. The State Police, though, had too much profile in the case, and as one of the lead investigators, I carried the ball. Human excrement ran downhill, and I stood at the end where it flowed the fastest.

We had been surveilling the apartment complex for over three hours when Ackert notified us he saw Pure's Lincoln Navigator briefly stop by the Stacks. A tall, thin, white male exited the passenger side of the SUV and then walked over to a group in the parking lot. The SUV quickly swung out of the lot. Ackert recognized the passenger as one of Pure's people, a dealer from north of the county who ran Pure's pipeline into the Capital District around Albany. Jordan Esterly, known as Slinky to anyone who mattered, didn't look like much, but he'd done two stretches upstate, both for serious assaults. One involved a stabbing; the other a shooting during a robbery attempt where another dealer tried to jack him of his stash. He was a hard case, not to be fucked with, and his easy acceptance into Pure's crew testified to his toughness.

Ackert followed the Navigator onto Kahl Road. When it drove north on Kahl, Ackert hung back at the intersection of Pekoes Avenue in anticipation of a return trip in his direction once the driver picked up Tamarah. As the Navigator pulled in front of building 2, Tamarah came out with a small rolling suitcase. She wore a powder blue jumpsuit and matching high heels, ready for a "party holiday," as Hartigan noted on the car-to-car radio. The driver never stepped out of the SUV. When Tamarah approached the passenger side, the door opened; she handed over her suitcase and then climbed in. It was past 7:30 p.m. and we still hadn't confirmed Pure drove the vehicle. A day had been spent looking, then waiting, and we only had a fifty-fifty chance of it being him.

We followed them south on Kahl Road for a mile and a half before deciding to stop the Navigator on a wide stretch of city roadway. Hartigan took the lead and put on his lights and siren while Adamo positioned his SUV at an angle to the left and ahead of Hartigan's car. Taglieri and Buchanan stayed to the right, and Ackert pulled in behind them. When the Navigator stopped, I came up along the left side of the vehicle, gun drawn, with Adamo off to my left as we formed a "V" with the vehicle on approach. Taglieri and Buchanan took the same approach on the right side as Hartigan and Ackert provided rear cover. Its tinted windows looked black in the fading light of the day. I was about to shout commands to the driver when the window rolled down and two open hands came slowly out the side. In a matter of seconds, we had the driver out of the vehicle and in handcuffs. A quick pat-down yielded only a wallet containing a license for Marshula Graham with a photo of the driver. We had Pure.

Adamo told him about the DEA warrant for drug sales. Pure exuded calm. Tamarah not so much. She spat out a string of rapid-fire curse-filled questions until Pure told her to stop. She relaxed once he gave her instructions on whom to call, first on the list being his attorney.

We drove Pure to the adjoining town's police station where, after being fingerprinted and photographed, the town held him for the DEA. We spent an hour with him talking sports and his planned trip with Tamarah to Foxwoods Casino and then the Rhode Island shoreline. While we talked, Adamo and I alternately nibbled around the edges of the topic we wanted to discuss, and we sensed Pure knew more than he'd ever let on and innately understood what happened. He remained personable and respectful without being contrite. Most of all, he showed restrained acceptance toward his present situation, a sign of someone who'd been through it before. Convinced of Pure remaining tight-lipped, we decided to head to the county impound yard to check progress on the search of his vehicle. When we stood up to leave, Pure halted us with a question. "Can I ask you something?" We had a momentary glimmer of hope. "Do you think this situation qualifies me to get a refund on my hotel deposits?"

Any anticipation he might offer something of value or look to cooperate vanished.

"You're the government," he said, looking at Adamo. "You got to have some pull."

Adamo returned a broad smile.

"Mr. Graham, unfortunately, when it comes to things like hotel refunds, even the Justice Department has no pull."

"Thought I'd ask." He stood in the holding cell watching us leave the room.

When we arrived at the county impound lot, Ackert, Taglieri and Buchanan had finished searching the interior of the Lincoln Navigator. As expected, not a trace of cocaine surfaced. Hartigan drew the unenviable assignment of taking Tamarah and her suitcase back to her apartment. She spent the short ride on the phone with Pure's attorney, then her mother. Hartigan called to update us and joked that Tamarah treated him like a chauffeur and expected him to carry her luggage to her apartment. He then signed off for the night. We all followed suit. I already had over eleven hours on duty and relished the idea of getting home before midnight.

The cell phone always sat to the side of our bed on my nightstand. Arriving home never meant I'd be there for long. After coming in from the street, I'd lie in bed for an hour listening in the dark for any sound beyond the hum of the air conditioner. Because my home was close to the areas where I worked and the security of the investigation troubled me, my usual hypervigilance was on steroids. Confidential information had a way of leaking out.

Intermittently, I'd glance over at my cell phone wondering if it would ring, summoning me back because the CK Mafia committed another robbery, or the gang prowled the streets looking for a revenge target, or they shot someone. They were nocturnal predators, and I was the game warden, keeping them from harming other wildlife.

One riot, one trooper. The boast they made us live by at the academy embedded itself into every trooper's psyche. Our training taught us to perform as a one-person command center in a maelstrom. We didn't weaken or topple. Except I wasn't the warden I envisioned myself to be. I was as much a nocturnal predator as they were, a lion to their hyena, natural enemies in the wild. They ran in packs, and I ran ahead of the pride looking to ward off attacks. We really weren't much different; we only had different motivations and justifications toward the game, which is what it was, a game, a dangerous one but a game nonetheless, and we each knew the stakes.

17
DOPE RODEO

The Feast of the Assumption brought a sticky heat. By 10:00 a.m., the temperature hovered in the mid-80s. The forecast predicted high 90s by the afternoon. I woke up early, for once more rested than usual, and went for a moderate six-mile run before breakfast on a trail not far from home and let loose on the wooded paths. On the trails, I ran freer, less constrained by the hard surface of the roads, and better able to focus. I relished the time alone, lost among the tall trees, sheltered from the growing sun and the day ahead of me.

Adamo had scheduled two meetings with potential informants. In the morning, we met with Hartigan and one of his street snitches at the city police detective division offices, and at noon we sat with Burghoff in the District Attorney's conference room with an inmate brought over from the county jail. Neither snitch provided new information. After the second meeting, we sat down for lunch at a restaurant across from the courthouse. On any weekday from early morning until closing, the place was crowded with lawyers, cops, court staff, and county employees.

"How about this afternoon we put this case out of our minds and go home early?" Adamo speared a pickle from his plate and devoured it.

"Sounds good to me." Thoughts of another run, this time an easy jaunt by the river, or a weightlifting session, invigorated me. "Dinner with my family two nights in a row would be nice," I added.

After lunch, we spent time across the river at the wire room catching up with the day shift and checking on the catalog of recordings. We had constructed a solid case over the past few months. We recorded over 22,000 cell phone conversations, made over 40 controlled drug purchases, initiated four gun buys, and closed two homicides. Burghoff said he had enough evidence to charge Sonny C with JJ Williams' murder and Manic for a murder committed the prior summer in retaliation for a slight in Club Aronal when someone bumped into him and didn't properly apologize. Manic later shot the victim as he walked to his car in the club's parking lot. We had probable cause to arrest gang members for seven other open shootings in the city. Burghoff said he and his staff needed another month and a few more targeted buys to include other gang members in the enterprise corruption charge before beginning grand jury presentations. I was desperate for the case to end.

We stayed at the wire room long enough for the next shift to arrive and updated them on the case progress. Guys like Jimmy Prieto, the young city cop who saved me from driving into Domino's ambush, and George Landers, a detective from the town, were mostly voices on the phone or radio directing us to trouble spots. Rarely did we get to see each other.

When we left the wire room, Adamo looked at his watch and decided he had a few hours before dark to hit some golf balls at a local range by his house. I looked forward to an evening run and being able to work off extra energy. A second run for the day and then dinner with the family seemed like a vacation. But first, I went to the afternoon Feast of the Assumption Mass with Joan, for no other reason than she wanted me there and it was a celebration of the Blessed Mother. Any pretense of a belief in God hovered over me as more of a superstition ingrained by years of Catholic education, yet I couldn't let go of the Blessed Mother, Mary. She held sway over me. Maybe it was because my mother gave me my first Miraculous Medal and introduced me to Mary, or maybe it was because she became a needed surrogate after my mother passed away. Even as a young adult, my mother's death left a deep, searing hole in my heart. Whatever the reason for my devotion, the Blessed Mother gave me comfort. I wore a small round medallion with Mary's image along with a replica of my shield around my neck, both of which were blessed by our parish priest. They served as my talisman against evil, even though I knew they didn't keep me safe.

After dinner, Joan and I sat on the back deck talking and watching the sun go down. Deirdre and Siobhan already had a movie in the family room DVD player, and Brian retreated to his room. The ring of my cell phone destroyed any hope for a normal evening. "Hey, it's Landers. Sorry to bother you . . . the phone lines have been going all afternoon since you guys left. They're up to something." "What's going on?" I went inside, walked to the bedroom, and closed the door. "Squid, Sonny, and Domino have been burning up the lines. Something's going down tonight for sure," Landers said. I sensed something else in his voice. "And? What else?" Landers continued, "I think they're planning a home invasion at Pure's girl's place." "Motherfuckers! They're going back to Continental Acres," I yelled loud enough that Joan heard. "They're meeting up at one of their stash cribs on Decatur," Landers said. I left the house and called in service from my car. I never doubted assessments about calls made by any of the cops or agents in the wire room. We had all become a team of players with different roles, and their role had the most impact on the case. Turning onto the cross street from our cul-de-sac, I glanced to the right, and looking across a neighbor's yard, saw Joan sitting alone on the deck. We should have been there together enjoying a normal evening after dinner.

Adamo and I met up at city police headquarters, along with George Lattner, a State Police investigator assigned to the wire. Lattner was an extra body scheduled for the overnight shift whom I called. "Bring your vest and raid jacket and make sure you have both spare gun magazines," I instructed while driving north to the city. The three of us arrived on Collins Street by the corner of Decatur in my unmarked car.

To a practiced eye, signs of gang activity are visible while driving in daylight through the city streets: the shot-up school crossing and stop signs; the unpainted wood filler along doorways and windowsills where bullets lodged into the soft, rotting frames of once immaculate single-family homes converted into illegal two- and three-family dwellings; the discarded forty ounce bottle of malt liquor at a corner and the trail of empty crack vials leading toward an alley or park. In certain sections of the city, these signs dominated as did the unmistakable way old and neglected gabled porch roofs sagged like the hope of residents who remembered how the neighborhood had been. Poverty and gangs replaced jobs and neighborhood civic associations. At night, both came out in full attire.

Diagonally across the street from us, a resident stood over a barbecue grill in the front yard of a house. Blue flames from the charcoal flickered in the dark, and the overpowering smell of butane poured over the coals cut through the night air. Loud chatter and laughter filled the street. Two stray dogs cautiously approached the grill where sausage, onions, and corn wrapped in aluminum foil were cooking. The street pulsated like a Saturday afternoon at the beach.

Squid greeted different gang members in front of a two-story white clapboard residence with a concrete front yard surrounded by chain-link fencing. His baggy white t-shirt and black knee-length basketball shorts consumed his thin frame. Halfway stood off to his left in a hoodie two sizes too big for him. He likely carried something larger than a handgun under the hoodie. As they gathered on the street, I watched their rituals upon seeing one another, and my mind flashed back to similar signs of respect and hierarchy I witnessed when surveilling Mafia social clubs over a decade earlier. Manic and Kango rolled up in a white Chevy Yukon and joined Squid in the small yard where he sat on a fold-out lawn chair. Those in the tight CKM circle stood inside the fence; the others milled about outside like a modern retinue of soldiers, emissaries, jesters, and visitors to a royal court.

I sat on the driver's side, watching. Something brewed. Manic and Kango, both hard hitters for the CK Mafia, came in as added muscle whenever the gang had to get rough with rivals. The Yukon was likely loaded with weapons. If we moved on them while Manic and Kango were out of the car, I believed we'd catch everyone by surprise and seize heavier firepower from them. I badly wanted to take them down, grab several weapons, and dump them on Quade's desk the following morning.

The CK Mafia had gotten away with many crimes prior to our investigation. Multiple shootings, robberies, drug sales, and murder filled their collective resume. They were a year older, more organized, and more brazen. They exhibited the latter by rapping about their criminal exploits. "I go through the streets like Billy the Kid," Halfway rapped in a CD released to the neighborhoods where CKM slung their product. "Strapped with my bitch on either side of my hip / my muzzles be itchin' if I get any lip / you see a blast from the furnace / you know it done rip," he continued rapping to Dope Rodeo, track number five on their first CD release, *Our Blingdom*. Burghoff later presented those lyrics and others as evidence to corroborate Halfway's role as an enforcer for the gang and as an example of one of the CK Mafia's methods of neighborhood intimidation. To quiet any doubt, CKM liked to hand out compact disc recordings touting their lethalness and power. Aside from being drug dealers and violent felons, they were aspiring rappers. I spent a good part of the early months of the investigation going through their three self-released CDs and knew the lyrics to all thirty-four of their rap songs by heart, many of which were used as corroborating evidence to build probable cause in the affidavits for eavesdropping warrants. Their rap lyrics contained a clear message—they ran the city, not any other gang, and certainly not the cops. Sonny C confirmed this belief a few nights beforehand in a conversation with Domino captured on the wire: "the cops don't know shit." If Halfway and the rest of the gang wanted to posture as self-professed Billy the Kids, they soon had to learn about Pat Garrett and his takedown of the Kid.

Captain Quade's recent edict placing responsibility on me for any killings by the gang stung repeatedly. I was trapped between two overly demanding, unrealistic bosses. How could any dropped body be my fault when they didn't give me street support? I couldn't control what others did. All I could control were my actions, and right then I wanted to gear up and take them down. Squid was strapped. The wire confirmed he kept a gun tucked in his waistband. "Nina's kissing my dick," he cooed to Sonny C in an earlier call. Nina was a 9mm Beretta in the CKM arsenal. Others carried too. The CK Mafia was always in a feeding frenzy, ready to rob and take other dealers' drugs and cash for themselves. This time we knew the target.

A few days earlier, when they hunted Pure, Quade ignored Heinrichs and me when we requested more personnel for the street work. Quade downplayed the gang's violence and organization. Now I wanted a takedown of the group and Squid's gun more than anything. Lattner leaned forward from the back seat, listening to Adamo and me go back and forth as to what to do. Adamo, ready with a Heckler & Koch MP5 submachine gun on his lap, cautioned about stray gunfire. Despite the late hour, people still milled about on the sidewalks and front stoops escaping the sweltering heat of their apartments. A few children rode back and forth on bicycles. I listened to Adamo without hearing a word he said. I wanted blood. Theirs or mine. Either way, the bosses would be forced to listen. It didn't matter to me anymore. All the bullshit ended tonight.

I was confident the takedown would go in our favor. We had the element of surprise; we also had the superior firepower—Adamo with the MP5, Lattner and me with our Glocks and three seventeen round clips. But my assessment was unrealistic; the CK Mafia had more soldiers on the street and more weapons. "I agree with Adamo. It's too risky. More can go wrong with the plan than can go right if we confront them," Lattner said. Adamo quickly expanded on the last part of Lattner's assessment. "Right now, we got an eyeball on them, and we have the five phones we're monitoring. They don't take a crap without us knowing about it. Let's get a few marked units to swing through the area and see what it does for us."

Tactically, they were right. Both made sense in their assessments. The pace of the past few days had frazzled me and piled onto what I'd previously dealt with in the investigation: gangbangers bagging up crack over State Police uniforms in a trooper's house; an investigator's fifteen-year-old gangbanger son pulling off an armed robbery with a gun he stole from his father; a retired trooper looking to trade a police ballistic vest for a gun with one of our CKM targets; the prior intel from confidential sources and the County Drug Task Force that a local cop dealt drugs for a known drug supplier; and the ongoing issue of the trooper suspected of trafficking drugs in the county. I couldn't let any of it go. The incidents and information ground me up inside and clouded my judgment.

Rage has a way of depriving your senses of what is rational. Mine had hit a scale beyond measure. The desire to get even blinded me. With whom, though? Fuck the bosses. I had felt this way many times in the past. What differed now? They had pissed all over my shoes before, and whenever given the chance, I wiped them dry on their pant legs. Except in this instance, pure rage, which usually follows betrayal, guided me.

A ring from my cell phone broke into the conversation between the three of us. Hartigan had returned to the area from a prisoner transport, and he'd checked in with Landers at the wire room. Hartigan told me he'd make a very visible ride through Decatur Street where Squid sat in the front yard with his crew. Hartigan's black Impala and his big bald head behind the wheel were well known in the area. By the time I hung up on him I'd come to my senses. "We'll sit tight. You guys are right."

We spent another hour in the car watching Squid and his crew. Landers called Adamo from the wire room to update him on the call activity. Squid spotted Hartigan when he drove down Decatur. He also saw my car parked half a block away, which, he told Domino during another call, looked like the one Domino spotted three nights before.

"I told you it coulda been the Ds out that night . . . you didn't want to believe me," he chided Domino.

"See, I saved your ass," Squid boasted.

Domino sucked his teeth into his phone.

"Man don't give me your bullshit . . . you saved me. Only ass saved be the motherfucker rollin' by in the hoopdie I didn't light up."

"Just the same, we done tonight. Too much heat in the area. A few uniforms also rolled by. Two of them were like ten minutes apart. Shit ain't right," Squid complained.

We watched the Yukon leave the area with Manic and Kango inside. Then Squid, Halfway, and two others got into a van parked across the street from the house. Hartigan followed the Yukon, and we took the van. After they made several stops and drop-offs, we saw Squid arrive back at his girlfriend's place. Hartigan let us know Manic and Kango were in their respective residences as well. We had the CK Mafia tucked in for the night. I didn't get a street takedown and the weapons I hoped to throw in Quade's face. Instead, I got to go home, flop into bed next to Joan, and fall asleep relatively early.

18
STRAY BULLETS

A stray bullet has no conscience. It doesn't detour when the original intent of its sender misses its mark. A straight line is all it knows. The scary aspect of a stray bullet is its stealth. There is no warning. Several weeks before our evening surveillance on Decatur Street, Adamo, Hartigan, and I experienced the frightening randomness of stray bullets. When we ducked for cover, our comically futile reaction was evident. The round had already passed. But we remained hunkered down in case a second round followed close behind. A trail of breaking branches to our right indicated we'd made a safe bet. One doesn't grasp the anonymity and wantonness of a bullet fired with no general purpose on a city street until ducking behind the protective metal shield of a car.

We had completed making an informant drug buy into Tommy Gunz, a/k/a Tomas Harden, a fleshy, lumbering baby-faced junior member of the CK Mafia, and we discussed the logistics of a second buy into him the following night when we heard the crack of the first round.

"D23 to Q1, shots fired, 500 block sector 3. Vicinity Pine," Hartigan called in while lying on his back by the front bumper of Adamo's SUV.

"Q1 copy . . . any units near sector 3 . . . shots fired, vicinity of Pine. D23 on scene, request backup," reported a female voice at the other end of Hartigan's radio.

"Request patrols check 500 block," Hartigan clarified.

We stayed put for a few more seconds in case a third round came whizzing by. "I think we're clear," Adamo said.

"These are goddam new pants," Hartigan huffed as he slowly rose to his feet. Adamo and I chuckled while Hartigan brushed himself off and lit a cigarette.

"At least you got some exercise," Adamo said, alluding to Hartigan's stout build.

"Yeah, fuck you too." Hartigan took a deep drag from his cigarette and walked to the back of the parking lot by the tree line overlooking Pine Street. "Let's see how long it takes one of those uniform humps to roll by and check the area."

Adamo, who I never saw smoke, asked Hartigan for a cigarette. "Whoa, that round came in low and close." "Pretty scary," I responded. "It came out of nowhere." Adamo leaned into Hartigan for a light. The sounds of gunfire, sometimes distant and other times too close, echoed in the streets at night. Joan worried about this kind of frequent and instantaneous violence. Only a week earlier, on a Friday night while tracking CK Mafia members at Club Aronal, a call with her ended abruptly when gunfire broke out across the street from where Hartigan and I sat in my car. A blur of bodies ran across the club's parking lot into cars and side alleys on that occasion of stray bullets piercing the night.

*

My anger often fired like a stray bullet, random and unannounced, not focused on any one victim, merely whoever was in the line of fire. Quade and Plummer fueled my anger, which made me no less impulsive than the CK Mafia. The night before, out on Decatur Street with Adamo and Lattner, anger clouded my judgment and pushed me toward wanting an ill-advised confrontation with the gathered gang members.

I'd resided within my anger for too long, treating it like a superpower. But it weakened me. I often acted no differently than a bullying street brawler looking to pick a fight to assuage his bitterness and hatred. Unfortunately, sometimes the victims of the verbal bullets I fired were Joan and the children.

This was my biggest regret as a parent and spouse. As a police officer, I loathed individuals who neglected their parental duties. Too often I dealt with mothers who allowed a live-in boyfriend or relative to sexually abuse or beat her child, a drunken father who threatened to shoot his spouse and children with a hunting rifle, or parents who disregarded the basic nutritional and sanitary needs of their children. I shouldn't have had to walk through apartments or trailers while stepping on garbage and human feces to find wide-eyed and wan children sitting on dirty, bare mattresses. Whenever called to one of those residences, it was in response to some tragically broken piece in the familial framework—domestic violence, sexual assault, neglect, sometimes homicide. The anger hung around at the end of a shift.

As a police officer, you move from bluff to bluff. You convince a raging hulk it's best to comply and let you put on the handcuffs; otherwise, it's going to be rough on him, even though you know he could take on the whole shift. Or you take down a dangerous felon at gunpoint and pretend your knees didn't shake. We put on the uniform, and it becomes a superhero cape—we can leap tall buildings in a single bound, or, like a streak of light, arrive at a crime scene right on time. We take up the mantle of invincibility people want to place upon us. We are spouses, parents, friends, children, lovers, neighbors, but first and foremost we are police—a 24/7 next-door version of a Marvel Comics creation. Soon we believe in our own hype and proudly assume the identity of a superhero. We are steadfast and brave, dependable and upright, virtuous and kind. Really, though, many of us weep inside for a variety of reasons, not the least of which is our built-up anger, and we carry it with us at work, in the community, and at home. Nonetheless, we continue to "fly over" the metropolis in search of danger, wrapped in our superhero cape, sustaining the bluff, and playing our role.

There are some police officers who give no thought to such insecurities. To them, introspection is for pussies and cowards. This officer chews nails, lifts heavy weights with one arm, farts fireballs, and fucks like a steam piston. It is also usually a bluff, the biggest of all, masking their insecurities. Often, most of us only want to come home, put our heads under the covers, and hide.

The average police career wades daily into the sewers of other people's lives. Over time, the wastewater becomes too hard to navigate, and some drown. The other hazard we navigate is the job itself and the organizational betrayal we regularly experience. But we don't talk about it, at least not outside of the organization; we bitch and moan to each other. Meanwhile, our anger incubates. This is the experience of working in policing.

*

Marathon runners know the feeling, late in the race, of being physically and mentally detached from all external stimuli except a vision of the finish line. I was locked into the final lap of the CK Mafia investigation. Burghoff impaneled a special grand jury to hear evidence. Despite still being a few weeks away from the case presentation, Burghoff, a master of preparation, had the grand jury ready in case of emergency.

I began the morning after watching the CK Mafia conclave on Decatur Street at the district attorney's office with Assistant District Attorney Marta Wilson to review video surveillance and catalog the street buys of our confidential sources. Wilson teamed up with Burghoff on the case. After two hours, I left to meet with Ben Caufield, chief of a small city police force nine miles south of our operational area, to review his department's "shots fired" complaints. His city had its own lingering gang problems as it gradually regentrified, including some incursions by the CK Mafia. The city's main thoroughfare, Bayview Boulevard, an east-west extension of the northern state route, ran to Exeter Avenue where it rejoined the southbound state road. Along this stretch, an area once known for its round-the-clock drug trade and active prostitute stroll, tiny bistros, craft breweries, bookstores, clothing, and antique stores had opened in formerly abandoned buildings. The city had quieted, and the area's prior disreputable denizens retreated to the neighborhoods off Bayview and Exeter, until their eventual exodus when young ex-pats from Brooklyn and Manhattan discovered the city and moved north. The city had a few unsolved shootings tied to the CK Mafia. Caufield gave me access to his agency files for leads.

I had recently closed an open shooting of a local Crip gang member by two CK Mafia soldiers, one of them the son of the female trooper whose house gang members used to bag crack. I'd found a reluctant witness, a female college student, who knew the victim, and a passerby who identified photos of the two shooters. Subsequently, I convinced the victim, who miraculously escaped serious injury, to come forward in exchange for the district attorney's office dismissing a low-level drug possession charge and accompanying probation violation. Burghoff included the shooting as one of several individual cases scheduled for the special grand jury when the enterprise corruption charge against CK Mafia members moved forward.

Chief Caulfield allowed me to drop in unscheduled. Despite his city's upward trend, it still had a high crime rate and operated with the additional burden of being under a US Justice Department pattern and practice consent decree for alleged unconstitutional police practices occurring under his predecessor's tenure. Minority profiling on car stops, excessive use of force, inadequate monitoring of problem officers, and overly aggressive use of K-9 patrols led the roster of charges lodged against the department. The city attorneys agreed to cooperate with the Justice Department, much like other police departments across the country when confronted with DOJ pattern and practice lawsuits. Cooperating avoided the resulting federal control when police agencies fought the lawsuit in court.

I was reading through the agency's gun reports up to July 2005 when Adamo called me.

"It's on! Sonny, Domino, and Doob are going to rob Pure's girl," Adamo excitedly blurted in my ear.

Doob, or Alan Grant, an older gangbanger in his late 20s, and Domino's uncle, acted as Sonny C's advisor. He assumed the equivalent role of a La Cosa Nostra consigliere, like the Tom Hagen character Robert Duvall played in Sonny C's favorite movie, *The Godfather*. We'd been monitoring Doob's cell phone since shortly after we began listening in on Sonny C, Squid, and Domino.

"Wh-when? Wh-where?"

The information jolted me back more than twelve hours earlier when we debated how to approach the CKM threat to Tamarah.

"Her apartment," Adamo said.

"The wire room's been busy the past hour. They've been talking about hitting her apartment while she's at work. Sonny believes she's holding Pure's stash and cash."

"What about Squid?"

"He's out with Manic getting new rental wheels."

We agreed to meet and muster the troops at a cement plant near Tamarah's Continental Acres apartment. Adamo had already gathered Hartigan, Ackert, Taglieri, Buchanan, and Detective Charlie Dreissen from the town police with three of his uniformed officers. Recent updates from the wireroom said Sonny C sought a fourth CKM member to join him, Domino, and Doob. The calls went unanswered. We knew the other gang members either had meetings with their probation officers, appointments with their attorneys, or visits with friends in the county jail.

"Fuck it. We're jacking up this bitch's crib today. No more waiting," Sonny C said in his phone call to Doob.

We set up surveillance zones around the apartment complex and near Sonny C's house. Once again, we waited. I sat in my spot in the parking lot of the strip club. My heart pounded heavily. The beats rose up through my ears and muffled every other sound around me.

Within an hour, a black Pontiac Sunbird driven by Doob pulled into the apartment complex and circled the building twice before parking by a dumpster. Ackert and Taglieri had the eyeball on the apartment from the back of a utility van parked nearby. We waited by our radios for the call to move in. The apartment was empty. Hartigan placed Tamarah still at work in a beauty salon at the other end of the city, and earlier Ackert had gone to the apartment door to see if anyone else roamed about inside. All our intel indicated she lived alone, except for when Pure crashed there, and we had him currently in federal custody.

We staged in the front parking lot and planned to give them three minutes inside and then move in as soon as Taglieri notified us they entered the building. From that point, time moved quickly, and apparently, so did the three CK Mafia members. Adamo, Charlie Driessen, and I ran up along a concrete walkway separating two freshly cut sections of grass near the building's entrance. Unexpectedly, Sonny C, Domino, and Doob sauntered out the front door. As soon as we spotted them, we charged forward. Adamo, to my right with his MP5 at eye level, began yelling commands, "Police, get on the ground!" Driessen, to my left, had his gun pointed at Doob, and I, with my Glock pointed straight at Sonny's torso, ran up from the middle.

"Show your hands, show your fuckin' hands," Driessen and I yelled in chorus.

I ran to Sonny C, who stood in a half crouch toward the ground, and, putting my right hand on the back of his neck, pushed him the rest of the way down and straddled his lower back.

"Yo, what's up? I live here," Sonny C protested.

"Shut the fuck up," I said while holstering my gun and handcuffing him.

Adamo had Domino cuffed, and Driessen turned over a handcuffed Doob to a uniformed officer who pulled him to his feet. Surprisingly, none of the trio carried weapons.

"My mom lives here, man. What the fuck you doin' to me?"

Sonny C's mouth kept running while Domino and Doob stayed quiet. Ackert came up to me after exiting the building.

"There's been a break. They tore up the place and left a television in the hallway," he said.

We stood over Sonny C and watched Driessen, a uniformed officer, and Adamo walk Doob and Domino over to a town police car. Ackert and I grabbed Sonny C from either side and lifted him to his feet.

"You're under arrest for burglary." Sonny C looked at me with a slight smirk.

"Whatever," he said.

For all the months of listening to him on the wire, following him day and night, and making drug buys from him, it was gratifying to finally meet face to face, flesh to flesh, and size up the gang leader, drug peddler, and murderer.

"You got nothin' better to do than harass a citizen?"

Sonny C displayed an expected bravado in front of us except for a shooting star of a second when we eyeballed each other as Ackert and I stood him up. Then I saw the scared look of a man barely past his teens.

When the three were placed in marked police units and driven to the town station for processing, Adamo, Hartigan, and I went to Tamarah's apartment to survey the damage. They kicked in the front door, tossed over the bedroom mattress, pulled out and dumped dresser drawers on the floor, opened the stove, ripped out the bathroom wall vanity, removed the toilet tank cover, and emptied the kitchen refrigerator contents onto the floor. They'd done this before, knew exactly where to look, and moved fast. They completed the ransack in less than two minutes after kicking in the door.

Since we were in the town's jurisdiction, Driessen took on the burglary case and the task of notifying Tamarah. Later, he sat across from Sonny C, Domino, and Doob to see if they wanted to talk. Each told him to go fuck himself. A crime scene technician processed the apartment for fingerprints and other evidence, like Doob's big boot mark on the door.

Adamo, Hartigan, and I stayed away from the town police station while Driessen dealt with the CKM trio. We didn't want them to be aware of the FBI, State Police, or city police involvement in the case. As far as Sonny C, Domino, and Doob knew, a neighbor saw them and called in the break-in. It was dinnertime when we left the apartment.

"You look like shit," Adamo said to me in the parking lot.

"Just tired."

"You should be the way you've been running after these guys the past few nights," he said.

Pulling out of the Continental Acres complex onto Kahl Road, I suddenly felt free. Other CK Mafia players still worked the streets, but we had locked up the main guy and one of his top lieutenants. I prayed the fast-paced activity of the past few weeks would subside and that my anger would too.

*

Joan and I ate a late dinner. Earlier in the evening, Brian took Siobhan and Deirdre to the local Applebee's and then to a movie at the mall. We sat on the deck, with a candle in the center of the table, a glass of wine beside each of our plates with the bottle in reserve, and talked. I couldn't remember when I last looked deep into Joan's eyes—her beautiful, soft hazel eyes.

"What?" she asked after sipping her chardonnay.

"It's been a while. The two of us talking like this . . . about things in general."

"And not talking about . . . ," she began as I held up my hand.

"And not talking about anything other than us tonight."

She accepted the conversational limits. The case went on, but three of my headaches were in custody. With Sonny C, Domino, and Doob in the county jail, the gang's momentum would slow down for a while.

"There's nothing to discuss other than how we end this lovely night," I said.

Tears welled up in Joan's eyes.

"I thought you forgot about me the past few weeks."

"Never," I reassured her.

If she'd ever given me an ultimatum of her or the job, I'd have retired without hesitation. She never did, and I always thought she showed more strength and self-sacrifice than anything I underwent.

"I didn't forget you; I just misplaced you. Maybe we can put things back in order."

She smiled, swiped her thumb and index finger across her eyes, then rose from her seat while holding her glass of chardonnay. She walked to the deck's sliding door.

"Blow out the candle, grab the wine, and follow me."

She then led me into the soft light and quiet of our home.

19
MANHUNT

The day after arresting Sonny C, Domino, and Doob, we executed search warrants at their residences and those of Squid, Halfway, and Manic. Amid the haul of drugs, guns, stolen property, and incriminating gang videos, we found blood-stained clothing in Sonny C's room.

Burglary charges against the trio and additional charges against Sonny C for the JJ Williams homicide were presented to the grand jury. Assistant District Attorney Burghoff also offered evidence of drug sales against Squid, Halfway, Blade, Manic, Kango, and gun sales by Sonny C, Halfway, and Domino. The investigation continued, and we had a buy operation scheduled with one of the gang's wholesalers.

Lawrence Kittles, otherwise known as Big Cat or BC, a behemoth of a man at six foot four inches and weighing over three hundred pounds, partnered in the drug business with Pure. He also supplied CKM's main source of powdered cocaine aside from their rip-offs of other dealers. Kittles and Sonny C had recently begun regular meetings, and we suspected Big Cat was behind the attempt to kill Pure. Kittles came into our investigation back in June when he put up Halfway's bail.

No matter how the case continued to move forward after the trio's arrests, I expected to see things slow down a bit. At least for a few days. That is all I hoped for since Brian and Siobhan were getting ready to begin their fall college semesters, and we were moving them into their dorms on Saturday. Both had to be on campus early for sports commitments. Deirdre was starting seventh grade a few weeks later. As a reward, and to fill the void created with both older siblings off to college, we decided to get her something she had always wanted—a dog. Kylie, a Jack Russell Terrier, became part of the family in early July and was a welcome diversion whenever I came home from work. We'd go outside for a half-hour, and she'd fetch a tennis ball thrown to different parts of the yard. She was still tiny but fast, and she would proudly prance back to me with the tennis ball clenched in her teeth by its fuzzy coat. Time in the yard with her reintroduced me to the simple pleasure of playing and finding joy in the moment.

The arrests of Sonny C, Domino, and Doob didn't expose the investigation or the wires. The trio suspected a snitch in their ranks, which worked to our benefit because of the paranoia it caused. During Domino's daily jail calls to Squid, they exchanged thoughts on who the snitch could be. Meanwhile, Sonny C and Doob used their jail contacts to find any information about potential snitches. The county jail, like any US jail, had its own information pipeline. Locked up didn't mean out of the loop. With Sonny C and Domino held on bail, and Squid trying to identify a snitch, Kango came out of the shadows after Labor Day to take control of the CK Mafia. We had a few drug buys into him and linked him with an old shooting, but he spent a lot of time across the river in a seedy hotel partying and having sex with hookers. We recorded him on various calls he made to the others. Even though we had probable cause to tap his cell phone, Burghoff decided to stick with the five phones we already monitored. We didn't have enough personnel in the wire room to undertake more phone lines, and we never got to listen to either him or Manic on their direct lines. Besides, Kango stayed on the periphery most of the time, hunkered down in the motel partying when not handling CKM car rentals or coming back to the city for enforcement purposes or to stay at his mother's westside residence.

Kango immediately began issuing threats. The first was against anyone the CK Mafia caught snitching. The second was against Adamo. Hartigan heard from street sources that Kango talked about locating where Adamo lived. We assumed someone called him by name during the arrests of Sonny C, Domino, and Doob, and one of the trio passed it on from jail. The FBI part of it we couldn't figure out because no one wore raid jackets during the arrests. There was a chance it could have come to Kittles from Pure, except he was in federal custody with limited outside communication. Kango also knew a state trooper was involved. We were more concerned with how Kango knew Adamo's name and that the FBI and the State Police were involved than with the threats. I flashed back to the Leak Investigation 15 years earlier.

Kango's threat, we hoped, held little to no substance, just more bluster and street swagger from someone we had grown accustomed to listening to on phone calls talk tough when speaking with Squid and Domino. We had Kango linked to shootings, and he served as CKM muscle, but his violent tendencies competed with his need to get high and seek out female companionship. Nonetheless, Adamo took extra precautions, like parking his government vehicle in the garage, taking his MP5 home, and keeping his exterior house lights on at night. Adamo declined his supervisor's offer to place an FBI surveillance team in the neighborhood for a few nights. He didn't think it was necessary.

My routine didn't need to change. Since learning of family connections between gang members and State Police personnel, I'd been checking for tails and taking different routes when driving home. I had also told Joan and the children to be aware of their surroundings and periodically woke during the night to noises I heard, or thought I heard, outside and inside the house. I'd been on alert since the case began. Criminal contacts within law enforcement caused my heightened awareness, and the gang ties to State Police family members especially concerned me. After learning of the threat against Adamo, I drove to troop headquarters to inform Captain Quade about Kango's threats. Heinrichs, uneasy about the threats, joined me.

I'd been in car chases, tracked and arrested fugitives at gunpoint in Brooklyn, Harlem, the East Bronx, and throughout the Hudson Valley. I'd chased and arrested robbery suspects in the Bronx and the east side of Manhattan, taken down knife-wielding assailants, jumped out of an unmarked police car late at night along the FDR Drive in Manhattan to arrest a wanted Mafia associate at gunpoint who refused to pull over, executed felony arrest warrants, and made no-knock warrant entries in Far Rockaway drug houses and Hell's Angels clubhouses, but never in any of those moments did I experience the foreboding and dread as when meeting with Quade at troop headquarters.

"Do we really think this guy Kango is as bad as he's made out to be . . . as bad as you're claiming him to be? Am I to believe he'd actually threaten a federal agent?"

Quade looked at me through dark soulless eyes sunk into his head. A new buzz cut gave him a more ominous look.

"Absolutely," I snapped back, bothered by his dismissive attitude. "He and the rest of the gang have been and continue to be violent."

"I've read the weekly reports. I'm familiar with your case," he said.

The conversation shifted to the investigation's length and my being needed back in the regular Major Crimes schedule. He wanted the case wrapped up. Quade said nothing further about the threats against Adamo or expressed any concern for my safety. His claim to have read the progress reports and to be up to date on the case while suddenly questioning Kango's and the CK Mafia's tendency toward violence infuriated me.

*

I dashed out our front door, in bare feet, shorts, and a t-shirt, my Glock pointed toward the ground while ducking along our SUV. I crept to the driveway's edge. A tall figure walked in the middle of the street, away from our house after coming through the yard and across the driveway. He wore a loose-fitting hoodie, hands tucked in the pockets. A black object protruded from his right pocket. I held my gun out of sight against my left buttock.

"Can I help you?"

He stopped. I tensed and eased the gun along the side of my leg, my body bladed to reduce exposure in case he had a gun. He turned toward me, and a melodic Spanish accent offered an apology.

"Sorry. Our dog got out."

A cocker spaniel pup swiftly bounded onto the street from the middle of a row of bushes on my right.

"I didn't clip his leash good enough, and it slipped off," the man said, pulling back his hood. He was my neighbor, someone I rarely saw because he worked long hours at the family business on the other side of town.

"No problem," I said with a wave.

I turned, concealing the gun from view, and returned to the house. My heart raced. I couldn't catch my breath. The suddenness of waking, then sprinting out the door to confront the possible threat propelled me into overdrive. I poured a glass of water, sat at the dining room table, and stared out the back deck door. Joan turned on the kitchen light, startling me.

"Were you outside?" She looked at my gun in front of me on the dining room table.

My hands trembled.

"There was a noise . . . someone in our backyard by the sliding doors . . . thought it was someone from the CK Mafia . . . who'd found our house," I explained between rapid breaths.

"Who was it?"

"The neighbor from across the street looking for his dog. I nearly shot him."

She eyed the gun again, then came close and wrapped her arms around me. My whiskers scraped along the satin sheen of her robe.

"You're wired." She ran her hands from the base of my neck along the edge of my shoulders while squeezing in a soft massage.

"It's nothing."

"It's not nothing. Talk to me." Joan had my chin cupped in her hands, pulling my head up to look at her.

"Please tell me you're going to be in the office today catching up on paperwork or something else." I shook my head "no." Kango had to be found.

We scoured the city, looking for Kango, including his mother's house and the two motels where he bunked down with various women. The County Drug Task Force also remained alert, ready to place an informant drug buy into him or catch him in possession. We urgently wanted Kango off the street for officer safety reasons.

Nearly eighteen hours after I mistook my neighbor for a gang member, Kango was dead. He had been in a Lincoln Navigator rental driven by his girlfriend when she pulled along the curb diagonally across from a house on Pine Street where a rival gang member, Hi-Hi Wiggins, sat on a porch with two others drinking beer. Kango got out of the Navigator with a cut-down AK-47 and fired several shots toward the porch. Hi-Hi hopped over the porch railing and, as he sprinted across the neighboring yard, fired three shots over his left shoulder from a revolver. In a fluke of random marksmanship he couldn't repeat if he tried, one of Hi-Hi's rounds whizzed across Pine Street, and, as Kango leaned into the Navigator, the round passed between the passenger-side front pillar of the open door frame and into Kango's right temple. He went down, his girlfriend drove off, and the AK-47 fell onto the sidewalk before quickly disappearing into the night.

The call from Adamo came a few hours after Kango's death. Hartigan had responded to the scene and worked on the case with his department's detective unit. As much as it was our job to prevent violence and preserve life, his death made me relax.

"Some guy named Hi-Hi Wiggins did it. Do you know him?" Adamo asked.

I never had any direct contact with Hi-Hi, but was familiar with his middle brother, Glorious, who received prison time for an attempted murder conviction, and I'd dealt with his older brother, Magnificent Supreme Wiggins. Several years earlier, Magnificent was a passenger in the car of a wanted felon who led me and a trooper on a wild chase through city streets until they crashed in the front yard of a local home after tossing a gun out the car window. When I searched him, Magnificent had an electronic monitor attached to his right ankle. He was on probation for a shooting.

A year and a half after the car chase, Magnificent joined his brother Glorious in prison on a twenty-five-to-life bid for murder and attempted robbery after he mistakenly shot his buddy during an attempted robbery of a drug dealer.

"Quite a family," Adamo said. "Hartigan is getting a search warrant for the mother's apartment. The city police picked up Hi-Hi an hour after the shooting. Meet me at her place." I wrote down the address, took a quick shower, and rushed out to the Wiggins apartment.

Hi-Hi's mother lived on the third floor of a crumbling multi-family building along a street of similarly clustered buildings. Lonetta Wiggins met us at the door in curlers, a house dress, and worn-down cloth slippers. In the living room, a half dozen single mattresses were spread across the room. On four of the mattresses, two sleeping children curled up at either end. Mrs. Wiggins lived on Supplemental Social Security income and cash from her unlicensed daycare service. Her face sagged like a basset hound. The lines and wrinkles around her forehead and mouth illustrated a lifetime of worry, sorrow, and pain, with little to smile about. Our search likely added to the list of many she'd dealt with whenever the police followed up on something one of her boys did.

"Mrs. Wiggins, we have a search warrant for your apartment. We're mainly interested in Hi-Hi's room," Hartigan explained to her.

He'd had prior dealings with the family.

"Hiram ain't been here this morning."

The mystery of Hi-Hi's nickname partially unraveled. By the end of the search, we learned his middle name, Hyacinthe, came from his mother's maiden name.

"We still have to search," Hartigan told her.

"Do what you must. Just don't disturb the babies." She motioned to the sleeping children and settled into a corner chair. An open Bible rested under her left forearm.

The sound of a dropped box followed by another brought Hartigan and me to the back room. Two officers flipped through personal items like scavengers sifting through a garbage heap.

"Hey, hey," Hartigan shouted, "handle this like it's your mother's home. Give her and her property some respect."

I had been in the same situation a few times before when younger troopers treated a search warrant as an open invitation to trash someone's property. When voicing admonitions like Hartigan's, I was met with the same quizzical look. Search warrants require not only a meticulous recording of where evidence is found but also respect for other people and their belongings, no matter who they are. Otherwise, it's sloppy police work and unprofessional.

Adamo and I joined another officer in a side room where Hi-Hi slept. Buried in a bottom dresser drawer under several folded jeans and sweatpants, we uncovered a .410 gauge double-barreled shotgun. In a top drawer under socks and underwear, we found a 9mm semi-automatic handgun, a .38 caliber revolver under the bed mattress, and in a back room closet, a sawed-off shotgun.

After the search, I drove north to troop headquarters with the seized weapons for eventual transfer to our Albany Firearms Unit for testing. Later results linked the .38 caliber to the shooting. On the way, I called Heinrichs with an update.

"The captain and lieutenant are waiting for you to brief them in person as long as you'll be at troop."

"Gladly."

Heinrichs sensed I was coming in hot.

"You got something?"

"More guns."

When I arrived, Heinrichs waited by the Major Crimes rear entrance and led me to the captain's office where Quade sat behind his desk and Lieutenant Plummer perched to his left in a side chair. I placed the guns on Quade's desk, saluted, and settled into one of two chairs opposite him. Heinrichs took the other.

"Is this all from the morning search already? That's quite a haul." Quade's unexpectedly friendly tone caused me to briefly look at Heinrichs, who responded with a slight shoulder shrug.

"Yes sir, direct from Hi-Hi Wiggins' bedroom."

"Excellent."

"Good job, T," Plummer piped in.

"Thank you, Lieutenant." My Cheshire Cat grin couldn't be contained. "Yes, excellent work . . . this whole case so far . . . excellent," Quade added. The change from his previous demeanor toward the investigation and me was fun to watch but confusing.

Three days earlier he'd only been interested in winding down the case and getting me back to the Major Crimes rotation. The threats to Adamo, and possibly me, and the concern I'd expressed about increasing violence were of no consequence to him then. Now, with a case target dead and other gangs involved—Hi-Hi ran with the Crips—Quade showed more interest. My guess was that he received a call from Albany after reports of the shooting. The next rung on his career ladder dangled before him, and he couldn't afford to slip on the way up. Quade took notes while I continued to brief him and Plummer.

"Lucky for us that Kango decided to first hunt down Hi-Hi instead of Adamo, or one of my investigators," Heinrichs said. She was a master at subliminal messaging whenever she felt the bosses needed a gibe.

"Very well. Great job. Both of you. Keep at it," Quade said, signaling the meeting's end.

"One more thing, sir." I couldn't help myself. "We can still use more personnel. The town police took back two of their people. It'd be nice to have more help from our end. You know, before more bodies drop."

Quade shifted in his chair.

"Otherwise, I'd only be hindered in doing everything in my power to prevent another homicide."

Plummer looked away while Quade assured us he'd send more people. I gave a quick salute, gathered the guns, and left with Heinrichs. A day later, Quade assigned two more State Police investigators to the case, one of them being Juan Limon. It had taken a gang-related shooting, a dead gang member, a missing AK-47, the seizure of four illegal guns, and the looming threat of more violence to get me help in the investigation. Mostly though, from my vantage point, it amounted to optics and protecting Quade's next promotion.

20
OFFICER DOWN

A silver hearse, followed by a black stretch limousine and a line of cars, pulled into the cemetery, then proceeded along a path to a resting place 400 feet away. Several SUVs and four-door sedans pulled in behind the limousine. Kango's final resting place, a dirt opening surrounded by a swath of brilliant green grass at the southern end of the cemetery, offered a bucolic setting much different from the streets he came from. Elm trees a short distance away formed a wall where the cemetery sloped through patches of spindly birches to the river. An unobstructed panorama of the opposite shoreline allowed for beautiful sunset views from Kango's gravesite. The beginning oranges and yellows mixed with the dark and light green of the distant foliage framed our surveillance photos.

I parked behind Adamo in the rural cemetery overlooking the Hudson River. The night before, we sat outside a local funeral home taking pictures of people attending Kango's wake. I grabbed my binoculars and settled into the passenger seat next to Adamo. His 35mm camera's zoom lens rested on the steering wheel as he focused on the gathering.

"Let's see if this goes off without a problem," he said.

Adamo took pictures while I served as a spotter, calling out known gang members present.

The young men arriving to pay their final respects dressed in an array of clothing styles. They wore dark suits with sharp collars, a few in bowler hats, some in turtlenecks with a sports jacket or leather coat. The women wore Sunday dresses and cloche hats. The younger men in crisp new jeans and oversized white shirts with Kango's photo across the chest looked lost. On their shirts, in graffiti style purple writing, blazoned the words "CKM Forever" and "Rest in Peace K." The graveside service lasted twenty minutes. A brief sermon, prayers, choruses of "Amen," and the sounds of a woman crying carried over to where we watched. Some men wandered away from the service to take calls on their cell phones.

In the past, I'd watched similar rituals outside of New York City funeral homes while photographing attendees at Mafia wakes. There were also police funerals, a separate kind of ritual for those who made the ultimate line of duty sacrifice. The same goodbye liturgy repeated itself no matter who went into the ground.

When the service ended, we watched and waited for the cars to exit. I let out a few loud consecutive yawns.

"Don't get too sleepy; we've got the informant buy op into Kittles later."

"Yup, I'll be ready."

I'd been waiting for the last buy into Big Cat, knowing this would bring us a step closer to wrapping up the investigation. We already had two felony buys into CKM's wholesale supplier. Burghoff wanted one more. Later in the day, several hours after Kango's burial, Big Cat sold two ounces of cocaine to an informant. This last buy cleared the way for us to arrest him once Burghoff obtained a search warrant for his house.

When I arrived home, Joan and Deirdre had just sat down for dinner. I washed up and joined them for lasagna and garlic bread. Deirdre finished her first week with the varsity cross-country team as a seventh grader, and we discussed her early season transition from the modified team to varsity.

"Are the older girls nice? Any issues with you being a seventh grader?"

"They are very nice. No problems. Sarah's been running with me at practice."

Sarah, a junior, took over as captain of the team once Siobhan graduated. Deirdre missed the chance to run with her older sister by a year because New York State athletic rules only allowed seventh graders to move up to varsity level. Deirdre watched as a sixth grader the year before when her older sister's team won the league championship for the first time in school history. Siobhan and three other seniors integral to that team graduated. As a seventh grader, Deirdre quickly moved into the number two spot on the team.

"Glad to hear things are going well," I said. Deirdre cradled her puppy Kylie in her lap. She petted Kylie between fork loads of lasagna. Her little Jack Russell Terrier squirmed to catch a taste of Deirdre's food. Watching them together made me happy. I wanted more evenings like this and for the crazy hours chasing after gang members to end. Soon enough it'd all be over.

It took Burghoff a week and a half to get us our search warrant for Big Cat's house. Two other city homicides, unrelated to gang activity, demanded his attention. We decided to neutralize Big Cat as a threat by waiting for him to leave the house and then pull him over a few blocks away on a traffic stop. When we had him in custody, the search team would get the go-ahead radio transmission to begin the search. Adamo and I rode together, Hartigan in an unmarked city unit, and Sgt. Buchanan from the County Drug Task Force in a minivan. Big Cat left late in the morning for a meeting we knew about through the wire. He sauntered down his driveway wearing a triple-XL white t-shirt and baggy basketball shorts with unlaced Timberland boots. Big Cat concentrated on his cell phone as he walked to his Escalade. The SUV frame shifted on its chassis under his weight. He pulled away, the cell phone to his ear, and after a couple of turns on side streets, made his way across the city's east-west arterial and headed toward the town. We decided to pull him over within the city boundaries using a nearby marked unit for the stop. The city patrol car pulled behind the Escalade and put on the overhead lights. We had no reason to believe Big Cat would run, but as soon as the lights went on, he swerved around cars in front of him and led us on a pursuit. We were the first vehicle behind the marked patrol car, and Adamo flipped on his dashboard and emergency grille lights. Buchanan drove close behind. Big Cat's vehicle roared eastbound through a mix of residential and commercial streets before coming to a sharp curve. Instead of riding the apex of the curve, his vehicle continued straight into a deli parking lot. The marked police unit shot past him and came to a screeching stop twenty-five yards from the lot. The Escalade bounced over the curb into the parking lot and continued toward a nearby house. I feared another chase ending with a crash into someone's front yard as Big Cat's vehicle accelerated straight toward the front door of a ranch-style home. Suddenly, the Escalade made a sharp turn, and its two right tires lifted off the ground, exposing the undercarriage and its stainless-steel exhaust muffler. We expected the vehicle to flip and roll into the house. Any other outcome seemed improbable given Big Cat's added weight on the driver's side. Instead, the SUV abruptly settled back on all four tires and came to a stop. Adamo pulled in at an angle in front of the SUV and Buchanan behind it. My adrenaline overrode common sense, and I jumped out of Adamo's Tahoe before it stopped. I fell out the door and crashed my right knee onto the pavement, quickly recovered, then ran toward the SUV. Adamo came into my right peripheral vision, and Buchanan, slightly behind me, yelled commands for Big Cat to exit and show his hands. Big Cat came out slowly, arms raised over his head. We held him at gunpoint until the uniform city patrol rejoined us. It took three sets of handcuffs to secure Big Cat's wrists behind his back.

I turned to Adamo.

"I'm hurt."

"You fell out pretty hard."

"Yeah, my wrist is a bit messed up too. My right knee's worse, though. It hurts to walk and bend it."

I had to call in the chase to Heinrichs and notify her of my injury. An investigation and an afternoon of paperwork, including workers' compensation forms, would take up her shift. I'd been fortunate in my law enforcement career not to have sustained significant injury. Other than scrapes and bruises from scuffles, whiplash after being rear-ended, a dog bite, and a duty-related hernia, I stayed relatively injury-free. This medical visit would be inconvenient and pull me away from the case.

The search of Big Cat's house took place without me. Adamo and Hartigan seized six more ounces of cocaine and $24,000 cash. Buchanan had already found two ounces of cocaine and another $6,000 in Big Cat's Escalade after the chase. The possession charges on top of the three prior felony drug buys assured us Big Cat would eventually receive double-digit state prison time.

Heinrichs met me at a local urgent care facility to get my knee checked. She appeared upset. "What's up? You look like a kid who found out there's no Santa Claus or Easter Bunny."

"Fucking brass," she said. "You know what they had the nerve to ask me?"

Heinrichs outlined the grilling she received at troop headquarters from Captain Quade and Lieutenant Plummer.

"They wanted to know why you got involved in a vehicle pursuit. Were you driving? Were you really hurt? How long would you be out of work? What impact would it have on the case?"

She fumed.

"Jesus Christ, I had a fucking headache by the time I left the place. It's a loony bin during the day when they're around."

"Was I really hurt?"

"Yeah, do you believe it?"

After x-rays and a scheduled MRI, the doctor released me with crutches, a prescription for Tylenol with codeine, and instructions to avoid weight bearing on my knee and take three days off from work. While signing release forms, I realized that the Chicago Marathon was in ten days.

"You're not running a marathon any time soon," the doctor said. "There's no fracture, and likely no tears, however, there's severe swelling, not to mention you have a limited range of motion right now."

"But it's ten days away and . . . ." The doctor cut me off.

"The fall caused damage based on the fact that you're sore. Pounding out twenty-six miles on pavement is only going to aggravate it, and then you'll have worse problems." His final judgment sidelined me from the marathon. Six months of training wasted in the span of a few minutes chasing a drug dealer.

I ditched the crutches and went back to work in the afternoon with my knee wrapped and took Tylenol for the pain. Three days later, my knee still hurting, I testified before the grand jury. Burghoff questioned me about the investigation from inception to the recent arrest of Big Cat. Since the arrests of Sonny C, Doob, and Domino, the grand jury met regularly, and Burghoff shuffled witnesses in and out. The sooner the case concluded, the safer it would be for the community.

"I feel good about this case," he said to me in the oak-paneled hallway outside the grand jury room. "The investigation came together nicely. Now all I have to do is convict the bastards." Burghoff's deep laugh followed him down the narrow hall as he walked back to the grand jury room.

Upset about missing the Chicago Marathon, I purchased consolation tickets for games six and seven of the National League Championship Series between the Mets and St. Louis Cardinals for Brian and me. His college wasn't too far away from the stadium, and we met for a pre-game dinner on Wednesday before game six. My knee bothered me, and the logistics of planning multiple arrests and searches weighed on me. But as soon as the game began, thoughts about the CK Mafia, Quade, Plummer, and the marathon faded away. The Mets evened the series with a 4–2 win to force a deciding game seven at Shea Stadium. We were thrilled at the prospect of a league title and World Series appearance for the Mets. I'd always rooted for the underdog, and the Mets were the perennial choice for like-minded New York baseball fans. The next night's game, however, ended in a way Mets fans had come to expect with the bases loaded, two outs in the bottom of the ninth, and Mets slugger Carlos Beltran looking at a called third strike on a curveball at the knees. Disappointed with the result, we stopped at the Airline Diner on Astoria Boulevard for a post-game meal.

As we ate, I wondered when Brian had become such an adult. He was always mature for his age and had developed an incredible entrepreneurial spirit in middle school. He continued in high school and college with different business ventures. Joan and I envisioned big things for him, as we did for Siobhan and Deirdre, but recently he'd told us he was considering a police career. This caused a lot of stress for both of us.

Perhaps I should have been flattered by my son's thought of following my career path. I knew colleagues whose children had entered the police ranks, and they were immensely proud. I would be too if Brian chose policing as a career. But I had reservations. The pettiness, corruption, incompetence, and dangers accompanying police work were negative attributes often outweighing the job's allure. There were a lot of positives, though: the friends and partners you work with, their integrity and bravery, and the satisfaction of serving the community.

I had no doubt he'd be a good cop. My fervent hope was he never became one. I didn't want him to follow my pathway. I was forty-four years old, fifteen years licensed as an attorney with a growing part-time law practice yet still running around the streets chasing after gang members while trying to solve past shootings and murders. I'd been selfish in pursuing my passion and felt I hadn't lived up to expectations. A growing cloud of regret hovered over me during the CK Mafia investigation regarding my decision nearly seventeen years earlier to remain on the job. I wondered if they'd been wasted years when I should have instead been practicing law. Brian had his whole future in front of him. I wanted it to be perfect. My regret would be compounded if he followed the police path.

Additionally, Joan would be a wreck. To our relief, Brian's entrepreneurial spirit and business acumen later led him on a different path.

*

After Kittles's arrest, I stayed busy coordinating more drug buys into Squid, Halfway, Blade, and Manic. We also strengthened the case against lower echelon gang members by making more drug buys from them. Gang members with the street names Turtle, Dirt, Uptown, Two-fist, and Threads hitched their way onto the enterprise corruption charge. We aimed to weaken the CK Mafia by snaring as many street players as we could. Disrupt and dismantle. I took pride in the way we'd adhered to the Safe Streets Task Force motto.

A week after NLCS game 7, I drove lights and siren in response to a radio transmission of a police officer being shot. The call came in a few minutes past eleven in the morning. CK Mafia involvement was my overriding fear as I sped to the public housing complex where the shooting occurred.

At the scene, police cars and officers from the local police department, sheriff's office, and State Police blocked vehicle and pedestrian access to the complex. I looked for the local police chief, Ben Caulfield. One of his uniformed officers told me he went to the hospital with the wounded officer. I didn't stick around; I had to check on the officer and find out what happened. Shortly thereafter, I was in the emergency room with Caulfield at the bedside of the wounded police officer, Travis Cooper.

Caulfield, a tall man with a neatly trimmed mustache and glasses, looked more like an accountant than a cop. He had invited me into Cooper's treatment room when I came up to him at the nurse's station. Officer Cooper's backup shot the perpetrator who doctors and nurses treated in the next room. Cooper, still in his uniform pants and boots but shirtless, lay on the gurney hooked up to a heart monitor along with other devices measuring his vital signs. An intravenous fluid bag hung over his bed, and white adhesive tape held the IV line in place along his forearm. Cooper's face and neck were cut in several places from the car window glass that shattered when the shooter opened fire from within his car.

Caulfield explained to me what happened. Cooper responded to a suspicious vehicle complaint at the housing complex. When he arrived, a sedan with tinted windows was parked in the lot with its engine running. As Cooper approached the car door, a shot blasted through the tinted driver's side window, striking Cooper's ballistic vest and sending glass flying into his face. Cooper fell to the ground, and his backup, Officer Berto Ramirez, fired several shots into the vehicle, striking the operator, twenty-year-old Derwin McAdams, a Crip affiliate with the street name D-Mac. Before leaving the emergency room to return to the crime scene, I looked in the neighboring trauma room where medical staff worked on D-Mac. Doctors and nurses stood over his open chest, trying to stabilize him for surgery.

McAdams' name never surfaced during the investigation, and the recovered gun, a .38 caliber Taurus, didn't match any of those held by the CK Mafia. No matter the circumstances, the shooting of a cop is bad, but I left the hospital relieved that the officer would recover and that the shooter wasn't one of the CK Mafia. The investigation had taken a lot out of me; I didn't need added flak from the bosses that enough wasn't done to prevent a police officer from being shot.

The hospital treated and released Officer Cooper later in the afternoon. He returned to duty the following week. Remarkably, D-Mac survived his gunshot wounds. Burghoff handled D-Mac's prosecution and obtained a conviction of attempted murder of a police officer and weapons possession. D-Mac received twenty-seven years to life in prison.

Neither Captain Quade nor Lieutenant Plummer questioned me much about Cooper's shooting. For all the times they'd hassled me during the CK Mafia case about other incidents, I thought for sure the shooting of a police officer by a gang-affiliated perpetrator would get their attention. "I've given up trying to figure them out," Heinrichs said to me in a phone call.

It was just as well. I had plenty to do as the month came to an end. The grand jury foreperson scheduled me for one more session the day before Halloween, and then I had meetings with Burghoff to review charging sheets on each defendant. Burghoff expected to have a grand jury vote on the indictments by the first week of November and wanted Adamo and me to coordinate search and arrest plans.

Aside from the case concluding, I also looked forward to the upcoming high school cross-country sectional meet. This was the annual qualifying race held to determine who would run in the state championships. For six years, Joan and I had watched Brian and Siobhan qualify to compete. Now it was Deirdre's turn. Since moving up to varsity, she'd been running well. She wanted to qualify like her sister did in seventh grade and every year thereafter throughout high school. Deirdre achieved her goal and ran at the state meet with her teammate Sarah a week later. In between those two cross-country races, New York held its gubernatorial election and Eliot Spitzer, the state attorney general, defeated the Republican candidate John Faso with almost 66 percent of the vote. A new administration in the state capital meant changes in the State Police hierarchy. For lower-ranking people like me, it didn't make much of a difference, except now being able to say I knew the governor.

*

A week before Thanksgiving, seventy-five law enforcement officers from various police agencies and the FBI executed early morning warrants at the residences of CK Mafia members. Fifteen suspects from the investigation were arrested, not including the four already in custody: Sonny C, Domino, Doob, and Big

Cat. Adamo and I, along with a four-person SWAT team, arrested Squid in the Westview Apartments where he stayed with his girlfriend. Hartigan and a State Police team picked up Halfway at his mother's house. Later, at the press conference arranged by the county district attorney, Walter Braden, a large chart with the photos of all the arrestees rested on an easel next to the podium with over a dozen media microphones popping hydra-like in front of the diminutive district attorney's face. An arsenal of seized guns sat on a table in front of the podium, along with stacks of cash and drugs in clear evidence bags. The district attorney and supervisors from the different agencies involved, including Quade, stood in front of the cameras with self-satisfied grins.

The CK Mafia investigation concluded, and trial preparation began. We had follow-up street work to do, but Quade expected me to report back to the Major Crimes Unit the following week. At their arraignments, the judge scheduled all CK Mafia defendants for a preliminary hearing five days later in state supreme court. Tight security cordoned off the courthouse for the hearings because we learned they planned to cause a disturbance and attempt an escape with the help of friends in the audience. Nothing happened, but we treated the threat as real and had SWAT teams deployed. After all, this was the Crazed Killas Mafia.

PART III

THE FIRE

21
FAMILY MASSACRE

I felt nothing standing over the three bodies. The firemen placed them on the black tarp in age order. More of a coincidence than design. Tony Jr., the oldest at thirteen, named after his father, who hadn't been located, rested on the left corner of the tarp. Then came Ryan, age ten, who looked as if he was still nestling in the sleep stolen from him. Finally, Adam, the youngest, six, placed to the right of his brothers. We later learned he died from smoke inhalation and not the blunt force trauma visible on his scalp.

Tony Jr. was the bloodiest. The medical examiner tallied eighty-three stab wounds. His left hand, unnaturally splayed backwards and nearly severed at the wrist, gave the first indication this was a homicide and not a house fire the occupants failed to escape. A walk-through of the boys' second-floor bedroom, its walls charred and blackened, indicated Tony Jr. put up a valiant fight for his and his brothers' lives. On the lone undamaged wall facing the front yard, his blood streaked in crisscross patterns and a handprint pressed into the wallpaper like a preschooler's art project hung on the refrigerator. Subsequent forensics matched the handprint to one of the killers.

Violent death had become routine for me, and by extension for my family. By the time Deirdre was in middle school, she had the habit of asking Joan, "who got killed?" whenever she woke to find me already out of the house. Looking over the bodies, I realized Tony Jr. was close to her age. I had left home shortly before 5:00 a.m. to stand over someone else's children, and yet, I was unmoved. Unlike some firefighters who stood on the periphery shaking their heads and wiping tears from their eyes, I remained stoic and focused. Those firefighters let emotion interfere with their job. Smoke still poured out of second-floor broken windows, and another body, burned beyond recognition, had yet to be removed. I didn't have time to feel anything. Work had to be done.

My only reaction was that my feet were freezing. I had returned to the Major Crimes rotation after the Crazed Killas Mafia arrests seven weeks earlier, and my dress shoes and socks weren't enough. The front yard was a mix of cold mud and gray slush from hoses the firemen dragged across to put out the flames. Flecks of black soot topped the areas of packed snow. It reminded me of chocolate sprinkles on scoops of ice cream. Another random thought to reflexively detach me from the carnage. I made a mental note to put on work boots. They'd look funny with my suit, but fashion had to give way to warmth. Fortunately, I kept extra gear in my car. From experience, I knew there'd be little time spent at home during the next few days.

Tony Sr. quickly became a suspect when we didn't find him. You often first look at those closest to the victims. However, the crime scene unit's work and the subsequent autopsy revealed the boys' parents had been shot and the father placed on top of the mother, then covered with a couch set on fire. The intensity of the fire made Tony Sr. indistinguishable from his wife, Tina, in a fused pile of flesh and bone. This discovery only deepened the mystery as to who killed the family. Violent death is rarely simple. I'd learned long ago not to be wedded to initial presumptions in an investigation.

A steady erosion from within had taken place over the course of my career. Its gradual effect finally reached the point where I acknowledged something had been carved out of me. I felt soulless. The Morey family homicide brought a key moment of recognition. It came too soon on the heels of the CK Mafia case, from which I hadn't recovered. Now a quintuple homicide started my day.

I'd been around death for most of my career and rarely gave it a second thought, never realizing my easy acceptance of it wasn't normal. I built walls and defenses to keep it at bay. In the past, my Catholic faith's belief in eternal life had inured me to death's finality, but I had a hard time believing in the hope and redemption theme of the resurrection while looking over the Morey boys' battered bodies.

Instead, memories of death looped, like a movie reel in a continuum of crime scenes and notifications to victims' families, like the explanation provided to the elderly parents whose thirty-six-year-old son overdosed in their home where he returned to live after losing his job; then the consolation given to a grown son whose father took a shotgun and placed it in his mouth before pulling the trigger, sending his flesh, blood, and brain matter in a widening spray from his bed's headboard to the ceiling; and a notification made to the wife whose husband died when his car swerved off the road and a heavy tree branch came through the windshield and impaled him. He traveled home a week before Christmas with gifts he purchased for his five children, each of whom proceeded to come downstairs from their rooms as they heard their mother's anguished cries. The youngest child, a four-year-old, sat on the stairway and cried along with her siblings.

Then, informing the sister of a missing woman, a drug addict and prostitute whose right ulna we recovered around a trash bin at an apartment complex, that DNA provided an identification, but we found nothing else of her sister to bury. Her mysterious demise we believed to be at the hands of a serial killer.

This notification was reminiscent of another prostitute's death a few years earlier, except her killer was in custody. He had murdered eight women and hidden them in the family attic and cellar. Each of these conversations with the victims' loved ones indelibly lingered. If death was merely a transitory act and the next day life reset, the memory of it would be less permanent.

The loop of memories continued: the mother at the wake of her daughter whose body we found wrapped in a carpet and tossed into the woods after being raped and strangled; the skeletal remains of an abducted twelve-year-old child who'd been missing for two years; the high school senior convenience store clerk shot in the face during a Mother's Day armed robbery; and the nineteen-year-old newlywed beaten and strangled in her apartment.

More images rushed by—the body of an eighteen-year-old prison inmate who, three days into his six-year bid, couldn't take it and hung himself in his cell, and the autopsy of a thirteen-month-old baby girl whose mother was suspected of smothering her.

Nothing made me as angry as when a parent failed to protect a child. This was the situation with the Morey family massacre. The father, a low-level drug dealer and addict, brought the violence into his home. He associated with bad people and made worse choices leading up to his family's murder. His wife shared complicity. She tried to control his drug use and hold onto the money he made from dealing by deciding to get more involved in his business. If he wasn't going to put her and the children first and continue to get stoned with his friends while spending money they desperately needed, she'd make sure they held onto some of the drug profits. She acted out of a misguided necessity, and it cost her family dearly.

A homicide investigator serves as an agent for the dead, their vindicator on earth. To be effective, one must be a voyeur into their past life. Many times, I judged the dead, an attitude justified by the intimacy we shared. During this case, I cursed Tony Sr. and Tina for what they'd done. Through silent whispers and internal monologues, I sometimes talked to murder victims, vocally beseeching them for help in solving their cases. Joan caught me once, forcing me to confess my conversations. She didn't know about their occasional visits to my sleep and their unrelenting demands of me until many years later when I could no longer hide it from her.

If I didn't have sympathy for the boys, I'd be no different from the monsters who slaughtered them, but I had none for the parents, as horrible as that seemed. Weariness placed me beyond the capacity to care about them. Parents who didn't protect their children disgusted me.

The Morey family massacre took a week to solve. Joan saw me in glimpses. Heinrichs designated Limon and me as one of two main teams tasked with locating and interviewing possible suspects and key witnesses. Andy Kamisky and Daniel Liguori formed the other main team. I worked with both as investigators outside of Major Crimes, and they were among the best. Heinrichs pulled them from their duty stations to assist.

The same morning of the fire, less than three hours after arriving at the scene, Limon and I picked up Charlie Gilleo, a friend of Tony Sr., and his brother Nicky at the trailer where Charlie lived, within two miles from the Morey house. When we pulled up to the trailer, Nicky stood by a parked car, and a pale, freckle-faced young woman walked toward him. A disheveled man in his early 30s approached to our left.

"Hey, remember me? I helped you catch my cousin Darren," Charlie greeted me as he walked across the snow-covered yard.

A few years earlier, Gilleo's cousin Darren had knocked on the door of a local house one May evening and at knifepoint abducted the elderly woman who answered. He had her drive him to her local bank ATM and withdraw several hundred dollars. Before running off, he pushed her to the ground, causing her leg to break. The victim was the mother of a prominent local attorney and former county prosecutor. For two days, we searched for Darren and finally caught him hiding in a local apartment. I interviewed Charlie where he lived at the time. He had tried to steer us away from his cousin, who we found not too far from Charlie's apartment. If Charlie now wanted to start our morning encounter with the fiction that he'd helped us, I'd go along with it.

"Yeah, I remember. Thanks."

I pointed toward a two-inch cut along his right forehead below his hairline.

"What the hell happened to you?"

"What d'ya mean?" Charlie ran his hand through his hair.

"The cut on your head there. Where'd it come from?"

"Oh, that's from quadding . . . must've hit a branch."

He made a motion with both hands as if holding the steering bar and gassing the throttle of a four-wheel quad.

"Don't you wear a helmet?"

"Yeah. Why?"

Charlie didn't get the question's relevance.

"You look like shit. Where've you been? Did you go out last night?"

Charlie stared at me through glazed and bloodshot eyes. He didn't appear to be someone who'd had a sound night's sleep.

Charlie lit a cigarette; he watched and listened as we talked with his brother Nicky and the young woman, Nicky's girlfriend. They all agreed to drive to the local State Police station to be interviewed. When we arrived at the station, it was a madhouse. Investigators and troopers came and went. Sue Heinrichs huddled in an office with the troop commander and the colonel in charge of statewide BCI operations, who came down from Albany.

We interviewed Nicky and his girlfriend, and Charlie went to Kamisky and Liguori. After an hour and a half interview, we had another person of interest to locate: Malcolm Boyd, a drug dealer friend of Tony Sr. and Charlie. Boyd had done time upstate for drug possession and sales. He wasn't gang-affiliated, though he maneuvered easily among groups on both sides of the Hudson River. His street name, Malice, suggested he wouldn't be especially receptive to the police. Limon and I spent most of the day trying to find him while following up on other leads. Meanwhile, Kamisky and Liguori identified another person of interest, Mark Serrano, a friend of Tony Sr., who Charlie used as his alibi for his previous night's activity. Kamisky and Liguori interviewed Serrano, a local waste company employee, at the station later in the day.

When I finally reached Malice on his cell phone, he was on his way to Atlantic City with his girlfriend. Our conversation wasn't pleasant. He was brusque and uncooperative at first, but I convinced him to return to the county and sit down to talk with us. A few hours later, he arrived at the station.

Malice, a six-foot-five-inch tower of solid muscle in his mid-thirties, glowered at us like a man who had no time for two tie-wearing police motherfuckers. His voice boomed when he spoke. When not scowling or contorting his face into various overwrought expressions, his handsome features stood out, notable among them being a nose with a broad, prominent bridge and downward turn bookended by high cheekbones.

"Ain't got no time for this," he snapped while pacing the room.

"Sit down, relax. Let's talk, and we can get you out of here," Limon soothingly said.

"Man, it's so fucked up . . . those kids," Malice said. "I didn't have nothing to do with that."

We assured him he was being interviewed as a potential witness, not a suspect. He eased up.

"Tony and me was tight. Can't imagine anyone who'd want to hurt him and his family."

Malice settled into a chair, and we spoke for the next hour. Although he cooperated, we knew he held back information. We let him go with instructions to stay local for the next few days. By late in the evening, the investigation had already yielded the statements of three key players in the Morey homicides. It would take the rest of the week to unravel the twisted timeline and connections the day's interviews brought.

Malice evaded us after the initial interview, and there came a point when we had to force him to sit down with us. There was only one way to get him talking. I contacted Sergeant Buchanan at the County Drug Task Force and told him what we needed. He had an informant who knew Malice and had made cocaine buys from him in the past. It didn't take much for Malice to get caught making two sales. The whole operation took a day and a half. The County Drug Task Force had Malice in custody at a town police station across the river. Buchanan found my business card in his wallet and asked Malice about it.

"He asked me to help him with a case," he replied. Malice, according to Buchanan, stressed over the arrest and worried about going back to prison.

"Can I call him, or maybe you can do it for me? I need to speak to him." Malice's request came as we hoped it would.

Limon and I, already parked down the road from the police station, decided to make Malice wait.

"Tell him we'll be there in half an hour," I told Buchanan.

I drove to Dunkin Donuts where we discussed how to play Malice. Then Limon picked up a coffee before heading to the police station. The desk sergeant led us to a holding area where he opened the cell and Limon handed Malice the coffee.

"I'm gonna be cryin' mad tears tonight if my parole gets revoked . . . can't go back upstate and do more time. My girl made me promise to do no more of this shit. We gonna be gettin' married this year."

"Why then are you still selling drugs?" I asked.

"'Cause we havin' another kid. Just found out a couple weeks ago. A man's got to provide."

"It's simple; you got to barter. Is there some info you have to trade."

He thought for a moment.

"What about Tony and the kids? You still looking at it?"

Malice, eager to please, bit sooner than expected. He got hooked easily. Limon made his move to bring him in.

"We're trying to get a complete timeline. There are gaps we need to fill in."

Malice looked down and shook his head. "Those kids, man, ain't no way you got a soul if you hurt kids."

We soon discovered the reason for Malice initially holding out on us. He detailed two drug sales he made to Serrano and Gilleo in a Walmart parking lot. By the second meeting, when he sold them an eight-ball of coke, they were both flying high and edgy. They even got aggressive with him, especially Gilleo, who had a large Bowie knife. Malice thought they might try to rip him off.

After Malice told this story, he provided a damning piece of evidence by relating a phone call he received from Gilleo the morning the Morey family bodies were discovered. Before any news release on the fire, and before we picked him up, Gilleo called Malice to tell him the family burned to death, and he provided details not released to the press. Telephone toll records and a later interview with Malice's girlfriend corroborated his story when she told us she rode in the car when he took the call and heard what Gilleo said on the speaker.

*

I had arranged with the County Drug Task Force to set up Malice for a drug buy and use it to squeeze him for information. Some might say this kind of conduct by the police is abusive and unnecessary, but they're the ones who live tidy lives and expect storybook endings. I didn't have a problem with what we'd done. Limon and I agreed it was the best way to ensure his cooperation. So too did Heinrichs and Major Doyle, who gave us approval to move ahead with the plan. Guys like Malice didn't deserve any consideration. We gave him an opportunity to decide whether or not to sell drugs. He chose to sell. Another fact I later learned about Malice was that he sold D-Mac the gun used to shoot Officer Cooper back in October. This occurred after several CK Mafia members ran up on D-Mac and his girl in their apartment. They threatened to shoot D-Mac and rape his girl if he didn't hand over money and product. Blade, Sonny C's bodyguard, led the raiding party. Four months afterwards, D-Mac shot Officer Cooper before being hit with four rounds from Cooper's partner. It was another twisted street tale almost too incredible to believe if it didn't happen. Bad things occurred whenever Malice showed up. He didn't deserve an ounce of sympathy.

Eight days after the Morey family massacre, their killers were in custody. Even though neither of them confessed, forensic evidence linked them to the crime. The most damaging evidence was a gun owned by Serrano, recovered from a nearby lake and ballistically matched as the murder weapon used on Tony and Tina. Other interviews, in addition to Malice, linked Gilleo to a large Bowie knife, like the one used on the two older boys. The cut on his head and statements to Malice sealed his fate. A uniformed trooper and I transported Gilleo to his arraignment, where the judge remanded him to the county jail. One of the court officers came up to us and shook our hands as if we'd done something special. This was the job. No handshakes were needed, though I appreciated the gesture.

The murders pushed me to my limits. I went home after Gilleo's arraignment and sat in the living room with Joan. We talked about the murders and the events of the past few months. I confessed to feeling nothing upon seeing the three dead boys. I couldn't muster an emotional response to the homicide scene. Compassion fatigue is a clinical term for no longer "giving a shit." Sympathy for others is gone. With the Morey case, I had bottomed out.

"I'm leaving. I'll work on a plan to retire by year's end."

"Really? Are you sure? I thought you wanted to do twenty-five years."

Joan couldn't hide her joy at the sliver of hope she'd been given.

"No, I'm done. I can't . . . I don't want to do this anymore."

I put my arms around her, and we curled up on the couch.

22
BIG T AND D

The mistake made by inexperienced police investigators is to assume that once arrests are made, the investigation is concluded. I'd seen cops make great arrests only to blow the case with poor paperwork or shitty courtroom testimony. Their lack of diligence and preparation doomed future convictions based on good arrests. I tended to overprepare. I hated to lose, but it sometimes happened, as it did years before with the Leak Investigation. The CK Mafia investigation still left us with interviews to complete, witnesses to track down, and weeks of trial preparation.

After the November arrests, Hartigan went back to regular detective duties, and Adamo kept working from the local undercover office the FBI rented. Everyone working in the wire room returned to their agencies. The summer following the arrests was a quiet one for the city. Many of the street dealers were stunned by the extent of the investigation and the length of the prison sentences. However, gang activity rarely goes away; it merely subsides like an early morning ocean tide before roaring back. A renewed need for the task force arose the following summer when business as usual returned to the city. We were still a long way from worrying about the future. Sonny C and Domino wanted to go to trial. They and Squid had the most criminal exposure as the CK Mafia leaders. They also had more serious charges pending against them. Squid, though, had an alternate plan.

Eight months after he hid from the police with Sonny C in the parking lot of Continental Acres while warning Domino not to shoot at my car circling the block, Squid sat ensconced in the county prosecutor's conference room. Burghoff let Squid listen to the recorded conversation from that August night. He had already undergone two proffer sessions, confessed to a multitude of crimes, and signed a cooperation agreement. In exchange for his testimony, Squid—who we now referred to by his birth name, Delroy, or just D—was assured a straight five-year sentence in prison. Delroy jumped at the bargain deal instead of the statutory minimum twenty-five years he faced. His court-appointed attorney, Harold Janowitz, an experienced criminal defense attorney, told A.D.A. Burghoff of Delroy's reaction when confronted with his potential prison sentence. While meeting with his attorney at the county jail, Delroy, without hesitation, told Janowitz to get him a deal. Amid laughter, the attorney related Delroy's end of the conversation, "Janowitz, I can't even spell twenty-five, ain't no way I'm doing those years." Delroy obviously kidded because he was smart with a keen sense of humor. He was also incredibly likable, if not for the fact he sold drugs and shot people. He was a dangerous individual when mixed in with his gang.

"Listening to the tape, I kinda saved your life, Big T," Delroy said with a smile. During our trial preparation sessions, Delroy considered himself part of our team. We were his new crew, and we all got nicknames. Burghoff became "Stan the Man" or "Boss B," he tagged Adamo with the appropriate moniker of "Atomic," and he called me "Big T."

"It's gotta earn me some more points."

"More than you already got?" I asked. "What're you expecting, for us to eventually let you walk out of here?"

"It'd be nice . . . just saying." Delroy once again flashed his electric smile. "I did save your life, T." I reached my arm across the table with my palm held up and we high-fived. Delroy sat back and then became pensive.

"Remember last summer, on Decatur, when y'all said you were watching us?"

"The night you were holding Nina, your 9 millimeter, and planned to rip off Tamarah's place?" Adamo asked. Delroy's expression indicated he had an unresolved question gnawing at him.

"Yeah, we had our bitches with us. Strapped as a motherfucker. You said y'all had a plan to take us down," Delroy continued. "Like what would've you done?"

I jumped in, remembering how I felt that night. "Atomic had a machine gun and another trooper and I had our Glocks. We were coming for you."

"What would you do?"

"D, as God is my witness, if you so much as moved toward your waistband and pulled out Nina, I would've placed two rounds in your chest," I replied.

"Damn, you're cold, Big T." Delroy seemed surprised and hurt by the response.

"What would have you done under the circumstances if you saw us coming? Be honest." He looked at Adamo then back to me.

"Fair enough, I get it." Delroy dropped his chin to his chest in a moment of reflection before once more flashing his smile, "We cool now though, right?"
"Better than cool, D, we're solid," I said, this time reaching out and extending my hand, which he shook.

After listening to more recordings, we broke for lunch, Delroy's favorite part of the debriefing sessions, closely followed by the stops we made at a local soccer park for Delroy to get in a smoke and watch parents and their children mill around at afternoon soccer practices. We always stopped at a town field east of the city prior to returning him to the neighboring county jail where he was held for safety reasons.

"This could be your life, Delroy," I said to him one day. "You do your time, learn a trade or go to college, then take your girl and move away. It's up to you. Nobody's going to help you."

He took a deep drag of his cigarette and then blew smoke into the air.

"Yeah . . . it'd be nice." He took another drag as he looked around.

"For real," he said while taking in the scene of upper-middle-class parents and their children descending onto various soccer fields. They were like an invading army alighting from minivans, oversized SUVs, and expensive foreign cars. Delroy had never experienced this side of life, even though we were less than four miles from the neighborhood where he grew up.

"Them people got legit money," he said.

"For the most part."

"What do you mean?"

"Delroy, even in the suburbs people are gonna play their games and do their dirt," I told him. "The difference is they tend to hide it better."

In between meeting Adamo at the district attorney's office for case preparation sessions with Delroy, I worked on my assigned Major Crimes cases, which included follow-up leads in the Morey family murders and two homicides. One, called in on my birthday, involved a fight between two roommates in their fifties. Heinrichs, knowing it was my birthday, gave me the night off and didn't call me in until the next day. She thought I needed rest and time with my family. The case was a ground ball. Juan Limon and I chased down leads while another pair of investigators located the murder suspect in a local motel. The other case involved two sisters who fought over their mother's jewelry. Their mother died six months earlier and left her dilapidated residence to her daughters. Both women, in their twenties, were drug users. During the argument, the older sister grabbed a large kitchen knife and threatened her sibling. Their argument was loud enough to be heard in the street, and neighbors called 911. Along with another BCI unit, we responded as backup. When we arrived, the older sister sat on the floor with her younger sister's head resting on her lap and the kitchen knife embedded in the younger one's abdomen. "She's gonna be alright, isn't she? Tell me she'll be okay," the woman pleaded over and over while paramedics attempted to save her sister. Both cases were straightforward, and the suspect's confession in each made it easier for the prosecution. As the trial preparation for the CK Mafia case ground on, so did the investigations assigned to the Major Crimes Unit. I balanced court appearances, investigations, and trial prep sessions with Delroy. Sadly, I also attended the burial of a trooper killed by gunfire while dealing with an armed barricaded subject.

Meanwhile, I earnestly worked on my exit strategy from the job. I rented office space and expanded my real estate practice to include public sector labor law. A law enforcement union client on retainer and individual cops hiring me to fight grievances and disciplinary cases for them bolstered my exit plan. As the year wore on, Joan kept a watchful eye on the calendar. No matter what came about, I had committed to leaving before December 31.

A week after the Morey family homicide, I applied for a full-time university teaching position in Connecticut and was called in for an interview several weeks later. If the university position came through, I told Joan, my retirement papers were as good as filed. Teaching invigorated me. I got to interact in a different way with people, mostly young adults planning future law enforcement careers of their own. For ten years, I had been an adjunct professor and thought doing it full-time would be a dream job. If the opportunity came through, there was no reason to delay retirement.

*

I rode a big wave of cases toward the end of my career. What more did I need to do? Twenty-two years of service were enough. One way or another, the year was going to end with my return to civilian life, if for no other reason than I had to do it for Joan. She was my world: partner, spouse, confidante, friend, lover, soulmate. Sometimes, I made it a challenge for her to want to retain any of those titles. She never gave up on me, or us as a couple. We could have easily been a statistic, another ruined marriage at the altar of the job. We weren't, though; we'd survived the storms that otherwise disrupted our smooth sail together. And our three children thrived, each maturing into caring, kind, and beautiful young adults. My plan was to chart out even calmer waters for Joan and me. Meanwhile, more police work needed to be done.

Delroy always ordered a cheeseburger, fries, and either a chocolate milkshake or a Coke for lunch. Sometimes he'd order both drinks and save the Coke for later in the afternoon. As we ate our lunches, Delroy and I often played a game reciting lyrics from one of the three CK Mafia album demos. One of us began a line of lyrics, and the other had to finish it. The lunchtime game between us served as a method of prepping Delroy to testify to the meaning of selected rap songs and how they corresponded to actual crimes. At two later trials, it wouldn't only be me testifying as an expert witness; it'd be Delroy as one of the performers and co-creators of the lyrics, outlining in vivid testimony how select verses were factual accounts of the crimes the CK Mafia committed.

By the end of the following year, all CK Mafia members had either pled guilty or gone to trial. Most received minimum eight-year to double-digit prison terms. Sonny C and Domino went to trial together. Domino, who had never been arrested before, received eighteen years in prison. Sonny C received fifty years to life. For his cooperation, Delroy earned the promised straight five-year term he served out of state in a federal prison. The last time I talked to Delroy was in the district attorney's conference room after he testified in the first CK Mafia case to go to trial, a two-year-old shooting I had connected to Blade and Manic. Delroy had been unflinching under cross-examination from defense attorneys. Later, he did even better at the Sonny C and Domino trial. When asked if he had any qualms about testifying against his former friends, Delroy was resolute. "Fuck them clowns. I got a life to live and get back on track." He gave me a broad smile and flashed two fingers when a correction officer came to bring him back to jail. "Peace, Big T."

*

The tacit reality of police work that every police family understands is the potential danger and how it shadows home life. Later in May, the unspoken risks of the job became clearer to my three children. For my work on the CK Mafia case, I earned the second-highest State Police honor, the Superintendent's Commendation Award for outstanding police service and bravery, at the annual awards ceremony in Albany. Surprisingly, Captain Quade, despite how much we butted heads during the case, put me in for the commendation. Brian and Siobhan came home from college to attend, and Deirdre was absent from middle school. We left our Hudson Valley home early in the morning to get to Albany for the breakfast reception followed by the ceremony in the State Police Academy's main lecture hall. Joan returned to the academy for the first time since saying goodbye to me on a Sunday afternoon nearly twenty-two years earlier at the start of my six months of training. When the first deputy superintendent read my commendation citation, he mentioned Domino's plan to ambush me and shoot up my undercover car. Also cited were the potential robberies and shootings I intervened to disrupt, often alone at night. My children looked over at me while he read the commendation, but the more visceral reaction came when we walked to the stage as a family, and they saw me stop and shake the hand of a uniformed trooper in the front row. I had worked with him when assigned as a station investigator. Everyone knew him as Pac Man, a nickname from his college rugby days. My children knew Pac Man from barracks picnics and local road races. They saw his right arm heavily bandaged after being shot and seriously wounded a few weeks earlier in a firefight in which another trooper and the suspect were killed. I had stood by his hospital bedside with Heinrichs and a few other investigators a day after the shooting. Next to Pac Man sat a State Police sergeant recovering from gunshot wounds suffered the year before in another incident in which a trooper was killed. The experience touched my children.

"Seeing Pac Man's arm all bandaged up . . . he looked really pale and thinner," Brian said.

"He'll be okay," I assured him.

"Yeah, I suppose . . ."

Siobhan cut in as Brian trailed off in thought.

"I never realized . . . never thought about your work like that."

"What did you think?"

"Not sure . . . I guess . . . you know . . . just assumed you'd always be safe."

Deirdre, as usual, absorbed every word before asking, "Will those two troopers be okay?"

"Yes, physically they'll recover. Mentally, they have a lot more healing ahead of them." I did not realize at the time, as fit and healthy as I felt, my own healing, from a different kind of wound, was still a long way off.

23
MEETING SAM

We waited over two hours for the interview. I neglected to check his date of birth in preparation for our visit. It was his fifty-fourth birthday. The reception room officer told me he had three visitors ahead of us. He expected them. After spending time with a minister and two ladies from the church, he would be brought into a room to meet me. The interview guaranteed an interesting end to his day.

Tim Wassler, my corrections department contact, Vinny Mazzura, my partner for the day, and I grabbed lunch and then drove around the area before returning to the prison. Eastern Correctional Facility sits off the appropriately named Institution Road in the Ulster County town of Wawarsing. The prison building, a meticulously maintained Gothic monolith, resembles an English manor house. A green copper roof caps the polished stone facade. Four medieval-style turrets frame the square main building, and two rectangular extensions on either side of the entrance hide the modern housing units squatting behind the massive stone structure and razor wire. Rondout Creek flows south, separating the prison from the nearby village of Napanoch. The largest employer in the area, other than the prison, is Walmart. If not employed by either of them, odds are the residents are likely to either collect food stamps or deal meth.

A cold case homicide brought us there for the interview. In January 1978, a motorist saw the bullet-riddled body of Charles Hirschmann along a Dutchess County road. The next day, Hirschmann's girlfriend, stabbed eighteen times, turned up in a vacant lot near Kennedy Airport in Queens. Nearly thirty years later, I waited within the prison to conduct an interview relating to the cold case investigation. The victim, Hirschmann, resembled the composite sketch of a suspect from an earlier 1977 Bronx homicide. We wanted to see if the man convicted of that three-decade-old murder could shed light on the slight resemblance between Hirschmann and the NYPD composite sketch of the suspect from the 1977 homicide.

When finally let into the interview room, we sat and waited for the prisoner. The room glistened like the rest of the facility. Other New York prisons I'd visited never looked as clean as Eastern did. The cleanliness surely might have something to do with the fact that every one of its inmates was destined to die there. They kept it so nice because Eastern was home.

"Should we sing him happy birthday before or after the interview?" I asked to break the tension. Vinny and Tim responded with nervous laughs.

"Do you know what you're going to say to him? How're you going to start?" Tim asked.

"Hello is usually best."

When the door to the interview room opened, the prisoner, escorted by a uniformed correction officer, entered, and cautiously looked around. He was a grayer, slightly heavier version of the man who terrorized New York City during my youth. I stood and extended my right hand, introduced myself to David Berkowitz, and gave my reason for being there. The Son of Sam, the notorious .44 caliber killer, shook my hand and sat down. For the next hour, I was the birthday surprise he didn't expect.

Berkowitz tentatively looked over the table at me with the same trapped expression I'd seen before on suspects' faces when confronted in an interview. I didn't suspect him of involvement in my case; he had already been in custody for the Son of Sam murders, but I'd uncovered a possible connection between Hirschmann and Berkowitz.

At the interview, two sons of the Bronx, a generation apart, sat across from each other. Berkowitz, one of the most infamous serial killers in the world, had become a Christian in prison, maintained a youth ministry, and on a religious website touted the Bible as the source of his strength and protection. I sat at the other side of the table, a lapsed Catholic with a police badge in my pocket that didn't protect me from anything. The inescapable irony swirled around the interview room.

*

The psychic injury resulting from a policing career is invisible. One day doesn't change you. It is an accumulation of days and incidents. Like aging, the shift is subtle until you look at an old photograph and compare it to the face in the morning mirror. Only when you have something to compare yourself against do you appear old and not the twenty-something you envisioned. Self-delusion is a form of vanity. You believe the image you project to the world has no flaws.

I acted for many years, playing a version of myself and rarely let the real one emerge. It was easier being this false person, one whom everyone expected to look assured and cool when entering a crime scene or dealing with murder suspects, gangbangers, or Mafia soldiers. I despised my actor's role, but displaying the least bit of weakness or hesitancy could be fatal in ways more complicated than physical harm. Reputation, as always, mattered. A career in policing is like a gradual exposure to radioactive material. It takes a while to realize you've been poisoned. Command presence—the way police officers are taught and expected to project authority, confidence, and control—hides the illness from us until long after we've been exposed. Meanwhile, we act as if nothing has changed within us.

The first time I saw a body cut open on the pathologist's table, God had left the room. I watched the pathologist remove organs, weigh them and, if not kept for forensic purposes, put them in a plastic bag and back into the hollowed-out shell of a former living being who laughed and loved. The pathology assistant then sewed the body closed. All pretensions of faith I held onto started slipping away, and with each autopsy, slid further away. Police work challenged my rationalization for the existence of a higher being and an afterlife. St. Thomas Aquinas posited belief in the rational soul, where our thoughts and feelings, our intellect and will, existed in a subsistent immaterial substance after separation from the body upon death. Autopsies refuted my confidence in an afterlife; all that remained was dead flesh, gray and decaying once deprived of blood, oxygen, and water. I now sat across from a devil of a man who believed in Jesus Christ's resurrection from death. Not a metaphorical or allegorical resurrection, but a flesh and blood risen Christ. Berkowitz's victims, though, remained dead and buried. He too lived behind a façade, no different than mine but more pathetic. I wanted to expose his hypocrisy.

An interview is like an autopsy, except the examination requires peeling back the person's lies and defenses until left with the exposed tissue of the mind. You probe their soul and rip it apart to scratch at the truth. The interviewee is as helpless as the body lying on the stainless-steel table in the morgue. Berkowitz's vulnerability and uncertainty quickly came to the surface. He had once lived in a fantasy world of devil worship and drugs, and then, after several consecutive life sentences, he traded Satanism for evangelical Christianity.

How could Berkowitz, the boogeyman of my youth, have found his faith in prison, while I struggled to hold onto mine? Sunday Mass had become hit or miss until I finally stopped going. I looked at Berkowitz and felt compelled to call him out on his act, his only means to live with the horrible things he did instead of hanging himself in his cell from a bed sheet. Three decades earlier, he had stood outside a parked car and shot Stacy Moskowitz in the head at almost point-blank range, and now sat hunched over in his chair, hands folded on the table, attempting to hide behind a piety I didn't find credible. Those same hands he clasped together in prayer once held the Charter Arms .44 caliber Bulldog revolver used to shoot and kill six people and wound seven others over two summers. I wanted to expose his lie.

*

"You're a Christian, aren't you, Mr. Berkowitz?"

"Yes, sir," he replied.

"When did you come to your Lord and Savior, Jesus Christ?"

"1987."

"And in 1987 when you found Jesus, you rejected all sin, deception, and evil, correct?"

"Yes," he responded.

"Then why in 1998 did you say in a magazine interview there were others involved and you weren't the only gunman in the Son of Sam shootings?"

Berkowitz froze, his face a shade lighter than the prison pallor from when he entered the room. His eyes darted around during the short gap between my question and the resumption of my attack.

"If you became a Christian in 1987, why did you say there were other shooters? Why did you torture the victims' families with a lie? Is that what a Christian does? Is it what your Lord and Savior would expect of you?" I wouldn't relent.

Berkowitz's eyes began to water. He leaned back against his chair, took a deep recovery breath, then softly said he had been confused at the time and had no answer for his transgression. "I was the only shooter," he whispered to the room. "The only shooter."

I'd taken it too far by going after his visible weakness and questioning his faith, convinced of the necessity to attack him. Emotionalism made me weak in the moment. I'd violated a credo kept since the academy. Later, I wondered if a desire to cause him some pain prompted my private act of vengeance. Was my interview method used as revenge for all those times three decades earlier when fear of him loose on the streets made my mother change her routine? Was it for all those other women who felt fear when they went out at night?

It was abusive the way I went after Berkowitz in the interview room. We were in an unequal relationship. He couldn't leave the room. I took advantage by pressing him on his past claim about other shooters. The line of questioning strayed from my purpose. Anger motivated me. What else explained my actions? Except the anger wasn't generated by the fact I faced the self-described "chubby behemoth" who terrorized the streets of New York City and chased women, like my mother, indoors on steamy summer nights. Nor did the anger result from the fact I investigated an unsolved murder from long before I put on a police uniform, a murder for which we had no viable leads. My anger homed in on the peace Berkowitz found in prison and his faith. He possessed a tranquility I couldn't come close to feeling while on the job. Another irony. The job, my mistress, had been a seductress. Could it be I had chased nothing more than a thrill all these years? Had I become the opposite of Berkowitz, from faithful to fallen?

When I returned to the real purpose of the interview, Berkowitz appeared honest and sincere in his responses to my questions. He said he'd been interviewed many times by author Maury Terry, whose book, *The Ultimate Evil*, had first made the connection between my victim Hirschmann and Berkowitz. Terry, consumed by the Son of Sam case, argued that Berkowitz wasn't the only shooter. Part of his theory relied on varying police sketches of the shooter from witness descriptions, including one that looked like Hirschmann. Several didn't come close to resembling Berkowitz. Based on ideas Terry had given him, Berkowitz told me he felt prompted to say other people shot some of his victims. Berkowitz said Terry manipulated him and prevented a planned meeting with Neysa Moskowitz, the mother of his last murder victim, Stacy Moskowitz. Berkowitz wanted to meet with her and apologize as part of his healing process and act of penance. She was scheduled to meet with him at Eastern Correctional Facility. Terry allegedly intervened and contacted Neysa Moskowitz and said it'd be best to televise the meeting. Berkowitz wanted a private meeting, just him and Moskowitz. When he balked at the media presence, Berkowitz said plans for the meeting ended. He broke off contact with Terry in 2002. Whether Berkowitz's account was truthful or not didn't matter. He seemed to believe it. My impression of him was that he was a malleable soul, one who had been forever lost in his attempt to fit in and be liked by other people. He was far removed from the evil gunman who stalked New York City streets in the mid-1970s, though I had no doubt he now resided where it was best for him and society. For the rest of the interview, Berkowitz looked at photographs of Hirschmann and close-ups of his different tattoos. He cooperated though he had little to offer.

Mazzuro and I didn't expect much from Berkowitz. We had a lead to follow and close. We'd done so. Investigative work is often a series of dead ends.

On my drive home, I sensed much more than closing a lead on an old homicide file had occurred. My law enforcement career had come full circle by meeting with the individual whose crimes motivated me to become a police officer. Three decades had passed since I first contemplated a police career. If given a second chance, would I do it all over again? I continued having the same doubts about my chosen path of employment that arose during the Crazed Killas Mafia investigation. For the rest of my drive, that question occupied my thoughts. By the time I returned home, the answer still evaded me.

24
FINAL SHIFT

What happens from the time a police officer steps out the door and returns home impacts the family. Everyone in a police household lives the job. A police officer's day can turn quickly. A quiet afternoon becomes a late night with you knocking on the apartment door of a murder witness. Or an early morning raid and call home to say you're safe is by lunchtime a quick apology with no time to talk because you're at the scene of a barricaded murder suspect, with a SWAT team preparing for entry, and news helicopters swirling overhead. All there's time to say is that you don't know when you'll be home because, assuming all goes well, you and your partner will be interviewing the suspect. It's on those days when the family sits down to dinner and you're not there, or you're coming home from a call out and they're finishing breakfast ready to head out the door, that they are living the job with you.

Most people have no idea what a police officer experiences on the job. They are equally clueless about the amount of pressure police investigators are under to close cases and how the stress invades home life. The only refuge at the end of my workdays was being home with family and putting everything else behind. This didn't always work. Too often, the job came home with me. Fortunately, I had other outlets. Aside from an incredible and understanding family, my adjunct teaching, law practice, and physical regimen of running and working out kept me busy with productive diversions. I had seen too many other cops get lost, and some of those outcomes were tragic. There were suicides, broken marriages, and addictions. Police officers are told there is a helpline, an employee assistance program; however, nobody wants the stigma of seeking help. Toughing it out is the way to cope. But there is too much left unresolved from a policing career.

*

A week after my interview with Berkowitz, I received a call from a Connecticut phone number after leaving a corporate conference room in Armonk, where I attended a two-day mass casualty crime scene management presentation. After 9/11, the scope of crime scene management changed, as did many approaches to policing and in-service training. We were now inundated with seminars on intelligence-led policing, international and domestic terrorism training, and inter-agency resource sharing, including access to previously unavailable federal databases. Police work had changed. The local could have global ramifications, and the global could touch the local. Police officers, especially in smaller agencies, could no longer afford to view their work as restricted to the municipalities they patrolled.

Exiting the sprawling corporate complex, I took the call from the chairperson of a university hiring committee. He offered me a job as a full-time tenure-track professor teaching law courses at Western Connecticut State University. Immediately, I accepted the job. It was early June, six months ahead of my self-imposed end-of-year deadline for retiring. Thoughts about the next few weeks, my last as a police officer, and the short window before the start of the semester in late August consumed my drive home. We had an upcoming family trip to London scheduled before heading to Dublin for Joan's cousin's wedding. The two-week trip meant shorter preparation time for my new faculty position as well as an expedited retirement filing.

The trees along the Taconic State Parkway whizzed by on my drive north amid daydreams of how my life would change. I didn't know what to expect. Like a prisoner locked away for decades, I'd been institutionalized and couldn't envision a normal life. The reverie caused me to miss my usual exit for the interstate, and I continued north along the parkway while mentally listing all the things I'd never have to worry about again—the scheduled shooting range qualifications, the annual inspections, caseloads, odd work hours, maintenance on my assigned unmarked car, gun and equipment care, and all the drama, tedium, and stress. But I'd miss a lot too—the people in my unit, the camaraderie of being on the job, working high-profile cases, and the satisfaction of arresting individuals who did bad things to other people. Thoughts of celebration soon turned into panic after glancing at the dashboard clock. It was our twenty-second wedding anniversary, and Joan's gift waited at the jeweler. I had barely enough time to get to the jewelry store before closing, stop for flowers, and pick up a bottle of wine for dinner. It really didn't matter whether I got to the jeweler or not. All she'd remember from this anniversary was that we had a firm date for my retirement.

*

Police work anesthetizes you. A disconnect from ordinary life gradually occurs. You no longer interact in public the same way as others; everyone is a suspect; every event is a potential danger zone. Eating out becomes a shuffle to get a seat with a view of the door. You scan the exits in every room you enter. Sharp noises and the absence of noise equally alarm you. Over time, you view the world only through the myopic lens of your work. Judgment of others is harsh. Workday events accumulate. You become numb to other people's pain and your own. Unfeeling is the mental state late in your career.

Nearing retirement, I hit a point in life, with Brian and Siobhan in college, and Deirdre in her last year of middle school, when a law firm partnership should have been secured after years of busting my ass. There would be partner money and partner perks, and none of the bullshit, deception, and disappointment encountered from the job. Instead, I traded it for something else that most people wouldn't understand. Despite earlier doubt and second-guessing on whether I chose the right path, I had no regrets, except for one.

I had lied to people throughout my career, deceiving them to obtain confessions and set up criminal suspects for arrest, and accepted it as part of the job. But I also lied to myself and to Joan by reneging on several promises that I'd resign after graduating law school and passing the bar exam. I didn't realize the dissimulation of my promises until reaching the twenty-year mark of my career. Joan had to know, and she must have felt helpless doing anything about it. She accepted my decision for all the good it brought and tried not to dwell on the bad.

We had little time during our early years together to assess where we stood as a couple and what we wanted out of life. Our children, our responsibilities as parents, and the one unwavering belief we always felt kept us on a solid path—our deep, abiding love for each other—sustained us. It seemed enough. The only reason I made it through the job, with my marriage and family intact, was Joan's unfailing support.

Joan anticipated my final day with the State Police. I still couldn't imagine retirement. A different experience awaited me, and I'd have to adjust, same as she did twenty-two years earlier. Uncertainty lingered. Law enforcement had been my life for over two decades. Capturing the same degree of purpose and fulfillment in another career seemed unlikely.

*

On a Wednesday morning, over two and a half months after the interview with Berkowitz and the call from Connecticut, I arrived early at work. I never had a problem getting to crime scenes before everyone or scheduled meetings with informants or raid briefings; only when I had to report to the office did my punctuality wane. This day was different. My retirement began as soon as my shift ended. I wanted to capture every last minute of my final day as a police officer, better yet, as a New York State Trooper.

I didn't wander far from the Major Crimes office during my last shift. Except for a trip to the local deli with Limon for his coffee and my tea, I remained a "house mouse" for the day. This wasn't a role I was accustomed to. During my twenty-two years, I disdained those who made a career of being a headquarters cop with only carpet fibers to dust off their shoes at the end of a shift. Mine told a different story. My shoes had stepped in human feces while creeping down the hallway of a single wide trailer looking for a cop killer, jumped piss puddles in city alleys, crunched crack vials scattered underfoot, waded in the brackish waters of the Hudson River to retrieve a body, and pushed through doors for entry. More recently, they had trod the black and gray ash of the burned home where the Morey family died. Through the years, my shoes often had to be discarded because they were too worn, tired, and soiled from their travels.

On this final shift, though, my shoes had the luxury of the carpeted hallways of troop headquarters and the comfort of its air-conditioned rooms. After an exit interview with Major Doyle and signing retirement paperwork in the administrative clerk's office, the last official walk my shoes made strode past the indoor range to the quartermaster cage to turn in my state-issued equipment—a ballistic vest, handcuffs, gun, magazines, and shield. Then a quick right to the automotive maintenance garage to drop off the keys to my unmarked car.

I didn't expect the sudden lightness of the return steps to my desk, gliding past the trophy case—where an award from the Kiwanis Club for the CK Mafia case sat—past the captain's and lieutenant's offices, and the forensic ID unit, to the back corner of the building where the rest of my unit waited with cake, a plaque, and congratulations before returning to their work and the cases I'd be forever leaving. I sat at my desk with my feet propped on an open drawer and surfed the internet while waiting for Joan to pull into the visitor parking lot to bring me home. The day equally belonged to Joan as her final shift too.

She arrived fifteen minutes before the shift's end. I watched her walk along the sidewalk from the parking lot by the side of the headquarters building toward a narrow, paved path leading to the rear entrance of the Major Crimes office. She carried a bouquet of flowers for Sue Heinrichs. Joan always joked it took a village to keep me out of trouble. She and Heinrichs agreed years ago they were co-tenants of the village. Heinrichs had become like a sister to me. She'd remain a dear friend long afterward.

Joan passed by the tinted window near my desk. She wore a nice pair of blue jeans, black ankle boots, and a new colorful top she purchased at the mall earlier in the week. She wore her honey-brown hair swept up in a ponytail with a gold-flecked black clip. For as long as possible, I craned my neck to see her walking along the sidewalk. The sight of the rounded back of her jeans, toned from years of running, took me back to college when I'd watch her from my morning class in Keating Hall at Fordham University as she walked between buildings to her biology class. I was always distracted for the few seconds when watching her from my seat in the back row on the far-left side of Room 105. I'd visually follow her, oblivious to the lecture. Of all the classes to get caught looking out the window, it was Fr. Grady's religion class.

"Mr. Dwyer, is there something out the window more majestic than the Gospel of John?" the elderly Jesuit asked after catching me.

"Sorry, Father, nature's beauty caught my eye."

"Very well. Please contain your nature-loving instincts while in class."

Every Wednesday of the semester, I didn't miss a moment watching Joan scurry off to class. By then, I knew we'd marry. This warranted some absolution for my wandering off from the course topic of the four gospels, sin, and redemption. If any clergy would understand, it'd be a Jesuit.

What mattered now on my last day as a police officer was my deep love for the woman coming to take me home. For the past twenty-two years of our marriage, she had been admirably accepting and considerate of my mistress—the job. She never complained. I didn't realize then the impact being a police spouse had on her, much the same way I didn't realize the impact my career had on me. We'd have time to figure that out. I was finally ready to step away from the allure of the Bronx rooftop I'd perched upon over a decade before when, on a hot, moonlit summer night, while searching for a murder suspect, I'd chosen the job over Joan. Never again. Watching her make the turn up the path to the rear entrance of the building, I felt like I did in college when I saw her walking to class, tingling with anticipation of our future together. Finally, I was ready to fully share that future with her, and only her.

25
RECOVERY

Recovery is an odd word to describe the experience of retiring from a police career, though it's apt. The formidable task of starting anew at forty-five after nearly a quarter century in law enforcement scared me. I had left a career begun while still in college. My recovery meant learning how to live outside of a profession that consumed me and the lives of my family for over two decades. Granted, I prepared myself well for retirement by securing a university faculty position and maintaining a law practice. Nevertheless, the profession institutionalized me in many ways.

The nature of police retirement hadn't fully dawned on me until running into an academy classmate in a local mall a year after my retirement. He had recently retired and greeted me as a fellow survivor. The comment perplexed me until he explained.

"We aren't retirees as much as we're survivors of the job."

He was right. We entered the academy unblemished and eagerly optimistic. We retired scarred and jaded. Retirement meant no more angst. At least that was what I thought. For a long time, I couldn't understand the motivations of cops who retired after a twenty- or twenty-five-year career and then joined another police department. Hadn't they had enough? The cumulative stress had to eventually get to them. But consider the irony of my post-retirement path.

A large part of my law practice focused on representing police officers. I took a special interest in cases wherein good officers were wronged by their departments and often found myself fighting the same battles as in the past as a sworn police officer—challenging official accounts of events and confronting corruption and wrongdoing. This pitted me against police agencies, including my former employer. In the process, I often exposed a cover-up or shone light on a flawed investigation when a police department sought to discipline or terminate a good officer. During one high-profile case, I represented an investigator and a trooper who were framed by State Police bosses for an offense a well-liked supervisor committed. "Look at what happened to my clients and look at what they did to two of their own. What if this was some member of the public?" I stated when interviewed by local news media. Injustice and favoritism offended me. As a criminal justice and legal studies professor, I had the opportunity to instruct a new generation of practitioners, and as a lawyer, I could make a difference in ways not possible while working as a police officer.

For fifteen years after my retirement, I represented police officers in court who were wrongly accused of disciplinary infractions or who sued their police departments for various forms of malfeasance and corruption. Protecting officers' rights and obtaining settlements for harassed and sexually assaulted female police officers and for minority officers who were discriminated against by their agencies became the bulk of my law practice. In each case, a supervisor's egregious violation of department regulations or the law victimized my clients. Many of them experienced the same sense of betrayal and hurt I did when on the job.

*

Moral injury is not often mentioned when discussing police officers' mental wellness. Its impact on officers is intensified by secondary trauma exposure. One example of moral injury occurs when an individual suffers a betrayal of what is morally correct by someone who holds legitimate authority in a high-stakes situation. Failure in leadership, rather than an individual officer's moral shortcoming, accounts for many of the cases. It is the unseen scar many carry from their police careers; one they are either unaware of or unwilling to discuss.

When I retired, police departments did not conduct follow-up mental wellness visits or offer counseling to check on how a retiree fared after the first year or two of retirement. Not even upon retiring did anyone inquire about my physical or mental well-being. There was an exit interview with my troop commander. It amounted to a perfunctory talk about my career and retirement plans, followed by a handshake. Trained mental health professionals, not police supervisors, are the ones who should screen retirees. Some police departments now provide retirement counseling and check-ins. More should.

Even though police retiree suicide is significantly lower than among active officers, the rate is higher than that of the general population. The numbers for active officers are particularly alarming when considering more police officers die by suicide each year than in the line of duty. Seven of my state police acquaintances died by suicide, three after retiring, including an academy classmate. Officers with post-traumatic stress disorder, secondary traumas, addictions, physical disabilities, and other less severe mental and physical health problems leave a job that forgets them once they retire. If an officer is lucky, they have family to pick up the scattered pieces; even so, family doesn't always know what to do. Outside help is then needed.

My counseling journey began indirectly when interviewing a former university colleague who is a licensed mental health professional. I contacted her about my research into moral injury and its impact on stress disorders. She is a retired law enforcement officer with an extensive resume of counseling police and other first responders. During our conversation, past events from my police career came up. She asked if I had ever been in counseling.

"No," I lied. "Why do you ask?"

"Because from what I'm hearing, you need to talk to someone."

A silly comment or joke followed to mask my uneasiness with what she had said.

"Seriously, do yourself a favor. See someone. I can find a law enforcement-specific counselor for you," she said.

What I hadn't told her about, aside from my prior brief experience with counseling, were my recurring dreams of being attacked. Of late, they had gotten worse. I'd scream in the night, pound my fists into the headboard, or wrap my arms around my pillow in a strangulation hold. Joan, startled and scared, had to call my name several times, place her hand on top of the bedcovers, and gently apply pressure to my back or buttocks to calm me. I'd go back to sleep as if nothing had happened.

In the summer of 2023, a year-long counseling journey began wherein I confronted the full range of my police career and the various stressors and traumas encountered. I participated reluctantly at first. Why confide in a stranger? What prevented them from exposing my secrets? The oath they took as a mental health professional and state confidentiality laws didn't entirely assuage my concerns. I had experienced too many violations of professional ethics and oaths in the past. But I had another reason for my reluctance: guilt. I hadn't fought in a war and been diagnosed with PTSD, and as a police officer, I never shot anyone, was directly shot at, or suffered a debilitating injury. Those who had were the ones who needed to meet with a mental health counselor; they had experienced trauma. What right did I have to sit with someone and complain about past corruption, investigations gone wrong, or the multitude of events I responded to and investigated over the years, not the least of which was violent death? In time, I became receptive to counseling and discovered my symptoms were not uncommon. My counselor's clientele included other anonymous police officers, including many State Police members, ranging from mid and late career officers to retirees. Their stories were not much different than mine. The more I learned about moral injury and secondary traumas, the more I understood my twenty-two year career and its impact. I read studies on police officer mental wellness, wrote about and advocated for officer wellness programs. One research study I found listed thirty-four critical trauma exposures a police officer potentially faces in a career, and based on the number of exposures researchers could gauge the extent of policing's impact on an officer. The incidents went from most severe at the top and descended to least severe, while accounting for multiple exposures to the same trauma. I read through the list and found I checked off eighteen of the thirty-four listed exposures, with multiples in some categories. This is by no means remarkable. I know of or have talked with retired police officers who would run down the list with a check mark next to most of the listed incidents. But I also know officers who would barely make it to double digits on the survey. Similarly, this is not to minimize those careers. Rather, it is meant to highlight a fact I once read about police trauma that I initially scoffed at. According to a study in the *Journal of Traumatic Stress*, the average police officer will experience between 178 to 200 critical incidents throughout their career, while the average person by comparison experiences two to three traumatic incidents in a lifetime. It took me years, and a lot of self-reflection, to finally acknowledge this fact. This is the problem many retired officers and those still active face, admitting the impact the work has on them.

*

Policing is a great career. I'm proud to have been a police officer and to have worked for one of the premier agencies in the United States. There is much good in American policing; however, there remains an unnecessary amount of bad that shouldn't be tolerated. Detailing the negative issues existing in policing could fill another book. My career left me with a distrust of organizations in general and less acceptance and belief in official law enforcement versions of events. It suffices to say that the existing bad in policing is a perilously perched stone which, when it falls can crush one's belief in an ordered society. This adds to the burden good officers must carry to protect the public. For a retiree like me, it adds to the love-hate relationship one has with the job. This duality of emotional attachment creates another kind of stress on top of the rest of the cumulative career baggage.

During my year of counseling, Joan and I talked about the job and its impact on us. We had never done so in the past. Our discussions were frank and emotional. They were also therapeutic. We understood each other's impressions and feelings about a period of our lives we each thought was buried in the past. Some of the discussions also centered around faith and my rebuilding of it. Again, I sought guidance by reading St. Augustine, the daily meditations of Pope John Paul II, and even the poetry of the English Jesuit priest Gerard Manley Hopkins. Institutionalized religion, like other concentrations of collective thinking, does not appeal to me. But never, in all my education and reading, did the concept of faith in God depend upon belonging to a church or going to Mass. Faith is personal; the rest is about community, and my experience with people gathered in a common purpose, like the ritual of the Mass, is not favorable. Having been on the job assures me that my attitude on this will not change.

Recently though, while watching news coverage of a major investigation and arrests made by the State Police, I confessed to Joan that, contrary to past assertions, I missed the job and would likely do it again if given the opportunity. Never had I felt so useful and alive in the moment as when either in uniform responding to a call or in the BCI investigating a violent crime. Watching news stories or talking with cops, there was always a tinge of envy.

"With all you now know, especially my feelings about the job, would you still go back?" Joan looked at me with a cross-examiner's glare. I knew my answer; the issue was whether to tell her.

"Yes . . . sorry but, yes. I think I would." Deep down, I held onto the belief that one person could make a difference and felt there was more work for me to do. Possibly this was a lingering self-deception. Why would I continue feeling this way? I had a wonderful wife, three incredible adult children, their spouses, and now grandchildren in my life. Still, the job called out to me. Maybe you never recover from a police career; you only miss it.

Joan clicked off the television, got up from the couch, and kissed me.

"Thought so . . . I wouldn't have expected otherwise." She noticed my look of surprise. "What? Did you expect a different response?" "Yes. Didn't you?" I said. "I'd have no reason to."

She then invited me to join her for a run, and in minutes we were out the door.

Remarkably, she understood, and finally, so did I. The badge between us had never been a wedge separating us. The badge was something we shared.

ACKNOWLEDGMENTS

Writing is a solitary art. Completing and publishing a book-length manuscript is a team effort. I am indebted first and foremost to my MFA program mentor in creative nonfiction, the indefatigable and unrelenting Dr. J. Michael Lennon, who understood me from the beginning and knew what I wanted to write. One would have to search far and wide to find a better literary mind than his. Without his guidance, this book would never have existed. Also, thanks to Robert Mooney, author and publisher at Etruscan Press, who helped me narrow my focus and find the story I first had to write before considering any other. His encouragement ignited something I'd been holding back. The input from my two beta readers, Dr. Bonnie Culver and my daughter Deirdre, was pointed and precise and helped reshape the original manuscript. Their input and notes made the manuscript better as it progressed. I am also grateful for my acquisition editor at Bloomsbury, Becca Beurer, who saw potential in the story I wanted to tell and gave me the leeway and time to craft it as it was meant to be.

Much love to the Wilkes University Maslow Family Creative Writing MFA program and the faculty who know how to energize individual creative magic and guide it to the page. Special kudos to Dr. David Hicks, whose leadership and mentorship proves that he is the Merlin behind the magic of the MFA program.

In life we are sometimes gifted with true blessings, and one of those blessings for me was meeting the incomparable creative nonfiction queen Beverly Donofrio at Wilkes University. Her instruction during two workshops, as well as private discussions about craft, provided invaluable guidance. She helped me find my ending and the important threads and subtext in my manuscript. Many thanks also to author and social justice activist Jessica Goudeau, whose insight on modern trends in the true crime genre helped me to hone in on how I wanted to structure my manuscript. And to Dr. Phil Brady, in whose workshop class I learned to craft powerful beginning sentences through a simple oral recitation and rewriting exercise. He is a wordsmith with few equals.

I am especially grateful for my MFA cohort members Greg Dutcher, Jillian Benedict, and Cory Massaro, who, either as a favor or in workshops, read through my work and made poignant comments and editorial suggestions.

Lastly, but most affectionately and lovingly, to my three children, Brian, Siobhan, and Deirdre, who always motivated me to be a better version of myself and gave me the love and joy of being a parent. I also appreciated their support when I joined a creative writing master's program at sixty, and not once questioned what the hell I was thinking. Their love means the world to me.

And, of course, thanks to my wife Joan, to whom I dedicate everything. You underestimate your impact on all that I do and have accomplished. My love for you is endless.

ABOUT THE AUTHOR

Terrence P. Dwyer retired from a 24½ year law enforcement career that included 22 years with the New York State Police. For 17½ years, he served as an investigator in the State Police Bureau of Criminal Investigation. During his career, he earned over twenty-five commendations for police work. Retired from a second career as an attorney, he now consults and is a professor teaching legal studies at Western Connecticut State University. He is the author of three textbooks, the most recent being *Homeland Security Law: Issues and Analysis*, a Public Safety Writers Association Gold Medallion award winner for nonfiction. Since 2008, he has been a featured columnist for Police1.com. He resides in New York with his wife, Joan, and in his spare time enjoys boating, exploring hiking trails around the Northeast, running, and spending time with family.